Emily Buchanan is an award winning journalist and broadcaster. Educated at St. Paul's Girls' School, Sussex University and City University, she has worked for the BBC for over twenty years. As a producer and correspondent for BBC News and Current Affairs she specialised first in politics and more recently in the developing world and religion. She has made documentaries for *Newsnight*, *Assignment* and *Correspondent* on BBC 2 and has presented Radio 4's *A World in Your Ear*. Currently she is a World Affairs Correspondent, living in London with her husband and two children.

D1023636

From China With Love

A Long Road To Motherhood

EMILY BUCHANAN

WILEY

Published in 2006 by   John Wiley & Sons, Ltd, The Atrium, Southern Gate
Chichester, West Sussex, PO19 8SQ, England
Phone   (+44) 1243 779777

Copyright © 2006   Emily Buchanan

Email (for orders and customer service enquires): cs-books@wiley.co.uk
Visit our Home Page on www.wiley.co.uk or www.wiley.com

This publication is designed to provide accurate and authoritative information in regard to the
subject matter covered. It is sold on the understanding that the Publisher is not engaged in
rendering professional services. If professional advice or other expert assistance is required, the
services of a competent professional should be sought.

Emily Buchanan has asserted her right under the Copyright, Designs and Patents Act 1988,
to be identified as the author of this work.

Other Wiley Editorial Offices

John Wiley & Sons, Inc. 111 River Street, Hoboken, NJ 07030, USA

Jossey-Bass, 989 Market Street, San Francisco, CA 94103-1741, USA

Wiley-VCH Verlag GmbH, Pappellaee 3, D-69469 Weinheim, Germany

John Wiley & Sons Australia, Ltd, 33 Park Road, Milton, Queensland, 4064, Australia

John Wiley & Sons (Asia) Pte Ltd, 2 Clementi Loop #02-01, Jin Xing Distripark,
Singapore 129809

John Wiley & Sons Canada Ltd, 22 Worcester Road, Etobicoke, Ontario, Canada, M9W 1L1

Wiley also publishes its books in a variety of electronic formats. Some content that appears in
print may not be available in electronic books.

British Library Cataloguing in Publication Data

A catalogue record for this book is available from the British Library

ISBN 0-470-09344-7 (PB)   978-0-470-09344-3

Typeset in $10\frac{1}{2}$/14pt Caslon by MCS Publishing Services Ltd, Salisbury, Wiltshire.
Printed and bound in Great Britain by T.J. International, Padstow, Cornwall.
This book is printed on acid-free paper responsibly manufactured from sustainable forestry in
which at least two trees are planted for each one used for paper production.
10 9 8 7 6 5 4 3 2 1

To Jade and Rose

*and the women who
gave birth to them*

Acknowledgements

My thanks to:

Gerald Slocock for his love, encouragement, constructive criticism and wonderful cooking. Florence Buchanan, Lady Charteris, Dr Sandra Buchanan, Caroline Slocock and Mary Pearson for their constant support. Tom Fry, Liling Huang, Jun Ding, Sally Yates, Professor Monica Dowling, Julia Lovell, Julia Fleming and Stevan Whitehead for all their valuable thoughts. The dedicated BBC producers who worked on the films mentioned: Tony Fallshaw, David Belton, Bhasker Solanki, Lucy Hetherington, Susan Stein, Alex Milner, Penny Richards, Giselle Portenier, Ewa Ewart and Jan Rocha. John Pawsey, my agent, whose idea it was that I should write this story down. Sally Smith at Wileys for her patient feedback. Kate Santon and Roger Hunt of MCS Ltd. Catherine Garner and Rowan Mitchell without whose loving and consistent child-care none of this would have been possible.

And to all those who helped but wanted to remain anonymous.

Contents

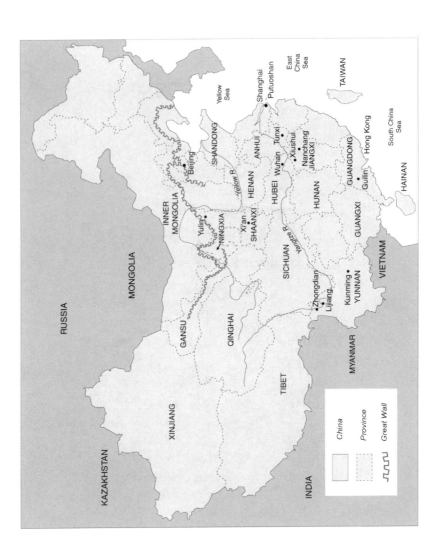

Introduction

It was one thing dreaming of a daughter. I had peered countless times at her picture, courtesy of the Chinese government: a small photograph of a five-month-old baby girl from the remote desert plateau of Shaanxi Province. I had fingered and stroked it, searching for the personality behind the still, sad eyes and the pale, motionless, chubby face.

Now my two-year 'bureaucratic' pregnancy was about to end. This moment, which had once appeared like a distant star, was accelerating towards us.

....

I watched the flat yellow earth blanketed by hazy yellow air stretch out ahead. The engines roared as the aircraft banked in preparation to land, and I could feel the pit in my stomach grow. Gerald and I were flying into Xi'an, China's ancient capital, to meet the child who would be ours, and panic was taking hold.

Our sharp-suited translator, with cropped hair, was there to greet us, bristling with efficiency. 'You are going to meet your daughter this evening,' she announced. 'In two hours time she'll be brought to your hotel.'

So this was it. I felt sick with anticipation. 'But I thought she would come tomorrow?'

'There's been a change of plan. The people from her orphanage will bring her tonight, so you'd better get ready.'

How we'd wallowed in big ideas of East linking with West, of the beautiful symmetry of abandoned child meeting childless parents, of love knowing no national boundaries. This miracle was perfect in the abstract, but the five-month-old baby in the photo was now eleven months' worth of flesh and blood. She would be brought to us and there would be no going back. Mother, father and daughter ... about to be bonded together as one family.

I had wanted to put off this life-changing moment until the next morning when we would be fresh, but no, it was about to happen and the minutes were ticking by. Our imaginary child was not only real; she was in this city, waiting for us. Waves of excitement and fear were washing over me. 'Please can I have a shower first?' I asked; I wanted to erase the grimy smells of our journey. I couldn't bear to think of my daughter being repelled by the first whiff of her new mother. She might take one look at this unfamiliar, freckled redhead and be horrified; the least I could do was smell clean.

We arrived into the marbled calm of the Bell Tower Hotel and were ushered into our room where we hurriedly unpacked. I felt hopelessly disorganised, unzipping my suitcase and taking the baby things out one by one and putting them on the desk: bottle, milk formula, rattle, wipes, nappies, bibs – they were like strange foreign objects. I stuffed some T-shirts, shorts and little dresses into a drawer, baby clothes of various sizes in case the measurements we'd been given weren't accurate. I remembered how buying these props had made me feel I was, if nothing else, playing the part of a mother-to-be. The role of 'mother' had eluded me for years and it still felt strange, almost unnatural. I'd often wondered if I was the 'mothering kind', yet here I was travelling to the ends of the earth to become one.

This whole journey had been full of contradictions: to prove to the British government that I was capable of being a parent when I was riddled with doubts, to take on another woman's child from a distant land when I knew virtually nothing about looking after children, to mother a baby when I had lost my own mother at an early age and been denied much of the experience of being mothered too.

When I wandered through the baby section of John Lewis, London's capacious department store, I had looked at the tired women wheeling sullen toddlers in their pushchairs, and had even begun to wonder if this longed-for state was really so joyful after all. I had got into a muddle about the kind of bottle to buy and which rubber teats went with it. Should I choose one that took disposable bags in case we couldn't wash the bottles in China? The shop assistant had looked at me strangely as I was obviously expectant, but not visibly pregnant. I didn't feel up to explaining that I was what's technically known as an 'elderly primigravida', an older first-time mother, but one whose daughter was already outside her body, thousands of miles away: a daughter who was waiting to rediscover the umbilical link.

....

Now, in this plain hotel room in Xi'an, a city that stood at the crossroads of the trade routes between Central Asia and eastern China, a place that was once at the very heart of Chinese civilisation, we were about to meet our daughter for the first time.

We held hands tightly and waited. I wanted to scream. The traffic from the gridlocked roundabout below hooted and roared. The neon signs flashed red and green through the window. There were footsteps in the corridor, then a gentle knock at the door.

Chapter One

A Tunnel at the End of the Light

'Hey Em, can you go to Sri Lanka today?' The BBC's foreign news editor, Vin Ray, strode towards me across the newsroom carpet, stained brown from dozens of spilled cups of tea and coffee. I sipped at my portion of tepid dark liquid in its polystyrene container, trying to keep my nerves steady as the adrenaline kicked in. He stuck the piece of news-wire copy in front of me. 'There's been a bomb attack in Colombo, the business district, dozens killed. See what else you can find out. We'll organise a crew. You fly tonight.' A suicide bomber had wrecked the Central Bank in Sri Lanka's capital. It was going to be carnage and I grimaced at the thought. Normally foreign correspondents have a kind of perverse excitement at the chance to get on air with a big news story. I covered the developing world, specialising in the conflicts and social issues afflicting many often-ignored nations. I loved my job, but that day was different. The ceaseless and often unpredictable travelling was playing havoc with my personal life. The needs of the newsroom were paramount; relationships had to sink or swim in the

My job was covering the aftermath of wars – tank graveyard, Eritrea, with cameraman Bhasker Solanki ...

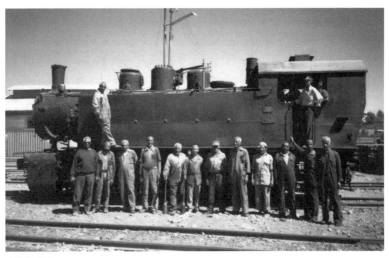

... And efforts for reconstruction. Restoring the old railway, Eritrea.

wake of urgent deadlines and long-haul flights from Heathrow Airport.

I slumped in the cramped aircraft seat next to Tony, one of our ebullient cameramen, crestfallen as he chatted merrily about the trip ahead, a glass of wine in hand. All I could think of was how the beginnings of a fairy-tale romance were now being shredded by the urgency of another country's civil war.

. . . .

The invitation had arrived like a ray of sunshine into my light-starved West Kensington flat. The paper had slid out of my fax machine to reveal the tantalising words: 'St Petersburg Ball at the Café Royal'. My seen-it-all, cynical heart registered a flutter of excitement. 'A Bal Masqué on the theme of the Ballets Russes of Diaghilev ...' Nijinsky leapt before my eyes, and then images from *War and Peace*: that breathtaking moment when Natasha enters the ballroom, bursting with youth and beauty, and almost swooning with excitement. She meets Prince Andrei, one of the best dancers of his day, her charm mounts to his head like wine ... I stopped my reverie: 'Don't be ridiculous.' This was London 1996, not St Petersburg 1809.

I was more than twice the age of Tolstoy's heroine, on the wrong side of thirtysomething, and had been exploring the seedy underside of the planet for five years. At any other time I might have binned such a frivolous invitation, but having just turned my attention to the seedy underside of my psyche with five days of intense group therapy, I was in the mood for a fresh start. This had been no wishy-washy chit-chat, but an excavation of my encrusted mental landscape. I was an expert at staying with unsuitable boyfriends out of a mixture of excessive loyalty and deep insecurity and I'd unloaded a cargo of emotional baggage, weeping more than I thought possible. To my surprise, I found that by the end I felt not miserable but elated, brimming with a desire to shake off old habits and find new friends.

A Charity Ball in aid of the Burns Unit of Children's Hospital No. 9 in Moscow seemed like a good place to begin. I felt a little uncomfortable at the contrast between the glamour of the invitation and the grizzly reality of children's suffering but a friend assured me that as a fund-raising event it had, over the past decade, raised tens of thousands of pounds for a worthwhile cause.

I'd never been to a ball. My fiercely anti-glamour, 1970s youth was spent at Sussex University learning about intellectual history, vegetarianism, feminism and gay rights and if anyone there ever went to such an un-PC event as a ball, they would never have dared admit it. I now realised there was a world of these smart charity events run by powerful, ageless women adept at persuading rich people to dress up in period costumes, turn up to church halls to practise dances like the polka, the schottische and the polonaise, eat a large dinner and then write even fatter cheques. My invitation said the dance practice for the ball was on the Tuesday, three days before the evening itself.

Rush-hour traffic thundered down the Cromwell Road while I ran past the domed grandeur of the Catholic Brompton Oratory down an alleyway to find the austere brickwork of its Anglican neighbour, Holy Trinity Brompton. I hugged my coat as the wind whistled past its shadowy archways, and eventually I found the hall: a modern, rectangular construction. I pushed open its squeaky wooden door. Inside, dozens of guests were already gathered, talking eagerly, many of them in Russian;

some had an exotic, Slav look about them, with bleached blonde hair and aquiline noses. I hesitated, wondering whether I should really give this a miss, when I was approached by a very tall handsome man with tousled dark hair and grey-green eyes. He emanated geniality and a slight air of melancholy as he offered me a drink. 'Something soft,' I said, nervous about my ability to follow dance steps at the best of times, let alone under the influence of alcohol.

'You'd better have a vodka then!' His smile was bewitching. I couldn't argue. This was clearly a ridiculous thing to be doing, so I might as well not worry about making a complete fool of myself.

The compère clapped his hands and called for quiet. Some jaunty Strauss music rang out of his tape machine while he demonstrated the steps of the polka. Soon we all followed, bumping into each other like dodgems. The mazurka involved some strange leg waving with a little hop, and then there was a leisurely waltz, a Chopin polonaise, and the chaotic helter-skelter of the gallop. I tried not to look at the dark-haired stranger, but caught the odd glimpse as he whisked a partner round the room. I couldn't even remember his name and knew nothing about him. He was going to remain a mystery, because I had to leave the dance practice early to go out to dinner.

....

That had been the night before and now I was heading for Sri Lanka. By the next evening, Thursday, we had to have a piece ready for the 'Six O'Clock News' in London. The ball was on the Friday, so I was certainly going to miss it. I berated myself for dwelling on the sorry state of my social life when there was an important story to report on. The *London Evening Standard* made grim reading:

> A suicide bomber drove a truck full of explosives into Sri Lanka's Central Bank ... High rise buildings burst into flames and the business district was thrown into chaos as raging fires prevented rescuers from reaching the heart of the carnage ... Dozens of people were trapped on top of burning buildings, waving for help ... Thick black smoke rose over the city ...

The attack was in revenge for the Sri Lankan military capturing the Tamil stronghold in the north, Jaffna. The Tamil Tiger rebels wanted an independent state and they were ready to die for their cause, perfecting the art of suicide bombing.

....

We arrived into the steamy heat of Colombo, and instantly it felt familiar; I was used to landing in a hot, chaotic place after a night flight and starting to work immediately. We rushed to the scene of the bombing. The police had cordoned off the devastation; the once-gleaming façade of the Central Bank tower block had collapsed. Its concrete floors were bent and broken, jutting out into the street above a sea of shattered glass. The whole street was covered with layers of debris, while smoke was still emerging from the blackened buildings. The skeleton of a car was lifted onto a pick-up truck as the painful clear up began. We spoke to one desperate woman who still couldn't find her sister-in-law but was barred by the police from entering the area. Another man bemoaned the loss of life and the impact on Sri Lanka's shaky economy. Then we headed for the nearest hospital to find it overflowing with the injured who were waiting on trolleys in the corridors. There was a noticeboard with lists of names of those who worked in the Central Bank; friends and relatives crowded around it waiting for news. We had a five-hour head-start on London, which gave us time to finish filming, editing and arguing with the surly guards at the government-run TV station and still make our deadline.

By now it was past midnight and, too exhausted to eat, I picked at the remaining curries in the hotel buffet, thinking about the wrecked lives in this futile civil war and wondering whether telling the world about such atrocities would ever make them any less likely to occur. My job depended on war and poverty, killing and misery, and I saw no end to the suffering. I was beginning to feel a pull back to another world, the world of marriage, families, children, domestic routine; a world that up until now had always appeared unbearably conventional and dull as I walked this high wire of global drama and tragedy. I felt a passing regret that I would now miss the Russian Ball that was going to take place in just a few hours time, over 5,000 miles from where I was sitting.

'Why not see if you can get released from the story and fly back? It's probably only going to run for one day anyway.' Tony was still incredibly perky after our gruelling day, and full of bright ideas. He was right. This kind of event, although huge here, would get little follow-up on our national bulletins, and other correspondents were now flying in anyway. 'Or you could spend the weekend watching developments from a nice sandy beach!' Now, that was tempting, and I could research stories for my brief: the sex trade, the current refugee crisis triggered by the war – there were any number of topics that needed investigating here.

I walked back to my room, to the debris of a frantic day: notebooks scattered on the table, sweaty cotton trousers and shirt in a tired heap on the floor with the remaining contents of my suitcase spilling out after my frantic search for contact lenses. I sat on the quilted bedcover and picked up the phone. 'Hello, I'm sorry – would it be all right if I come back to London?' I winced with embarrassment as this was definitely not the way to impress one's boss nor get on in journalism. It's a profession where enthusiasm and dedication are taken for granted.

'Well, if you really want to,' Vin said, obviously puzzled by my eagerness to return; most correspondents were hungry for the next story.

I dialled our travel agent. 'What time is the next flight to Heathrow?'

'At 6 a.m., Kuwait Air,' he said.

It was now 2.30 a.m.; I quickly packed and headed for the door, glancing back at the inviting bed I hadn't had time to use. The taxi took me straight to Bandaranaike airport, where I joined the long lines of Sri Lankan domestic servants checking into the London flight, going via Kuwait City. A second night in succession on a plane; this was clearly a kind of madness.

....

From the warmth and bright colours of Colombo I arrived into overcast winter skies over Heathrow – but the blanket of grey couldn't dampen my spirits. I raced home, threw on a 1930s black lacy dress – a relic of the Chelsea antique market – flung around it my grandmother's black silk shawl, and headed for the Café Royal in Regent Street looking like a babushka from the Russian backwoods. This was hardly the outfit to endear me to a new social circle, but at least, I thought, 'I am here'.

I was out of breath as I walked into the opulent ballroom, dripping with chandeliers and gilt carvings. I was greeted with a deep bow by one of Leo Tolstoy's descendants, Count Tolstoy, along with an array of other members of the Russian nobility, and had to pinch myself. I felt a complete stranger in this world and searched the sea of crinoline and cleavages to find my host. I squeezed past women in empire-line frocks with tiaras nestling into their perms; some fluttered their fans as they chatted to groups of men in Napoleonic uniform. Others held exotic, colourful masks over their faces, a token gesture towards the Diaghilev theme.

Luckily I was soon accosted by a wide, beaming woman whose long curls were tucked neatly behind her head in a bun sown up with pearls: 'I've just been to Russia to research a film about tattoos — absolutely fascinating — did you know it's a whole art form over there?' Before I could reply she waved her fan in the air as she spotted someone on the other side of the room. Taking my elbow firmly in her hand she hissed in my ear, 'Come and meet the most eligible bachelor here!'

I instantly recognised my dark-haired stranger — now in a bright red Cossack outfit with gold buttons. 'Shall we dance?' he said. I was struck again by his irresistible warm smile and twinkling eyes. I'd been catapulted straight from civil war in Sri Lanka to this other universe in a few hours, and now I was truly in culture shock. I tried to get a grip on the situation, to muse on the role of free will and fate, feeling intoxicated by a mixture of elation and jet lag, but any deep thoughts evaporated as Gerald hurled me round the room so fast that all I could focus on was trying not to twist my ankle.

....

I survived the polka, and subsequent encounters with Gerald. In fact our romance bounded on with more reckless dancing and numerous trips up and down Portobello Market. He knew virtually every stallholder in the area and took great pains to show me where I could buy second-hand clothes, books and tapes. He would rally a motley collection of opera singers, pianists, jazz musicians and Celtic banjo players, as well as rowdy rugby supporters revelling at the end of a good match, for his evenings of improvised music-making. Gerald was truly at the centre of a 'world wide web' and, after he showed me round the Travel Bookshop, we soon began our own *Notting Hill* romance long before Hugh Grant splashed orange juice over Julia Roberts.

We even survived our first rainy bank-holiday weekend away together in Cornwall. As we sat consoling ourselves about the weather with yet another portion of fish and chips, he said, 'I've won a free holiday. Would you like to come?' I had an image of a free weekend in a country hotel, or perhaps even Paris. 'It's to the country that had the best performing stock-market of 1994,' he continued.

I searched through my hazy knowledge of financial markets, and couldn't think ... 'Germany?'

'No.'

'Er, the US?'

'No.'

'OK, South Korea?'

'No, Brazil! All flights paid for. I won it in an *Observer* newspaper competition about a year ago, and haven't had anyone to take, so I just hung onto it until now.'

August came and we flew to Rio. We travelled up to Salvador, and the heartland of Brazilian salsa, before retreating south again to the tropical marshland of the Pantanal where we watched the loping gait of the capybara, a kind of giant cuddly water rat. We arranged for our canoe to be towed upriver; as we glided silently back down with the current, sleepy alligators caught unawares exploded out of the reeds and dived under our boat. Flocks of startled white egrets swirled like clouds round their nests and when we fished, our bait was gobbled by voracious piranha. Our adventures culminated beside the spectacular Iguaçu waterfalls, the widest in the world, where the Iguaçu River drops into a deep canyon. As we stood on a platform overlooking the plunging, churning falls, the air heavy with the sweet smell of jasmine, Gerald said, 'Will you carry me?'

It seemed a reasonable enough request after our large dinner washed down with plenty of cheap Chilean wine. Then it dawned on me that against the loud rumble of the falls and with his heavy cold he might have said, 'will you marry me?' I didn't bother to ask for clarification, telling myself that either way, the answer had to be, 'Yes!'

The next day we fished on the great Parana River, drifting near the concrete suspension bridge that links Brazil to Paraguay. I looked up from our little rowing boat to the place where, a year earlier, I had made a documentary about the trafficking of Brazilian babies to Paraguay, many of whom were adopted by unsuspecting couples from abroad. I could see the spot where we had struggled to film in the strong winds. I never thought then that I would be back in such different circumstances, nor that the currents of fate that were now sweeping me along would make that experience so important, influencing me eastwards, towards another continent many years later.

....

The land was in mourning. Skeletons of trees scratched the sky; burnt logs covered the blackened earth. I could see forest fires like blazing dots on the horizon. There was a constant smell of burning. At four in the afternoon the hazy red sun disappeared behind clouds of smoke. This was the heart of the Amazon basin and nowhere could have felt further from the intoxicating romance of our holiday. Gerald had gone home and I had stayed on to make a documentary about the landless peasants who were squatting on the corners of vast cattle-farming estates. Brazil has the most unequal distribution of land in the world, with 1 per cent of the population owning half of the country's productive land.

Tree-burning was the fallout from this fierce class 'war'. Both peasants and ranchers were setting light to the forest to clear the land for grazing or growing crops, encouraged by a bizarre government ruling which awarded land to those using it most productively. Dozens of peasants had been killed in clashes with police, while ranchers on their fine chestnut horses, herding their creamy-coated, long-horned cattle, lived in fear of a popular revolution.

We would prise ourselves out of bed at five every morning and drive over dusty, red-earth roads to the malaria-ridden camps, packed with ex-goldmine workers and others desperate for a living. Some were inspired by high ideals, others by the simple lure of a piece of land. A young woman we met had fled her life as a maid to a rich family to join this 'revolution'.

'The land should be divided as Christ did with the bread,' she argued, sitting on a log beside her simple wooden hut. Her leader was a man who flitted from hideout to hideout in the forest, carrying with him a bright red typewriter and pictures of his heroes Chairman Mao and Che Guevara. Giving the voiceless, like this young woman, a chance to speak to millions round the world was hugely satisfying. The discomfort and the sweat had to be worth it, even though it was hard to create a sense of real drama when the squatters took long siestas in their hammocks and displayed a very Brazilian-style good humour at their plight.

The hot days passed at a tortoise's pace. There were no phones, and I had no way of speaking to Gerald. As I lay sleepless in my simple bedroom, with its one fluorescent light in the ceiling, I began to wonder if our time together was just a dream. My confidence was withering like the plant life around me. Gerald had no doubt arrived home and by now had changed his mind. Who would want to marry someone who spent so much of her life on the road? But to understand a story from the inside needed weeks like this, observing day after day the squalor that so many people endured: it couldn't be done with a fleeting visit. Men could often get away with this lifestyle, but it seemed that most female television foreign correspondents were single; hardly any had children. I had spent years building experience and knowledge of issues that I thought really mattered, yet now I could feel my inner magnet switching poles. It had been wavering already: the commitment required for intense, sometimes harrowing, stories was taking its toll, but now homesickness was seriously beginning to outweigh the burning desire for adventure. Here, amongst the dregs of Brazil's gold rush, I was discovering that

© Emily Buchanan

The burning forests of the Amazon.

© Emily Buchanan

... where ranchers were rallying against the landless.

for me in-depth journalism and lasting romance, like oil and vinegar, just didn't mix.

....

By the following summer Gerald and I were married. The hawthorn hedges were in full bloom, the pheasants and rabbits cavorted in the grass verges as my uncle accompanied me to St Catharine's Church in Chipping Campden. The golden Cotswold stone glowed in the afternoon sun, while the priest inside asked God to bless us with children. I couldn't imagine otherwise; surely this was a match that fate decreed. Certainly, if goodwill alone could create offspring we would have a tribe of them. Our friends and family were effusive, perhaps displaying that extra joy and relief when people, who are not in their first flush of youth, finally marry. I still had to pinch myself that this happiness was really mine as we drank our toasts, ate and danced into the night in the cavernous fourteenth-century tithe barn at Stanway House.

Nature smiled on us the next day as guests teamed up to play cricket in brilliant sunshine. I glanced at the thatched pavilion designed by the author of *Peter Pan*, J. M. Barrie. He'd written about a boy who didn't want to grow up, and I too would have been happy that day for time to have stood still. Life was perfect. This was how fairy tales should end: and they lived happily ever after.

....

Not for us. There was to be a long and rather tortuous epilogue.

Four months after the wedding, I discovered I was pregnant. 'That was easy,' I thought, as the joy of it sunk in, and I felt inner bubbles of satisfaction. I pored over 'Mother and Baby' books, charting the size of the foetus, making guesses as to how many centimetres long this little person inside me would be. I continued to work, haloed in the warm glow of expectant motherhood, and hoping I wouldn't have to travel anywhere soon. I enjoyed being pregnant; it had such a sense of purpose and inevitability about it. Also gestation was so easy and so much the opposite of my working life; I didn't have to make phone calls, organise anything nor fly thousands of miles to achieve it. Fertilisation, hormones, cell division, chromosomes, they were brilliantly programmed to know what to do. I could become just like any other mammal and let the miracle of life take over.

Then, one Friday, I was cycling home and felt suddenly exhausted and depressed. I couldn't explain it. That evening was the annual dinner for ex-pupils of Stonyhurst College, Gerald's old boarding school in Lancashire. I dressed up to go, feeling strangely numb. I couldn't concentrate on the conversation or the canapés, and as I was being introduced to yet another long lost pal whose name I was struggling to retain, I suddenly felt a twinge of pain; I was starting to bleed. I excused myself and headed for the toilet. There was a spot of blood which I stared at in disbelief. After the drinks, the speeches and the dinner all ended, we went home and I checked again. There was no more. As we chatted about the evening, I told Gerald I was a little worried about the pregnancy, but we agreed that some rest would set things right.

At three in the morning I was woken by severe cramps in my abdomen, like period pains, but exacerbated by a rush of anxiety and fear. I ran to the bathroom to find the bleeding had increased, and there were even tiny clots. I started to panic and woke Gerald. He tried to calm me and encouraged me to lie down and keep still, as we hoped that with every second that passed the blood would stop flowing, that my body would go back to how it had been before. This brilliantly engineered biological process had suddenly stalled and I had no idea how to restart it. I lay under the blankets, closed my eyes and prayed that the next day this would all seem like a bad dream. Eventually I managed to sleep, fitfully, and in the morning I found the bleeding had stopped.

....

Daylight, and the familiar plain grey façade of Queen Charlotte's Hospital in Chiswick was reassuring. I had driven past it countless times, thinking of the thousands of babies who had been born here; I myself had been one of them. My mother's blood group was rhesus negative and to prevent risk to my life, I had to have all my blood changed at birth. As I walked the pale yellow corridors past the maternity wards I was sure that today, nearly forty years later, their expert teams of gynaecologists would be able to explain what had happened to my baby and be able to help a threatened life.

The doctor went over and over my abdomen with the scanner, saying he could detect a tiny foetus but couldn't see any activity, and no heartbeat. Then, in that gentle voice which medics seem to reserve for bad news, he said, 'I'm sorry to tell you that you aren't pregnant any more.'

I lay on the treatment couch staring at the screen. The black hole where a baby should have been mocked me. Something had stopped gestation in its tracks; it was as if God had slammed on the brakes, calling a halt to this tiny life. I thought of all my excitement over his or her future, my optimism at the idea of having a baby. How absurd it seemed now. I was back to square one.

I was admitted for a d. and c., a routine operation to clean out the womb. The anaesthetic felt like a welcome drug. Thankfully they kept the miscarriage patients on a different floor from the maternity ward: two worlds, the miserable and the deliriously happy just a short lift ride from each other. The nurse explained, 'It's often the body's way of getting rid of a child who isn't quite right, it's very common, one in four pregnancies end in miscarriage. You've just been unlucky.'

I kept asking myself why it happened. I was just 39: old, yes, but not too old for children. I'd never smoked, nor drunk myself into oblivion. Yet as much as I tried to rationalise that this was just a biological event out of my control, I still felt totally responsible. I had lost a baby, and somehow it must be my fault. I had let Gerald down, so I was not only leading a bizarre life of overseas travel, but I wasn't really a real woman after all. If I had been just tired from housework and looking after children, that might have felt more acceptable, but the fact that my job was demanding, and that I had chosen it, made me feel even more guilty.

The trouble with miscarriages is that without a medical explanation, any number of theories abound. Perhaps I hadn't followed the perfect pre-conception diet closely enough, had not taken the right vitamins or meditated to calm my spirits. I arrived home and tossed aside those half-read books with their pictures of serene smiling pregnant mothers enjoying their latest yoga pose. One was called *Taking Charge of your Fertility*, as if I could take charge of anything. I felt powerless and utterly out of control. Perhaps if I had avoided every risk factor, things would have been different, but my whole life was, according to these books, a risk factor: looking at VDUs, stress, pollution, in fact every aspect of urban living. It was a wonder that any babies were born in London at all.

I inwardly rebelled against the supposition that I could make myself perfect in order to be a mother. It was surely absurd to think that the small amount of stress I experienced in my affluent, secure, peaceful nation with its ample supplies of food could be such a killer. There were millions of women around the world living on the very edge of survival. I thought back to those who, even under extreme duress in refugee camps, seemed to be able to have children. In Goma, Zaire, I had spoken to mothers who'd been driven out of Rwanda after the genocide there, and were now living on

© Bhasker Solanki

The Goma refugee camp.

aid-agency rations, enduring intimidation and rape by the murderous militias crowded in with them. They were getting pregnant in large numbers, and some were even rejecting their babies. An Italian sanitation company had discovered unwanted newborns thrown down the mobile latrines. It was one of the most depressing and stressful places I'd ever seen, and yet human biology seemed remarkably unaffected.

In my search for an explanation, I wondered if my baby had died because it had been conceived shortly after returning from a couple of weeks examining rampant tuberculosis in Siberian prisons. The remote gulag near a town called Minsk held 2,000 prisoners suffering from TB and the sporadic use of antibiotics meant that some men there had the drug-resistant strain of the disease. Petty thieves found their brief punishment turned into a life sentence; their drawn, blank faces had the look of the doomed as they lay coughing in their dilapidated, overcrowded dormitories.

It had been disturbing, but I had also felt very inspired by the local army doctor who dedicated her life to treating them, putting herself at risk every day from the disease. Having lost my suitcase somewhere between London and Novosibirsk, this lieutenant colonel and one-time enemy of the West had not only put us up in her small flat, but lent me her spare clothes, even her underwear. I asked her why she didn't just get a more comfortable job in Moscow. 'I can't, I must stay here, I love my patients, and they need me,' she had said. With women like that in the world, I couldn't believe I was so weak that I had to put my feet up, do yoga and take buckets of vitamins the moment I got pregnant.

I found myself weeping sporadically. Everywhere I looked calm, pregnant women smiled contentedly. They seemed to ridicule me with their swollen bellies: 'Look what I can do, and you can't.' I tried to avoid them, as they unwittingly turned the knife in my grief.

Even so, a few days after the operation Gerald and I visited Xiaodi, a Chinese friend. She had just had a baby and was still in hospital. I made myself go, even though I privately dreaded it. We walked into the ward, and I sat down on the bed, looking down at the baby's pink, squashed-up face. 'How lovely she is,' I said. 'I'm so happy for you.' Her tiny hand curled round my finger, and she moved her head a little from side to side. She was gorgeous, but then I couldn't see her anymore. I blinked and my tears fell on her soft blanket. Her mother glowed with happiness. I ran out, gasping for breath.

A few days later an old friend wrote me a card: 'I am pleased to announce the birth of my honeymoon baby.' By then, I wasn't even able to write back. My grief was turning into a meanness of spirit, I was angry and insanely jealous.

'Give up your job,' became a refrain from many well-meaning friends. The trouble was that my job now felt like a refuge. It was a relief to be able to throw myself back into the big issues that belittled my own problems.

....

So I went back to work and buried myself in the widespread and largely invisible crisis of malnourishment in children across the world. UNICEF was highlighting how half the 12 million child deaths a year in the world were just due to a lack of food. Some former Soviet republics were discovering severe shortages for the first time in decades. Moscow used to ensure everyone had enough to eat but now outlying republics, like Kyrgyzstan, were left to fend for themselves. Once it had

Scandinavian standards of social care, but without the umbilical cord to Moscow it was struggling to feed its population.

The dawn sun gave a pink and mauve glow to the Tien Shan peaks; just looking at their staggering beauty felt cleansing. We drove away from the capital, Bishkek, passing an Arctic fox, a solitary buzzard, and a herd of long-haired chestnut horses pawing the snow for food. A farmer with a ruddy Oriental face, woollen coat and fur hat trotted by on his shaggy pony, his boots brushing the snowdrifts. We saw a hillside on which a vast swastika design stood out entirely made of fir trees; it had been planted as a practical joke by a German prisoner of war in the 1940s. He'd been sent out to plant the trees as a punishment, but no one at the time had noticed the shape he had made until long after the war when the trees had grown

© Emily Buchanan

Horseman in the Tien Shan Mountains.

© Emily Buchanan

Meagre supplies in the market, Kyrgyzstan.

up. At the end of a deep gorge we were greeted by a giant wrought-iron silhouette of Lenin's head perched on top of a rock. The faster Kyrgyzstan moved to a market economy, the less likely it seemed that anyone wanted to take it down. People talked longingly about the past, showing no desire to obliterate an era when at least they had had enough to eat.

Naryn Town – and its standardised, Soviet-style blocks of flats – was crammed into the flat ground between the mountains. Doctors from the local hospital, who routinely saw babies born underweight, welcomed us. In spite of the local shortages, they entertained us with a huge meal of roast yak, ham, potatoes and Russian salad, washed down with copious amounts of vodka. Then, with both the light and our energies fading, we visited the chief physician of the region. He recited a litany of depressing figures − 60 per cent unemployment, 60 per cent of women with anaemia, less than half the funds needed coming from the government, 5 hours a day with no electricity ... and as his voice carried on the room grew steadily darker. Soon he was almost invisible behind his large desk. There was no power that day; the temperature outside was plummeting and an icy wind whistled under his door.

It was −20 °C as we climbed the next morning towards the worst-hit villages at 4,000 metres, just a few miles from the Chinese border. Eki-Naryn was perched on steep, snow-covered slopes. At first there were no obvious signs of hunger: horses were pulling carts heavily laden with straw, children were tobogganing before they ran into school. Two rosy-cheeked boys took us to their simple wooden house, strewn inside with brightly woven carpets. They and their five brothers and sisters lived on bread, noodles, potatoes and buckets of tea. Fruit and vegetables were too expensive to buy, especially during the seven months of winter. Their father, wearing his traditional black fur hat even indoors, complained that they were killing their cattle one by one just to survive.

Down the mountain, back in Naryn Town, hospital health workers showed us the results of this diet every day: people lacked energy and were unmotivated, babies were born premature, underweight and anaemic, and children became stunted mentally and physically. In the maternity ward there was no joy. Mothers and their babies looked listless, their skin a sickly yellow from anaemia. One of the doctors swaddled a scraggy newborn girl until she was wrapped up tight like a parcel. My eyes filled with tears of regret and longing. Then I thought of the plump, well-fed babies in the West and our obsession with healthy diets for pregnant mothers. These listless women were powerless to take 'ten steps to the perfect pregnancy', too poor for 'the optimum pre-conception diet'. They were lucky if they had the strength to walk outside for the vital firewood needed for heating and cooking. What's more, no one told them to give up their job, when their job was survival.

....

In the end I did give up my job; at least, I gave up the Developing World brief to cover Religious Affairs instead. The issues could be addressed closer to home and I could see that interviewing vicars in the Home Counties would be a more sensible and safer option than hurling myself to the four corners of the globe.

It seemed that God and my body agreed. After a few weeks of immersing myself in a colourful array of beliefs, I found I was pregnant again. It was Easter; the sense of new life was everywhere, there was even the signing of the Good Friday peace agreement in Northern Ireland. Perhaps this time I was allowed to be a little optimistic.

On my way to work, the rays of morning sun lit up the blue ceanothus buds and the daffodils, making the normally drab Shepherd's Bush Green look beautiful. Once a place where farmers used to bring their sheep to graze on the way to Smithfield Market from the West Country, now it was blighted by a constant stream of heavy traffic churning and jostling for position before heading off across West London. As I walked into the circular sixties structure of Television Centre, I felt unusually light-hearted and happy. I had a job more suited to a settled life, and was feeling well.

I greeted Ian O'Reilly, my friend and producer, and we sat down to finalise plans for a feature for the 'Nine O'Clock

News' about the future of the Catholic Church in Ireland. As we flipped through our itinerary, I felt something, a small discharge. My stomach tightened like a vice, I felt sick, and this was no morning sickness – I actually enjoyed morning sickness, seeing in the discomfort a sign that I was healthily pregnant. No, this was pure nerves. I stared at the computer screen, attempting by sheer willpower to stop the bleeding. It worked, there was no more.

The next day we were on a plane to Knock, the shrine in the west of Ireland that was attracting 1.5 million pilgrims a year – and where I hoped that a few well-placed prayers might also keep my baby alive. Knock was the only parish in the country where attendance at weekly mass was rising. It was buoyed up by the legend that a 120 years ago on a wet Thursday evening, the Virgin Mary, kneeling in prayer and clothed in white robes with a brilliant crown on her head, had appeared to a small group of worshippers. They had watched the apparition for two hours, reciting the Rosary. I looked at the vast glass windows of the impersonal modern basilica and whispered, 'If there really was a vision of the Virgin and if she has any power, let her help me keep my child. Fruit of thy womb, Jesus ...' The words of the Creed kept going over and over in my mind. What of the fruit of my womb? Catholicism was so steeped in imagery of procreation. The big questions always seemed to be about contraception and abortion. Did it have anything to say about lives that wondered whether to exist or not, babies that toyed with life, who teased their mothers, 'Here I am ... for a little bit – but I won't be staying long?' I tried to stay calm, worrying that worrying could harm the baby.

This was a part of Ireland soaked in religious belief. Just a few years before a couple of girls had sworn they'd seen the

Virgin Mary on top of a hedge as they walked home from school. A small shrine had sprung up, and now there was a steady stream of visitors. Surely if anywhere was going to have a healing effect this would be it.

. . . .

Back in London, I was relieved to find there were no more adverse symptoms and I cultivated my comforting sensation of morning sickness. I kept looking at my tummy hoping that it was actually growing, that the bulge was due to the presence of a child, not to too much Irish black pudding. Of course the foetus would only have been a few centimetres long and hardly likely to influence the swelling of my abdomen. I even started eating more desserts just to make sure that whatever happened my stomach would appear more rounded.

Then it was time for my first check-up. The gynaecologist peered at the ultrasound screen. There was a long silence and eventually he said, 'We just can't tell, we'll have to give you a blood test to see which way your hormones are going. In ten days you can come back and then we'll know for sure.'

Ten days of not knowing. This was ridiculous. Ten days of wondering whether there was life or not inside, of not saying anything to people I worked with, pretending I felt fine.

After ten days they took more blood, and when I returned to get the results, the answer was stark. The tests showed my hormone levels were dropping: that was the death knell for my child. It was final, there was no pregnancy, and another d. and c. had to be booked in the next day. I was stunned. How often was I going to fail? Why couldn't I do the simplest thing? I could feel myself going into a downward, self-destructive spiral.

Ian called. He was in a car on his way home from the airport after filming in Kazakhstan. 'Hello, how are things? We've just had a really interesting trip ...'

I could hardly speak. 'I've just had a miscarriage, I'm devastated.'

'Oh, I'm so sorry ...' We talked for a while, and then he began to tell me what he'd just been filming. 'A few days ago we were in a hospital in Aralsk, it's right beside the Aral Sea, at least what was the Aral Sea, because now the water is sixty miles from where it once was. The Soviets diverted the water to grow cotton, they drenched the earth with chemicals and fertilisers and now the whole area's an environmental disaster. Toxic dust clouds swirl around infecting the local people. We've just been talking to women waiting to give birth. One in four babies who are actually born die, and the rate of miscarriages is astronomical. One woman we interviewed said "this is my ninth pregnancy, and I have yet to give birth".' Ian went on to say how the community's body and soul were being slowly destroyed.

I thought of how I was feeling after just two miscarriages, living my comfortable life in London. I felt embarrassed at my level of despair when there were women whose bodies were being eaten away by poison. There's nothing like a dose of global perspective at the right moment.

. . . .

That weekend Gerald and I drove through the winding, leafy roads of south London to a dinner party with friends whom we'd last seen when we were both newly engaged. They were now married, had a lovely little girl and boy, and they naturally glowed with happiness and contentment: 'Come and look at our new garden design, the boards will make it safe for the children, and we've built in a sandpit as well!' There was the pretty playroom stacked with toys, the games that littered the living room floor.

'How wonderful it looks,' I said, trying to sound enthusiastic. I put on a fixed smile as I was shown round the house.

The doorbell rang and other guests arrived. A round husband and his wafer-thin wife appeared, also burning bright with parental pride. 'It's so lovely how children bring such an extra dimension to one's life, don't you agree?' said round husband.

I kept my smile firmly on. 'Yes, I suppose they do.' We sat down and I was grateful to be sipping the pumpkin soup, its warmth was delicious.

The conversation carried on. 'I never thought I'd want to rush home from work and see my children. I used to be such a workaholic, it's just amazing. And there's nothing like a walk in the park on a Sunday with them. It's just such fun!' our host said, grinning broadly, and looking misty-eyed into the distance.

I found myself lapsing into silence. I was being eclipsed by all this joy, and I felt small, ragged, sour and inadequate. How could I pierce this bubble of happiness with my sad little tale?

The thin mother waxed on about how easy her pregnancy had been. 'Why do women make such a fuss about being pregnant? Nothing could be easier. All that sighing and panting that they do, honestly it's just for effect!'

'Really, is that right?' I nodded in acquiescence, crushed by the easy confidence of a successfully completed conception. I felt my soul shrinking inside, reflecting my limp, empty womb. It didn't seem to matter that I had made a dozen documentaries and learnt so much; ultimately I was a non-woman, reproductively inert, and without any apparent value in this strange parallel economy. Here I felt the currency was children, and the more you had the wealthier you were perceived to be. Those without children were poorer and had to be gently pitied.

I excused myself to go to the toilet, and stared with horror into the mirror as my eyes overflowed. My upper lip was going pink, and I wondered how I was going to organise a dignified re-entry into the dinner party. Holding in the grief was making me feel faint, but I couldn't bring myself to raise the subject at table because I knew the floodgates would open. I pushed the emotion down with the brute force of a jackboot and returned to the party. I sniffed, complaining of a bit of hay fever, and finished my soup. The roast pork was a comfort, as were the several helpings of mashed potatoes. Maybe I should have been an actress; I don't think anyone suspected a thing.

'Now, my little Arabella has just auditioned for a part in *Harry Potter*, I wonder if she'll get it.'

'I wonder. It must be very competitive.'

'She's so natural, you see, that's what they like, so we're pretty confident. The school has been marvellous about it, and says she can have the time off if she needs to.'

'That's great ...'

'Of course she's ahead with her schoolwork too, so they aren't worried. As long as she does enough work before her entrance exam for St Paul's, that's all I'm worried about.' St Paul's is a top London school that has become a byword for achievement, as much for the parents as for its pupils.

'I'm sure she'll do very well.' I heaped another spoonful of lemon cheesecake onto my plate, feeling better at each mouthful. My emotional tide was slowly subsiding, and I even managed a genuine smile at the enchanting exploits of little Arabella. I hoped I wasn't going to become bitter and twisted and unable to enjoy parents' conversation. Yet I saw dinner parties stretching out into the future like minefields where I was going to need body armour. It had been hard enough returning from some war-torn place and reinserting myself into London middle-class preoccupations, but now even my attempts at a 'normal' life were making me feel as distant from these people as if they came from a far-off country.

By the end of the evening we were emotionally drained. Even the ever-stoic Gerald said it was tough, and we were relieved to be out of that hothouse of family bliss. No one there knew about the miscarriages, so I couldn't blame them, but even so I felt nauseated by their air of smugness. Giving birth to children was a gift from God and biology, so why was it seen as such a personal achievement?

....

I began to tell myself that *not* having children was just fine. Perhaps I should join the ranks of the 'child free' and just enjoy it. But the losses were gnawing into me, eating away any sense I had of my own value. Even though childlessness had been built into humanity, and must therefore have had a useful function since the dawn of time, I still felt worthless. I had tried and failed, which was worse than deciding not to have children. I looked enviously at friends who had made the decision to remain without offspring, feeling almost as jealous of them as I did of the pregnant ones.

I subscribed to the Miscarriage Association, and when their journal fell through the letterbox, I found grains of comfort in dwelling on the misery of other mothers. I began to realise I'd been lucky; I could have lost the baby so much later and then the pain would have been multiplied. There were stories of babies born only a few weeks too early, whose mothers had put the foetus in a tiny grave, and still visited it year after year. My little babies were barely more than a speck inside a blood clot, so they had just gone out with the medical waste. I recalled eyeing the hospital bins at Queen Charlotte's with a combination of suspicion and horror.

Gerald remained firmly optimistic that we would eventually have a family. And I lost count of the times we were told 'it's all very natural'. I read the book by the country's leading expert on miscarriages, Professor Lesley Regan from St Mary's Hospital in London, and she was also full of reassuring statistics. She wrote that only 2 per cent of women have a couple of miscarriages in a row. And the chance of then having a third is minute. Most women who have recurrent miscarriages go on to have a healthy child, and until I had a third miscarriage, the doctors could offer no solutions.

By the end of the year, I found out I was pregnant again. This time I looked on the blue line of the pregnancy test with deep suspicion. I tried to ignore it, and as the weeks went by, kept my hopes firmly in check. 'I'm not interested until you stick around for at least three months,' I snapped at my only-too-flat stomach, terrified of the emotional let-down if I lost another child.

....

I was planning a story in Thailand about how cooperation between Catholics and Buddhists was helping to fight HIV infection, and this time Gerald was free to come too. Thailand was then a model for how to fight AIDS, and the Catholic aid agency, CAFOD, had researched the way new cooperation between priests and Buddhist monks was transforming results.

In the lush hill country of Phayao province in northern Thailand, the ravages of HIV were at their peak. Villages were being torn apart as parents died leaving grandparents and children to fend for themselves; there was a funeral every day in some communities. Sister Mercedes Placino, a dynamic nun from the Daughters of Charity, took us to one small village where AIDS stalked like the Plague. She opened up a hand-drawn plan of the village, showing each household that was affected marked with a red dot; the map was littered with them. We went to one small wooden house where a skeletally thin woman lay on a mattress. Her husband was already dead, victim of the prevailing habit of visiting prostitutes. Her gaunt face was covered in tears while her twelve-year-old son tried in vain to interest her in a bowl of watery rice. He was about to join the ranks of Thailand's 80,000 AIDS orphans. I looked at him staring at his dying mother; it's a sight that will haunt me forever. The only sound was the woman's weak cough and a fly buzzing by the small window. The room was so quiet, yet screaming with tragedy. Sister Mercedes told us that the village elders were in despair: 'There is too much loss and no one knows how to solve it.'

We drove to the nearby Buddhist temple to see the front line of the fightback. In its spacious grounds a little hut now housed a medical centre, where a nurse was handing out condoms to anyone who turned up, even if they were just complaining of a headache. The monks outside continued their meditative walk, while the smiling golden Buddhas seemed to see the irony of their hallowed ground being used to provide sex education. This initiative was knocking down the local infection rates dramatically. It was all being cleverly organised at arm's length by an independent-minded Catholic priest, though he was forbidden by the Church's policy from advocating the use of condoms. I loved ingenuity like this, everyone working around the dogma for the good of the local population. In fact I was becoming increasingly attracted to stories in the developing world which showed ingenious solutions to intractable problems.

I too began to think outside the tramlines of my own biological pregnancy. I was pregnant, but this next one could fail too. Perhaps we should reach out to a child abroad, even from a place like this.

Sister Mercedes took us to see some of the orphaned children in her care; they ran up to us, showering us with their enchanting smiles while we were told of their tragic stories. Their parents had died from AIDS and many were passing time until they were old enough to earn their own living. One ten-year-old girl took my hand and told me that her mother was in prison for possession of heroin, and as she had also been infected with HIV she might never come out. I wanted to take that girl home there and then.

....

We travelled on to Sydney where I was to get my first check-up of the pregnancy. New Year's Eve was a blaze of fireworks over the harbour; Gerald and I hugged each other and fizzed with high expectations for 1999. The next day I edited the piece about Thailand's AIDS crisis and fed it to London where it ran that night on the 'Nine O'Clock News'. I was happy that editors still liked my obscure stories, and the following morning

I had a spring in my step as I entered the courtyard of the King George V Hospital for Women.

The ultrasound soon put an end to my elation.

'There's no foetus there,' the young Californian woman doctor explained. 'Just a "yolk" and empty space around it. We can offer you a d. and c. tomorrow if you like.' Just like that. My carefully restrained but secretly nurtured hopes fell clattering to the floor. Perhaps I was only ever to have phantom pregnancies.

Gerald picked me up after the operation and we went for a short walk along the harbour; the same place where just days earlier we had watched the fireworks with such an imminent sense of new beginnings. The sky was bright blue, the sea perfect, but I felt inwardly wounded and exhausted. The whole business of having our own biological child was becoming an emotional roller coaster and I wanted to get off now. No more of these false hopes, these hints of life that shone briefly and then were snuffed out at the first whiff of an ultrasound machine.

'Shall we adopt?' I said. 'What do you think? Or at least let's start to look into it.'

'Of course,' replied Gerald, the emotional rock as ever, offering a rescuing hand as my soul was being dragged under by my plummeting hormones.

Chapter Two

The Long March to Motherhood

The No. 23 bus lurched forwards, its exhaust rattling. I ran to catch up with it, springing onto the platform as it was pulling away: an element of risk about to be phased out with the shiny new vehicles and their automatic doors. For now, though, there was a touch of self-determination to this simple action, and that's just what I needed as the secret behind my mysterious biology continued to elude me.

The idea of adopting a child was taking root, but even so I still harboured hopes for the next pregnancy. I certainly hadn't got to the stage of 'accepting' my inability to have a child, which is what social workers want you to have done before adopting. 'Have you fully grieved your infertility?' was one of the earnest questions I'd heard other adoptive parents had been asked during their assessment. I didn't know what that really meant. Does grief over lost babies ever disappear? For sure, my answer was then 'no', and as for adoption, it was an idea that still felt distant and just as difficult to achieve.

The bus chuntered along Westbourne Grove, the few remaining antique shops now almost crowded out by the unstoppable momentum of 'fashion and froth' − boutiques with overpriced clothes and coffee bars for the growing numbers of tourists and young, high-earning residents − past Queensway, a Mecca for immigrant families, before we swung right towards Paddington Station.

I couldn't look at the magnificent iron-girder roof without being transported back to childhood trips, journeys by jet-black, belching steam train to a Northamptonshire village called Woodford Halse and then, after the branch line was ripped up, by new diesel engines to Banbury. Every holiday I would stay with my mother's former nanny and her carpenter husband in an idyllic village called Eydon a few miles away; it couldn't have been better named.

This kind, elderly couple were the salt of Middle England. They were called Margaret and Eric, but my two-year-old tongue could only manage Mar and Eggie and the names stuck. They became like surrogate grandparents and their rambling sandstone house next to a rick yard full of chickens, overlooking miles of rolling pastures, was my paradise. It was there that as a sheltered city kid, I learnt that milk didn't come out of bottles, nor eggs from egg-boxes. I learnt, too, those vital skills of rural life in the 1960s, how to make small knotted carpets for the Women's Institute fair, embroidered handkerchiefs, crocheted needle-holders and thick yellow sponge cakes. We cut flowers for the church, and I watched the bell-ringers rehearse, thrilled and frightened by the possibility that I could be lifted by the heavy ropes high up into the stone tower. I dug tunnels in the wood shavings which covered the floor of the carpentry workshop and listened to endless stories about the children, the 'evacuees', who stayed with the family during the war to escape the German bombing of London. Twenty years later I became another child from the capital finding a refuge in Eydon, and strangely I never for a moment missed home. If I ever thought about where I was truly happy when I was small, it was there. Even after Mar and Eggie were long dead, I still missed them terribly. Today, that safe, uncomplicated world based on the simple certainties of Sunday School seemed to belong to someone else. Here I was, in what felt like another century, on my way to St Mary's Hospital.

Now that I had endured three miscarriages, the National Health Service deemed me unfit enough to be referred to the country's leading expert, Professor Lesley Regan. I had to wait five months to see her, avoid getting pregnant and in the meantime have some investigations. It all felt unbearably slow; I needed no lessons in the fast forward of my biological clock, and was tired of those people, usually elderly women with a dozen or so grandchildren, who seemed to revel in telling women of my age, 'You'd better get on with it, tick-tock, tick-tock!'

I leapt off the tired, creaking bus and was just searching for the hospital entrance when my mobile rang. It was the news organiser at Television Centre. 'Where are you? We need you to find out what's been going on in Kosovo. You've heard about the allegations of rape, are you up to finding out if they're true or not? We need a female correspondent and a camerawoman. There's an aid flight to Tirana this afternoon.' For several days there'd been pictures of Kosovan refugees pouring out of Serbia over the border into Albania. Amidst the horror there were stories emerging of Serb soldiers raping Kosovan women. These allegations had been hotly denied.

I could feel the magnetic force of my work claiming me and taking me from this long-awaited appointment. I ran to the hospital, panted into the reception area and asked to see the nurse. I was soon shown into a small side room, where she took a blood sample; the syringe was barely out of my arm before I tore out of the treatment room, down the stairs and took a taxi home — no time for another sedate ride on the bus. My flight was leaving in three hours.

. . . .

At the Heathrow check-in desk I met up with Sue, one of the few camerawomen to work in foreign news and we both just looked at each other and raised our eyes to heaven. We were in no doubt that this was a bizarre assignment, doomed to failure — to expect deeply traumatised Muslim women to speak to foreigners about the most taboo subject in their culture was wishful thinking in the extreme. We risked becoming a laughing stock, just like the tactless British TV reporter from the 1960s who was sent to the Congo and famously shouted out, 'Has anyone here been raped and speaks English?'

The only flight into Albania was organised by aid agencies, and it was waiting on the tarmac. We climbed in to join a handful of volunteers and journalists occupying the first three rows, while all the other seats were stuffed with a couple of hundred sacks of grain donated by the World Food Programme. Each sack was the size of a person and was strapped in with its own seat belt. They sat like rows of dummies down the full length of the fuselage, their jagged tops just peeking above the level of the seats.

Sue and I quickly found ourselves discussing the logistical headache of combining our jobs with the role of being a mother. She already had a baby, and we agreed it was little short of miraculous when women working in foreign news got married; if they had a family they needed to be almost superhuman.

....

Tirana had to be the poorest capital in Europe. From the airport we drove past dozens of strange round nuclear bunkers nestling into the countryside, a legacy of Enver Hoxha's paranoid dictatorship. Everywhere buildings appeared to be crumbling: their concrete had a fragile, pockmarked look about it. Into this country, struggling against poverty on the edge of Europe, were now pouring hundreds of thousands of refugees, not to mention the world's media.

For the next three days we questioned aid workers who'd been monitoring the accounts of atrocity and torture, and scoured the refugee camps. One was sprawled round Tirana's public swimming pool which had to be emptied as it was being used for washing clothes. We began to build a grim picture of families uprooted and terrorised at gunpoint out of their homes, of women assaulted before enduring a forced march that lasted for days until they reached the border and collapsed with exhaustion. Some had even had to watch their children being murdered. Predictably, we couldn't find a single woman who admitted that she herself had been raped.

Then we encountered one family in a makeshift camp inside Tirana's main sports hall. The mother and father were sitting on dirty mattresses, while a group of children listlessly kicked a ball of rags between the beds. Their grown-up daughter, whose thick brown hair hung to her waist, was pleading with her mother to eat. The family was in shock. They'd been driven by Serb security forces from their village in western Kosovo and forced to walk for four days and nights, without rest, to the Albanian border. The father, a civil servant, was in tears: 'We were thrown out of our house on a religious feast day. The soldiers massacred almost everyone. And wherever the Serbs found nice-looking ladies, they raped them. Two soldiers even forced me to watch.'

His daughter, a 29-year-old shop worker who spoke some English and called herself Drita, said she knew of girls in her village who'd been raped and survived. 'But they won't talk,' she said emphatically. We sat with them on the mattresses and heard more about the living hell they'd just endured.

The next day, we went back and found them outside on the steps. I sensed Drita had more to tell us, so I invited her to come to our hotel where she could have more privacy. We left the camp and she followed us half an hour later, so no one would see her walking out with us.

In the quiet of our hotel room and silhouetted against the window to preserve her anonymity, she slowly began to speak, her hands clenching and unclenching, her long hair draped over her shoulders and falling around her face. In a low, barely audible voice, she described how four masked soldiers had broken into her family's house. 'They started shooting everywhere – at the windows, at the floor – and screaming at us, "Where are your women, where are your girls?" Then one of the soldiers had taken off his mask, and she'd quickly recognised him as her Serb neighbour. She had grown up with him, gone to school with him, although she hadn't spoken to him for ten years since the Serbs began preventing Kosovan Albanians from attending school or holding decent jobs. 'When I saw him, I wanted to kill him, but I had nothing in my hands to do it. I killed him in my mind, though,' she said.

The soldier began hitting Drita and the police captain said to her father that his daughter would make a good Serbian wife; Drita was dragged towards the door, and her father tried to follow, but they hit him too.

Then she described how one soldier held her down in the doorway. 'The soldier who was my neighbour had sex with me, another soldier hit me, some of the others kissed me. My whole family was there. And at that moment, I started thinking that God didn't exist. Because if God existed, he wouldn't have allowed this to happen.' Afterwards, the soldier told her they were going to burn her alive, but they didn't. 'For me it would have been better if they had just killed me. I wanted to kill myself. What do I have to live for now?'

She finished speaking, and there was silence. The horror of what she'd been through slowly sank in, as did her enormous courage in speaking about it. She asked to have a hot shower, her first since her ordeal began. Then we took her to the hotel restaurant where she devoured a meal, and she left to go back to her family in the camp.

....

Sue and I left Tirana by car, driving south towards Greece. At the border it felt surreal going from a country scarred by poverty into a gleaming Greek tourist resort, bathed in spring sunshine. The shadow of the war we'd left behind slowly lifted. It was May and the countryside was achingly beautiful: between us and snow-capped mountains in the distance were fields of bright red poppies broken up by olive groves and lemon trees. We had completed our assignment, but I felt sickened thinking about Drita and all those other women tossing and turning in their tents, blighted for the rest of their lives by this senseless brutality.

I was able to keep in contact with Drita for several years afterwards. I put her in touch with a rape counselling centre in Tirana, where she obtained help for herself and trained to counsel others. When I returned to Kosovo a year later, she was back in her home district of Pec, living in one half of her burnt-out house and running an advice centre for hundreds of other violated women. She would walk miles every day visiting homes where victims lived, women who were too terrified to speak to anyone except her. Life continued to be hard for Drita; her father died soon after and the husband who had married her after the war later asked for a divorce because he couldn't live with the fact that she was 'unclean'.

I returned from Kosovo chastened; it had been a salutary reminder that our settled lives, with hot water and warm beds, were precious things not to be taken for granted. I thought too about all those women, marched into refugee camps. How many of them had been pregnant and then miscarried along the way, paralysed by the shock of what they'd seen and facing at every moment the possibility of being raped?

. . . .

How lucky I was now back here again, in the quiet, sterile waiting room of St Mary's surrounded by leaflets on pregnancy loss, books on the vagaries of spontaneous abortion; here was a department where behind the medical language they understood women's silent, private grief. I could ask about allo-immunity, progesterone deficiency, polycystic ovaries, fibroids and all the other myriad reasons why babies don't thrive in the womb, and I would be understood.

Lesley Regan is one of the very few doctors to have deeply researched miscarriages, perhaps one of the most depressing aspects of gynaecology. 'I can't imagine why I've chosen to specialise in this area,' she said, as she straightened the papers on her desk. 'I see so many women here in such a desperate state.' I sympathised, finding it impossible to speak about the loss of my babies without tears forcing their way down my cheeks. I couldn't imagine dealing with all this raw emotion as a job, day after day. Professor Regan passed over her desk the results of the tests which showed I didn't have anything wrong: 'You are fine, absolutely normal.'

Having nothing wrong, meant nothing could be done. I'd hoped at least I'd have to take aspirin to thin my blood, or anything. 'Surely there must be *something* wrong? What's causing the miscarriages then?'

'We don't know, I'm afraid, with you it looks like just bad luck.'

I stared out of her window at the blank, featureless sky. Bad luck. Just that. The difference between being a mother, having a lifetime's relationship with a child – family life, sandcastles on the beach, trips to the park, grandchildren, everything – and having no child, boiled down to just two words, 'bad luck'! Luck had been on my side all through marriage and getting pregnant, and then it had waved me goodbye, disappearing like the spirits of my unborn children into the ether. If it was all down to luck, then having a real child instead of an imaginary one was still as elusive as ever. The only bit of luck I could see was that I was alive, apparently healthy and as conception was not the problem, I didn't have to get on the expensive medical treadmill of IVF. I don't think I could have coped with more statistics stacked against me.

There can be few subjects that become more obsessive to women than their own fertility. Being 'without child' has been a stigma passed down from one generation to the next, ever since the time of the Old Testament believers were taught to 'be fruitful and multiply'. I, on the other, hand was 'barren', 'sterile' or 'infertile', empty and void or, in medical language, a *nullipara*.

Yet I still felt a natural urge to pass on my genes; we all talked about members of the family and how one looked like another. I had my mother's hair and my father's freckled skin; Gerald had his mother's build and gregarious personality with his father's height and stamina. My aunt, who in her youth had resembled the Hollywood star Katharine Hepburn, had passed her high cheekbones and elegant looks on to her children and grandchildren. So the idea of having a child by adopting one born of another woman seemed, at first, like an insurmountable emotional leap. Adoption meant breaking out of the family-centred way of thinking. It meant seeing other people's children as potentially our own. Parenting had to leap the genetic divide, and shake off the residue of social taboos associated not just with infertility, but with adoption itself.

....

In the UK, adoption had for years been a subject if not hidden, then spoken of in a hushed whisper. It had once been associated with the plight and the shame of illegitimate children – a product of the lack of birth control and stigma surrounding unmarried mothers. For hundreds of years these children had been left to die or passed discreetly to new parents. A survey in the 1870s showed that 30,000 of the 50,000 illegitimate babies recorded died in their first year. Eventually the 1926 Adoption Act did at last give adoptive parents the same legal rights as birth parents, but it wasn't until 1949 that adopted children had any right to inherit, and until the mid-1970s the prevalent view was that a child who was adopted should forget they ever had a past. They were seen as being a blank slate coming into a new family, and the subject need never be mentioned. There were many cases of adopted children who weren't told about their origins until they were adults. It was only in 1976 that adoptees in England and Wales could legally apply for their birth certificate and adoption records.

I had no first-hand experience of domestic adoption, although I was aware that birth parents now had far more rights to keep their child. This was as it should be, but it also meant that children ended up staying in care, sometimes for several years, while the courts decided whether they should be adopted or not. The pink bundle taken from the poor single mother and placed in a new family with no questions asked had now become the older child carrying with him or her a suitcase of emotional issues. It was a fairer, more modern system, much better for the birth mother and child if they ended up together, but often a lot tougher on adopter and adoptee. I heard that in some areas one in five domestic adoptions broke down, which I could only imagine meant untold trauma for both the child and the adoptive parents.

I had heard that Gerald and I might already be too old to be considered for a very young child, and the older the child the harder the adoption can often turn out to be.

So we began to think of looking abroad where children abandoned by their parents were more likely to be put up for adoption at a younger age. The trouble was that I knew it was a minefield of a different kind, and I had caught a glimpse of it when I'd made a documentary about international adoption in Paraguay.

....

I had first gone to this South American country in 1993, as it was emerging from half a century of military rule under General Stroessner. The police department's secret archives had been discovered, miraculously unshredded, revealing hard evidence of the misdeeds of his tinpot dictatorship. Amongst the drawers of dusty filing cabinets in the capital's imposing, marble-fronted Ministry of Justice we found documentary proof of friendly links with the apartheid government in South Africa, the sheltering of Nazis and money-laundering by the United States enabling Washington to conceal its arms trade with Iran.

While we were there we stayed in a small hotel in the centre of Asuncion, the capital. Every morning I would rush down the stairs to breakfast, always in a hurry with a full day's filming ahead of me, and invariably I would trip over American parents playing with their newly adopted Paraguayan babies. I vaguely wondered why there were so many of them, but was too busy to give it much thought.

It was another two years, before I found myself back in Asuncion. We'd come to hear of allegations of corruption in the overseas adoption process: Paraguayan newspapers were carrying stories of police raids on orphanages and of mothers claiming to have had their babies stolen from them.

Paraguay was a place where nothing was quite what it seemed. It appeared to have emerged peacefully from military oppression into democracy, but you only had to scratch the surface and the veneer soon cracked. We were staying in the colonial elegance of the Gran Hotel del Paraguay with its Italian-designed spacious courtyards and fountains. We couldn't have been closer to the story; everywhere around us were couples, mostly American but some British, carrying their newly adopted children. The vast dining room with its hand-painted bouquets and ivied trellises, its tropical plants and busy waiters was a happy scene; at each table a family sat with their new baby perched in a high chair, the babies' cries often drowning out the sound of the mackaws in the hotel zoo.

I thought it strange to see so many orphans in a peaceful country where there was no war, no famine and no cultural reason to abandon children: where, on the contrary, there was a strong Catholic sense of family. I wondered where these children were coming from. The country was poor, but I'd seen many poverty-stricken places where children were adored and kept within the community.

We were taken to see one of the smart, showcase orphanages where infants were looked after before they were adopted. In a series of rooms, we saw row after row of gurgling babies, with the name of the lawyer who actually owned them stuck on the wall above each cot. These were lawyers who were cashing in on an increased demand from foreigners for babies and were exploiting a poor population long made submissive through years of dictatorship. The lawyers expected to earn $10,000 per baby, and sent their intermediaries into the countryside to persuade young mothers to give up their children. Some did so willingly, and we met one mother who felt that offering a better life to her babies abroad was preferable to having an abortion.

But there were others like Veronica, whom we found in the slums of Asuncion, lying on her bed in a small shack in tears.

Her newborn son had been taken from her just after the birth while she was still in hospital. Now, six months later, she'd given up all hope of finding him again. The knowledge that he might by now be in the United States was no consolation.

Then there was Dionisia, with her thick, dark, curly hair and ashen face whom we found as she filled her bucket in a muddy well on the outskirts of the capital. She finished washing her clothes, rubbing them against a flat stone, before standing up to show us around the simple brick hut where she, her husband and her five children all slept. She dragged a wooden chair outside, sat down with her three-year-old son Rodrigo on her lap and described the fateful day two years earlier when a strange woman had appeared at her door. This woman announced that Dionisia's husband had suffered a terrible accident and been taken to hospital. She offered to take Dionisia there and told her to bring Rodrigo, who was then a ten-month-old baby. At the hospital the woman took hold of Rodrigo while Dionisia rushed in to look for her injured husband. He wasn't there and when she ran out both the woman and Rodrigo had disappeared. Dionisia was distraught and hunted everywhere for her child, ending up walking the streets day and night and making appeals by radio. She even read out on air a letter to her son: 'Are you all right, Rodrigo, are you thirsty, hungry, are you crying, are you upset because we aren't with you?'

Her agony lasted two months until one of the police raids on a clandestine nursery. They found twenty-nine babies and small children packed into cots in small, dark rooms, waiting to be adopted. Rodrigo was there, so thin and pale that his mother only recognised him because of a birthmark on his back.

She lifted up his clothes to show us. Then she began to cry. 'I am very poor, but I have so much love ...' I told her that the American parents we had talked to said they thought they were rescuing children from poverty. She looked at me intently. 'There's no better life for a child than being with his own mother. We didn't choose to be poor, and maybe one day we can escape our poverty.'

Next we drove north-east over a hundred miles of straight, red-earth roads to San Pedro. On the way we passed a priest surrounded by a group of women talking in the shade of a big tree. It turned out he was giving a human rights lesson, raising awareness, helping the women to understand that even though they were poor, they had the right to look after their own children, and not have them taken away. The scale of the criminal activity was beginning to dawn on me. It was in these remote areas that the lawyers' intermediaries came to procure babies, by persuasion or bribery.

We drove until we came to a little group of wooden houses set back from the road. There we found Luz Marina, an attractive bronzed girl with a round, genial face and curly brown hair. As we sat in the shade of her porch, she told us about the horrific ordeal she experienced at the hands of the adoption mafia. She had become pregnant and gone to work as a maid in the capital to pay for the birth. It turned out that her employer ran a nursery which supplied the international adoption market. At seven months pregnant, when she was seventeen, a nurse suddenly took her away to one of the clandestine nurseries. An adoption lawyer apparently needed a baby urgently, so they tied Luz Marina's arms and legs and forced her to have a caesarean with only a local anaesthetic and no sterile equipment: 'I screamed for help, don't do this to me,

I'll never give up my baby! But they wouldn't listen. Then I felt a terrible pain as the knife went in ...'

They took the baby and left Luz Marina to die. Luckily the police happened to make a raid on the nursery, and in one of the rooms they found her lying unconscious. She had to have four operations to save her life. I gasped out loud as she lifted up her red cotton shirt and showed us the wide jagged scar that stretched from her solar plexus to below her navel. 'I want my baby back — it's tearing me apart,' she said wiping the tears from her cheeks. The woman who had forced the operation on her was now in prison, but the lawyers involved were still free.

Until now Luz Marina hadn't been able to afford to go to Asuncion, so she travelled with us to the orphanage where her baby, now five months old, had been kept since her traumatic birth. We watched her wander amongst the cots, until the staff pointed out her child. She stared and stared at this wriggling little girl lying on her back without showing any emotion. I had expected something more, that she would sweep her up in her arms, but Luz Marina had had such a traumatic start to her relationship with this child that bonding was going to be a slow and painful process.

Back in the hotel in Asuncion, I felt more determined than ever to warn adoptive parents about the lengths that the crooks were going to procure babies, but I had never had so many doors slammed in my face. No one was speaking to us. What adoptive parent, after years of coming to this moment of finally being matched with their child, wanted journalists poking their noses in and asking awkward questions? So we tried to show them that it wasn't just us making these claims: that these stories were all over the local newspapers, that UNICEF was campaigning against the baby trade and that there were frequent demonstrations against baby theft at the Palace of Justice, but the foreign parents didn't want to know. For them it was too late: they had travelled too far, spent too much money to question the system now.

Adoptive parents had been led to believe they were involved in a bona fide legal process, each of them having paid $15,000 to an adoption agency back in the US. They would show us their officially stamped documents as proof. What they weren't told by their agencies was how for decades Paraguay's legal system had been at the beck and call of General Stroessner, and that now, even with a new democratic government, the country was a long way from having a strong, independent judiciary. Where there was money to be made, there were always lawyers ready to oblige with the appropriate paperwork.

It wasn't only Paraguayan parents and children who were suffering. Adoptive parents found themselves sucked into this murky world, sometimes having to pay more and more money to their lawyers. One couple had thought they were coming to Asuncion for a week to adopt two babies, but ended up being stuck there for over five months. One of their lawyers had been charged with baby theft, and the legal wrangling had delayed their paperwork. They'd run up $70,000 in costs and remortgaged their home: debts which they thought they would never be able to pay off. The kindly husband sang us a heart-rending lullaby to the tune of 'Summertime' as he tried to rock his two little girls to sleep:

Paraguay, where the lawyers are sleazy
Papers get shuffled and nothing gets done
Manaña, manaña
Is all the español we hear

Your mummy and pappy,
We cling and cry.

....

Our investigations led us to the offices of the prosecutor charged with cleaning up the legal system. It wasn't lost on us that his office was far from the law courts, and instead was stuck in a few rooms beside a hospital morgue. He was convinced that only 30 per cent of children available for adoption were given up voluntarily; the rest were probably taken from their mothers in an underhand, criminal way. What was even more disturbing, was that in this sinister marketplace there was a sliding price scale. Top price was for a fair, blue-eyed baby and bottom of the range was the dark-skinned, dark-eyed child.

....

By a strange coincidence, when we got back to the hotel my sister Florence telephoned from her home in New York. 'We are thinking of adopting a baby from abroad,' she said.

I couldn't believe it as I looked at the adoptive couples arrayed around the swimming pool, and thought of the potential problems: 'Just, for heaven's sake, please don't do it from Paraguay.'

Florence and her husband Steve already had a biological son. After five attempts at IVF, including a painful ectopic pregnancy, their fertility doctor had suggested, in that easy-going way that Americans approach new ideas, that maybe a family member could help. So Steve had asked his sister to be the 'gestational surrogate mother'. 'Could we borrow your womb, Anne?' he had asked, or words to that effect. Anne being a kind, obliging woman had simply said, 'Sure, I was wondering if I could help you guys in any way. I'd be prepared to do that for you, no problem!' The sister-in-law from heaven.

So after one attempt with three freshly grown, frozen embryos which didn't implant, Florence and Steve's two leftover fertilised frozen embryos were thawed out and inserted into Anne's womb. The pregnancy became fertile ground for jokes. Anne and her husband would go to church on a Sunday with Anne very visibly pregnant and people would inquire about the baby. She would say 'It's not mine,' and her husband would chip in with 'It's her brother's!' – much to the astonishment of the small Massachusetts community where they lived. But, as she frequently pointed out, growing the baby inside her was not the hard part: 'It's being a parent that's hard!' How right she was.

Having one child like this worked out well, but it was a lot to ask even the most generous of sisters-in-law to do the same again. Before Florence even asked, I was quick to rule out myself. Even supposing it had been possible, I couldn't imagine having a child and then giving it up. In fact, at that time, having children, biological or otherwise, was not on the agenda. There was a film to be finished, lawyers to be pursued through the corridors of the Palace of Justice, and corruption exposed.

·················

After our documentary was aired the Paraguayan Congress, under pressure from human rights campaigners, voted to suspend international adoptions. Adoptive parents already with children from Paraguay tried to stop the programme being shown, angry that it tarred them all with the same brush. I could see their point; we had no wish to damage any adopted child's life, but we still felt criminal activity had to be stopped to safeguard future parents and children.

Now, four years later, I was looking into the possibility of adoption myself, and that experience hung over me, flashing red warning lights not to let my desire for a child be exploited by ruthless traders. I felt so vulnerable, knowing that I would be an easy picking for the con men once I started down the overseas adoption route and raw emotion took over from journalistic detachment.

....

'No potatoes please.' Ian said, turning to me as we stood in front of the shimmering platters of the BBC canteen buffet. 'I'm on the "food combining" diet, no carbohydrate with my meat − it's been marvellous, I've lost a stone in a month ...' We sat down in the cavernous room, with its floor-to-ceiling windows, a place where actors rehearsing the latest costume drama would mingle with technicians and news hacks. Ian tucked into his steak and salad, while I delved into a comforting, brick-like structure that had been labelled shepherd's pie.

'Ian, we're thinking of adopting from abroad ...'

'Really? What an idea ... can I give you some advice? Be really careful if you're thinking of Romania. I've been researching a story there for Newsnight, we hope to have it done by the end of the year. Some people are saying there's a kind of mafia that's infiltrated the international adoption system and that babies are being bought and sold for thousands of dollars. You can go there as a Westerner and get a baby with no questions asked. I've even heard there are women who sell their babies in what's being called "the industrialisation of the womb".'

'How tragic when there are so many children there that genuinely need adopting.'

'Yes, it taints the whole business, and I'm sure the children themselves are adorable.'

....

Soon after, my sister called me with her latest announcement: 'We've decided, we've chosen China.'

'China! Why?' I asked, relieved it wasn't Romania or Paraguay, but unable to stretch my mind to such an unfamiliar country, which was only just beginning to open up to the West.

'There are countless numbers of little girls being abandoned in the streets because of the One Child Policy and the cultural preference for boys. We really want to adopt a sister for Harrison to avoid the competitiveness of another boy, and because we simply want a girl. It's unbearable to think of so many children without parents when here we are wanting a child. From a global perspective it seems the perfect way to balance things just slightly.'

This was the mid 1990s and international adoptions were getting underway in America. Unlike in the UK, there were few cultural hang-ups about them as they fitted in with the great melting-pot philosophy of a country built on immigration, along with the inbuilt confidence that anyone was lucky to become an American. An array of private adoption agencies were springing up to help adoptive parents, mostly aging baby boomers, with the paperwork and China was becoming a popular destination.

....

About 100,000 babies each year were being abandoned across China, although no figure could possibly be accurate, given the hidden nature of the act. Abandonment had been a centuries-long practice, as had female infanticide, but since 1979 and the introduction of the One Child Policy, Chinese families − desperate as ever to have a son − were using whatever means they could to ensure that a daughter didn't take the place of that much-needed boy. China is a country without pensions or social security, making a son vital to the well-being, sometimes even the survival, of the family. A boy could grow up and till the land, continue the family business, and according to tradition he would look after his parents in their old age. On the other hand, a daughter would marry into another family and have her responsibilities there. The new birth control policy just tipped the scales further against the chances of a baby daughter being born or surviving into adulthood. Some of the statistics were depressing. During the 1980s male infant mortality declined, as one would expect from a growing economy and rising living standards, but at the same time the rate of female infant deaths increased.

In 1984, the One Child Policy was relaxed in the countryside so families who had a girl as their first child were allowed to try again for a boy. It still meant, though, that second and third girls were at risk of being abandoned, aborted or killed.

As it became clear that Chinese orphanages couldn't cope with the growing numbers of abandoned babies, the Chinese government passed a new adoption law, in 1991, which restricted domestic adoption of foundlings to childless parents over the age of 35. This cut out thousands of potential adopters inside China, but the government's priority was population control born of the deep fear of not being able to provide enough food for its growing nation. It didn't want birth parents to arrange adoptions for their over-quota daughter so they could keep trying to have a son.

What the Chinese government did do to alleviate the crisis was to encourage overseas adoption, and my sister was an eager participant. She and her husband had a couple of visits from a social worker, filled in a lot of forms, had their fingerprints taken, and then waited eight months while their application was processed in China. The whole process took a year, and once they were matched with a child they travelled to Henan Province, to the city of Luoyang, to pick up their daughter. They called her Octavia, as she was born in the eighth month of the year, and she had grown into a beautiful three-year-old. For them the whole process had been relatively pain free.

But while Americans have their hands held, in Britain couples were left to chart their own course through a sea of bureaucracy. I began to make inquiries, talking to friends and reading anything I could find. It wasn't an edifying prospect.

A friend gave me a copy of the official handbook, *Adopting a Child*, issued a few years earlier by the British Agencies for Adoption and Fostering and I nearly admitted defeat there and then. First, I wasn't surprised to see that we didn't have much of a chance to adopt a baby in the UK.

> The husband is expected to be well under 40, sometimes under 35. The wife is expected to be under 35 too.

Well, that ruled us out for a start, and probably most other couples who'd been through the rounds of infertility clinics. And then, as if anticipating the question, 'So why don't we adopt a baby from abroad?' the booklet's authors were equally discouraging:

> The Home Office doesn't encourage the adoption of children from abroad ... their priorities must of course lie with the many children here who need families. So inter-country adoption has to be approached as a personal thing – very expensive and very time consuming ... red tape can turn an individual's efforts into a nightmare of bureaucracy.

The message was clear: basically, don't expect any help. I contacted other adoptive parents and began to put a picture together of the mountain ahead of us. To climb up it you needed the skills of a goat, the determination of a terrier and feline patience to match. Or, as one adoptive parent told me, 'You have to be bloody-minded, a bulldozer to get through. I found it the worst preparation for parenthood, and it didn't help at all when it came to the first nappy change.'

....

The in-depth assessment by local social services departments is known as the Home Study and is intended to vet potential adoptive parents. The procedure is a far cry from the American model. There, to want to adopt is seen as a 'good' thing: if you have the money and can pass certain basic ground rules you are accepted. In the UK overseas adoption sets off alarm bells, there are instant suspicions about whether would-be adopters have the right motives.

I heard that it was a strange process in which any aspect of a middle-class life could act against you: lifestyle, type of job, level of education, attitude to religion, even the number of pets you had. Potential adopters had been turned down for being a bit depressed, for suffering from a chronic illness or for having unresolved issues about religion; others were criticised because they were too fat, too busy, too bright, too well read or, incredibly, whose existing children appeared too well adjusted. In other words it was a Kafkaesque world where anything, absolutely anything, could be used in evidence against you. On these grounds few biological parents would qualify to have their own birth children, but we soon found that logic like this was irrelevant.

One North London couple had been refused by their borough because they were told they were 'too well educated and might have too high expectations of their child'. Their social worker had once said disapprovingly, 'You are "books", aren't you?' They appealed and eventually were allowed to adopt, but only after years of struggle.

Another couple from South-West London, Jonathan and Jane, had been told that because Jane was a solicitor and Jonathan a teacher that meant they obviously had controlling personalities, and might have problems being parents. When Jane said she wanted to work full time, while her husband worked part-time, the social worker had said, 'Well, Jane, I'm surprised after all you both have been through that you don't want to be a mum.' When I spoke to Jonathan he was still visibly upset by the ordeal of being interviewed. He felt their social worker had not only probed deeply their every emotion, but had also had a cruel streak. She had threatened to recommend long-term psychoanalysis before they could be passed for adoption. One day Jonathan lost his temper with her: 'There goes our baby,' his wife had said to him. 'At last you're in touch with your anger,' the social worker had said, smiling. In the end she did pass them, but the stress of it remains with them to this day.

Overseas adoption was also a post-code lottery. There seemed to be no independent arbiter. Everything depended on the particular attitudes of each local authority's social services department. For some couples the process was fast and efficient; others faced foot-dragging and resistance at every step. I heard how one London borough would not return calls from prospective adopters, and once they had started the paperwork would inject so many delays that it took several years to complete the process.

Infuriated at the lack of regulation, parents were turning to the newspapers to vent their fury. Matthew Engel wrote about his adoption of a Russian girl in *The Guardian*. He had been enraged by intimate questions about his sex life as well as having to do a pre-adoption course oozing with political correctness:

> This country has turned the adoption of a child into something very close to a crime: the perpetrators are harried, if not actually punished.

....

One adoptive father I later spoke to who has been active in liaising with government departments on the issue put it like this: 'The government has got new legislation in the pipeline which may improve things, but basically I think many officials see domestic adoption as removing a problem, while adopting from overseas is potentially bringing one into the country. They don't want children from poor countries, perhaps with special needs, coming here and using our overstretched public services.'

And when it came to lobbying for change, he felt that adopters didn't have much chance, compared to the massive financial clout of the fertility industry. He had adopted a child from Central America, but only after he and his wife had been through eight cycles of IVF costing £50,000. 'The doctors knew full well we had little chance of conceiving. After the IVF failed they talked about donor eggs and donor sperm, but at no point did anyone say "Have you thought about adoption?". It's just too lucrative for them. So, on top of official resistance, the powerful fertility industry doesn't help. Adoption is always seen as the last resort, low down the food chain.'

On the other side of the fence, the social services felt they had good reason to be resistant to overseas adoption. They were understaffed, struggling to protect abused children and coping with emergencies and finding places for British children, many of them difficult cases. It was hard enough to arrange domestic adoptions, so overseas adoption was pushed to the bottom of the list. Inter-country adoption was also the prerogative of better-off families who were never going to be a priority. Given that potential adopters made a substantial contribution – upwards of £2,000 – to their social services in order to be assessed, I wondered if there was much more to it than a simple question of money and resources.

I wanted to get some frank views from social workers on what was at the root of the official foot-dragging. One agreed to speak to me anonymously in a small café off the Finchley Road in North London. She had long experience of international adoption and was becoming gradually more sympathetic to it. But, as she stirred her coffee, she explained that attitudes had been shaped in the 1960s and 70s by the unhappy experiences of some black children who had been placed with white families. 'These children had sometimes felt they were "public property" and didn't fit in, either in white or black culture,' she said.

I put it to her that it was strange that adoptive parents were endlessly grilled to make sure they weren't racist, yet social services themselves defined families on racial lines: white parents should only adopt white babies, Asian parents only Asian children, etc.

'This has to be a high priority,' she answered. 'It is a huge burden to put on a child, to put him or her in a family that is clearly of a different race. It means everyone always knows he or she is adopted.'

I could see that for a child it could be hard, but then what about mixed-race couples? There were plenty of white mothers raising mixed-race children who didn't look anything like them. What's more the statistics clearly showed that inter-country adoption had a high success rate. I put it to her: 'Overseas adoptions hardly ever break down, while the failure rate for domestic adoptions is 20 per cent, so there must be other reasons why some social workers are so against them?'

'Yes, that's true, but in the past we did have some overseas adoptions that broke down and they were disastrous.' The social worker shook her head, recalling some sad cases she'd been involved in. 'Historically overseas adoption has been linked to high levels of corruption. Romania is a prime example. I remember times when we simply could not trust the documentation, people used to bring these children into the UK and then they would just disappear. The children were often very damaged, having been deprived of proper care for years in orphanages. We had one family in my borough that dumped their child when he was eight years old. Parents were not properly prepared, and at that time there was far less vetting, they often didn't know what to do about the child's cultural heritage. Some adopters might even have a negative attitude to the country the child was from, and deny their heritage altogether.'

'But that still doesn't explain the hostility today, now that everyone has to go through very strict procedures. Is there really, as many people suspect, an anti-middle class bias underneath it all?'

'Well, most middle class people who contact us about overseas adoption have got what they want, like home comforts and a good job, and they find this impotence, this inability to have children, demeaning. They feel a tremendous loss of power. Certainly I used to see overseas adoption as being all about wealthy families paying to fill this gap, to get what they wanted, and we didn't want to make things too easy for them. I've become more positive about it recently as the vetting has become more rigorous and parents are better prepared.'

So it was true, there was a class bias. Most parents seeking to adopt from overseas were in stable jobs, had stable homes and would have no other reason to seek help from their local social services department. Social workers were not used to dealing with them, nor they with social workers.

. . . .

A few days later, I sat on the fading kelims of a suitably multicultural Moroccan tea bar in Queensway with another former social worker. She had eventually decided to adopt a child from China, but still encountered hostility from her colleagues. She said that when she was trained in the 1970s there had been no mention of inter-country adoption and she'd received no training in it during the rest of her career. 'The trouble is, we in the UK suffer from a kind of post-Imperialist guilt. In many social workers' minds the history of overseas adoption starts with slavery; it goes on through the abominable deportations of children to Australia which went on into the 1960s. In Australia itself there was also the taking of aboriginal children from their parents to be given to white families, and they became known as the "Stolen Generation". The whole gamut of past injustices tends to get mapped onto present-day adoption. There's something distasteful about poor children in poor countries being snatched up by wealthy parents in rich countries.'

I thought of Paraguay, and had to agree. 'But what if those children weren't just poor, what if they would actually die if they weren't adopted, or live out their whole lives in an institution, as is the case in China?'

'That makes no difference to many social workers. If a child came up for adoption in the UK who was South American or Chinese, they would always look for South American or Chinese parents to adopt him or her, so they would say why do you think you can break the rules by going abroad?'

'Even if it meant that child languishing in a care home because there wasn't an adoptive parent of the right race to adopt him or her?'

'Then that child would just have to wait.'

'For years?'

'As long as it takes.'

'What if the child was in China, say, and might die if not adopted?'

'That's seen as an issue for our Department for Overseas Development, an aid issue, not for social services to worry about.'

There was madness underneath all this logic. For a start it was so UK-centric: devoid of a sense of universal values, of children who might actually prefer love and a family to wallowing in a culture that had rejected them. Turning one's back on these children and simply hoping that one day policies would change or sufficient aid would get through to them seemed like cloud cuckoo land. It felt like an ostrich approach: let's all pretend these children don't exist, and let their own country deal with them.

I went home and turned with renewed determination to my adoption handbook, but was firmly put in my place.

> Sometimes pathetic photographs or details of suffering children from poorer nations make people in this country anxious to help them. But there are many problems associated with this. First and most importantly, children have the right to remain in their own family and their own community ... most governments prefer to have help on the spot rather than sending their children to be cared for in an alien country. Children are, after all, the future of a country.

If they were, then why in China with its bubbling optimism and booming businesses, were babies, especially girls, still being abandoned in vast numbers? There was clearly a gulf between social work policy in Britain and the reality of a child's life in China. There babies, especially girls, were *not* treated as if they were the future of the country. The government's priority seemed to be population control, not saving the lives of the nation's infants.

I remembered watching a documentary, 'The Dying Rooms', screened on Channel Four in 1995 which painted the bleakest picture of life inside Chinese orphanages, even going as far as to say that there was a deliberate policy of neglect. Conditions in many orphanages were now vastly improved, but still the problem of abandonment was endemic. It was a crisis that had a profound impact on us and on our friend, the poet Frieda Hughes, who sent me a piece of paper on which she'd typed these words:

The Dying Room

Mother, father, no child,
Made the space between them
Into a hard thing.
A boulder in the bedroom, washed clean
Where they cried. Secretly, and separate.
Each afraid of the other.
Of their invisible baby.
That rock, their burden should have been a daughter.

And in the dying room, the children gather.
Where death does not need the language,
But picks his nails and cleans his nostrils
With shin bones small enough to knit with.
He knows they will come easily,
Because the cold seek warmth,
And even in his rot and tatters
He wants them most.

Dressed meat, their moons shine.
Tiny girls, not to know
Why brother lived. Never loved,
They grate until they stop,

Little clocks all run out and empty.
They clatter in their graves like hollow tins
And mother, father, no child,
Polish up their stone again.

. . . .

Over several months, I tried to pick up the phone to my local social services department. When I eventually did, I stammered out that I was interested in adoption and got put through to the Kensington and Chelsea Family Placement Unit. After all I'd heard, I expected an unfriendly voice from someone not wanting to be bothered with a low-priority inquiry.

The reality was much kinder. We had struck lucky in the post-code lottery. The lady on the other end confirmed that although age was less of an impediment than before, there were very few white babies put up for adoption, and unless my husband was Asian we couldn't adopt an Asian child. We would be eligible for older white children but we would need to feel confident of being able to handle more complex emotional issues. They had a positive outlook on overseas adoption, but first we would need to be interviewed by a social worker. I'd done it and I was still alive. I hadn't been put down nor put off. Things were looking up.

At our first meeting with our social worker, a young Indian woman called Rana with a long mass of raven-black hair and a winning smile, she told us she had never handled an overseas adoption before but was keen to try one.

I began to explain why we wanted to adopt a Chinese baby. The choice was gradually becoming more obvious: already having a Chinese adopted niece, the existence of strict Chinese government regulations over the entire process which the

British government recognised, and most of all the existence of genuinely abandoned children.

I had never been to China, but I did have some knowledge of the plight of the girl child in other parts of Asia. Suddenly, for the first time when it came to becoming a mother, my work could act in my favour. There was one documentary in particular which had taken me to the heart of the crisis of female infanticide in India. As we sat at the round wooden table in the pastel calm of our local-government office the burning heat of Rajasthan and Tamil Nadu came flooding back. What I had seen there, in the tribal deserts of the north and the languid villages of the south, was now influencing my own path to motherhood years later.

....

We had driven for hours across the desert, along the dusty hot roads out of Jodhpur to a sprawling mud-brick village surrounded by sand dunes. It was a big day, crowds had gathered along the road to celebrate the visit of a highly unusual young woman. Returning with her husband for the first time, she had been the only girl to have survived in her village. Their tradition was to kill all the baby girls. As she sat in the shade of a courtyard, I asked her how it was she had been allowed to live. 'I was born the day my father was shot,' she told me. 'He was told that it would be good luck if I was allowed to live. So they didn't kill me, and he recovered from his wounds ... my younger sister was not so lucky and she died.'

Her husband, sitting in his colourful turban, twirling his long moustache, seemed unperturbed by the story: 'We used to simply put a sandbag on a baby girl's nose or give her a double dose of opium. It is a social evil, but what can you do about it?'

© Bhasker Solanki

Indian Bride.

In these harsh, tribal lands, where women were seen as useless in battle, it became a tradition to kill them. Today things had improved slightly, but even so out of the hundred children in the village only fourteen were girls.

What most shocked me was not so much that this old custom had survived into modern-day India but that, as the society developed, it was actually spreading. Down in the south, in Tamil Nadu, we had met a young couple who openly admitted to having recently killed their second baby girl. The young husband spoke without any remorse. 'We poisoned her with the milky juice of a plant. My mother did it, just as you would feed milk to a child. The baby screamed for fifteen minutes and then she died.' He earned just fifty pence a day thatching roofs, and he could barely afford to keep their first daughter. A second would have condemned them to serious poverty: 'We can't feed her, and we have to consider the greater unhappiness she would suffer if she was allowed to live.'

Social pressures were turning mothers into murderers. We were told that four out every ten girls born were killed. In a little health centre in the middle of flat scrubland, we found lines of women waiting to visit the ante-natal clinic. We eavesdropped on a consultation. Eighteen-year old Vellayama was eight months pregnant. She had her three-year-old daughter with her as she sat opposite the nurse. The nurse asked, 'What are you going to do with the baby when it's born?'

Vellayama answered nonchalantly, 'If it's a boy, I'll keep him, but I am very poor. If it's a girl I'll kill her.'

There was no hint of shame. This was the grim reality in her village, where having a boy meant a family was guaranteed wealth as his bride would bring with her perhaps some cows, a television, or the luxury of polyester shirts. A girl was merely a burden; she had to be fed and watered, she couldn't do much manual work, there was the worry about getting her married, and then when she did find a husband her parents would have to find a dowry or she'd be left high and dry, unmarriageable and a shame on the family for ever. Once married she would go away and look after her husband's parents: hence the saying here 'bringing up a girl is like watering a neighbour's plant'.

As she sat cross-legged under a tree beside her soft white cow, I asked Vellayama how she intended to kill her child. 'I will feed her unhusked rice, and she will choke,' she replied, as if responding to a question about the weather.

We had also travelled north to the prosperous city of Ludhiyana, where India's new wealth was rapidly turning the unwanted into the unborn. The rise of the ultrasound clinic was accelerating the trend towards disposing of girls. In the name of population control, instead of a mother having ten to a dozen girls before she finally had a boy, doctors could now offer her the ultrasound test. She could then abort girl after girl until she had a boy. A local doctor summed up the attitudes: 'The first daughter is seen as bad luck, the second a disaster, and the third is an utter catastrophe as if the whole world has fallen apart.'

We accompanied him to the post-natal ward in the city's main hospital where we watched as a woman lay impassive and depressed, her mother-in-law beside her with a stony look on her face. I asked whether something terrible had happened. 'Yes,' said the doctor, 'she gave birth to a healthy little girl.'

In the next bed was a woman surrounded by her family, grown-up daughters and her exultant husband handing out sweets. Beside her in a cot was a gurgling little boy. The proud father told us that although he loved his three daughters now at last he had a son to whom he could hand on his business and he felt complete. Even more importantly, he now had a boy to light his funeral pyre, the only way in the Hindu religion that he would ever reach heaven.

We drove through streets, shimmering in the intense heat, to an abortion clinic on the outskirts of town. There the red-turbaned doctor presided over a waiting room full of women holding little boys. He boasted to us that he had identified 30,000 female foetuses and most of them were aborted. He justified sex-determination testing on the grounds that it kept the population down, and he didn't see any prospect of a new law to make it illegal being enforceable: 'Most of the ministers and politicians come with their daughters and daughters-in-law to have the test, the doctors they come, and the social workers ... So who is going to stop it? Only society can stop it, but it is society that supports it.'

The wholesale disposal of girls, whether from infanticide or the death knell of the ultrasound verdict, meant India was then missing an estimated 25 million women.

A year after the film we made, 'Let Her Die', was broadcast we received a letter from a couple in the United States. It said simply: 'We watched your film and we decided as a result to adopt a baby girl. Here is the picture of our Indian daughter.' We had already influenced one family's decision to adopt, and now this same documentary was going to play a lasting role in my own life, and that of Gerald too.

. . . .

By the end of the meeting, Rana agreed to begin a Home Study with us. The first hurdle was over.

'Home Study' sounded so mild, like a bit of homework. But this kind of home study was one in which the UK government became one's psychoanalyst. We had to lie on the couch, so to speak, for four months of intense questioning, while we were examined to assess our capability as 'prospective substitute parents'. I wondered how many parents-to-be felt qualified for the job when their first pregnancy took shape.

Everything about being assessed stirred up all the doubts and insecurities about my worthiness to be a mother. What right had I to be one? After all, if biology fails, then why should I be allowed to take on someone else's child? That must be nature's way of saying I wouldn't be up to the job.

I couldn't begin to unravel the complex emotions that were running as I opened the door to Rana on that first late afternoon. As she laid her papers out on our kitchen table, questions and uncertainties crowded into my mind, while my hands broke into a cold sweat. The ominous Form F lay like a silent prophet on the wooden surface. It would either prove to be an insurmountable obstacle or a passport to parenthood. Fifteen pages of bureaucracy were now taking over where biology had left off. The most daunting part was Part II, the descriptive report which would decide our fate.

We had to write a profile of our family, our accommodation, neighbourhood, access to local amenities and a description of ourselves. We had to compose a genogram, slightly ironical as we were now going to be stepping outside our family genes; this basically meant a family tree. And then there was the obscure Ecomap. This wasn't anything to do with eco-tourism, but a series of circles, like planets in orbit, swirling around a larger circle representing myself and Gerald. Inside this strange universe we had to write down our support networks: neighbours, close family, extended family, church groups, doctors, clubs and friends. The point was to see what networks would help support us once we had a child. It was more relevant for us than most, perhaps, as we had lost both sets of parents, and we would probably need to rely on a hotchpotch of connections to help with babysitting.

The 'clubs' section caused a stir in the politically correct mindset of our social worker: the mention of two cricket clubs to which Gerald belonged, and the London Irish Rugby Club, perhaps conjured visions of a whole team turning up to change nappies, or of our daughter being ridiculed by hordes of beefy blokes in muddy shoes. Anyway Rana asked, 'Looking at these clubs, isn't there rather a gender bias there?'

Gerald and I looked at each other, dumbfounded. We couldn't think of anything to say except, 'Yes, the teams do tend to be made up of men, and the women watch.' I wondered if this was going to scar my daughter for ever with a sense of inferiority. Rana appeared perplexed and I feared a black mark against us.

Another black mark would come if I decided to continue working full time – definitely not approved of – and Rana was relieved to find I was going to opt for shorter hours. I wondered what I would do if my employer didn't agree.

Over the weeks the questions and the discussions continued in extraordinary detail. I began to feel there was little the British government was not going to know about our life. We became adept at fielding questions such as these: How do you express emotion? How strong is your marriage? How well do you think you understand children? How would you punish a child? What experience or understanding do you have of racial discrimination? We also had the inevitable, 'Have you grieved your infertility?' and the awkward 'Tell me about your previous relationships,' which had the potential to be embarrassing. There were times when I felt we were doing well, particularly when it came to Gerald's family background and childhood. He scored points talking about the way his mother would gather in stray children and foster them in her home in Yorkshire. He recalled how, aged twelve, he had taken a sixteen-year-old pregnant mother to watch Manchester United play at Old Trafford. They'd sat at the Stretford End where the rougher home fans congregated. He had also set up a charity for disabled children while at school, and taken handicapped youngsters on healing pilgrimages to Lourdes. Rana was clearly impressed.

Over the weeks we discussed and debated parenthood, and there were even times I enjoyed it. When I forgot about how intrusive it was, it felt supportive to have so much interest taken in us. I did wonder, though, at the possible hidden traps, the gaffes we might commit without realising it: to think that a wrong word or phrase could bar us from being parents. Then there was the question I had been dreading. 'Tell me about your own mother. How were you mothered?' Rana asked one afternoon, her pen poised. I took a deep breath and looked out into our garden, the wind whipping up the autumn leaves and sending them scurrying in circles, her words slowly unlocking my mind to a time I preferred to forget.

....

I am nine years old, at school. One of my teachers tells me I'm going home early as my aunt has come to pick me up. 'This must be a treat', I say to myself. Perhaps I'm going to visit her for lunch. When she arrives I rush up and throw my arms around her. She bends down, and I feel her cool, smooth cheeks, and touch her red curls, she smells of elegance and soft armchairs.

In the car I sit on her lap chattering about school, when she says gently, 'Emmy darling, listen you must be brave, you know your Mummy hasn't been well ... well, today she had an accident and she died.' I am silent, I just don't believe her.

'What do you mean, an accident?' My mother had been fine when I'd rushed out of the flat that morning in a hurry to get to school. I hated being late, and I was used to travelling on the tube on my own.

'You know how she used to lean out of the drawing-room window to see who was coming to visit? She must have slipped on the polished wooden floor, and she fell. She didn't have a chance.'

I often used to hang on to her skirt as she hurled that window open; even I could see that leaning a long way out of a fifth-floor window was hazardous. I can't imagine that she had actually fallen. I strain to remember if I had said good-bye, what had been my last glimpse of her. 'She must be alright?' I ask, beginning to panic, still not wanting to believe what I'd heard.

'She's gone for ever, darling, she won't be coming back.'

We drive home in silence. I stare out of the window at the bright June sunshine. This had started as such a beautiful day. I had walked past the hydrangea bush next to the school and played with the ladybirds, letting them walk up and down my fingers. The sparrows had been chirping and I was looking forward to starting my new Doctor Dolittle book. Only the day before I'd been clattering my scooter down the same pavement I can now see stretching away, grey and hard ... clunk, clunk as the wheels hit each paving stone.

Now as we turn down past Victoria Station and into a side street, I look at our block of flats standing motionless and silent. We take the lift up the fifth floor, its metal gates clanking shut, and I rush to our front door. There is the familiar figure of Mar, the woman who had cared for my mother as a child nearly fifty years ago. I fall into her arms, sobbing into her shoulder, clinging as if my life would suddenly vanish as quickly as my mother's had. Then I tear myself away. 'Mummy!' I call nervously, barely able to think of her not here. I run through each room searching, stopping in the living room and staring at the offending window, at the slippery polished wooden floor. I decide to hate that window forever.

My sister arrives home minutes later, her eyes red and we hug tightly; all our usual bickering and jealousy evaporate in that dark moment. The rest of the evening has been erased from my mind.

The morning after, I go to school. Inside the daily routine, I feel my secure, ordered world breaking up. I tell myself to keep going, and I begin to construct my defences. In the playground some girls are talking about me. They peer in my direction and I overhear one say, 'Did you know her mother had a fatal accident?' 'What does that mean?' asks another, and gets the reply 'I don't know, something horrible.' I run away from them, feeling so ashamed. I don't want to be the odd one out; the odd one whose mother had a 'fatal accident'. It's so embarrassing and I don't want to talk about it.

When a kind teacher approaches me as we file out of the class room at break time and asks me if I'm OK, I answer like lightning, 'Of course I'm fine' and rush away down the stairs to the locker room. I promise myself this will be my secret, and I'll do all I can to pretend it never happened. Somehow I get through that first day.

. . . .

Only now, when I read my miniature schoolgirl's diary, can I see how it betrays the turmoil under my conscientious exterior. I always wrote down each evening a list of what I had done. For that fateful day, 6th June 1968, there is a heading: 'Mum died', followed by: 'Morning. Went to school. Had geography, French, break, maths, English. Afternoon. Prep, gym came home early with aunty. Cried. Evening. Homework, TV, bed, cried.'

The next day my diary continues almost without a hiccup. 'Morning. Went to school. Maths. Swimming. English. Prep.

Afternoon. Prep. Speech and Drama. Home. Mucked about. TV. Evening. Dad came back. Got some things. Tired. Bed.'

. . . .

My father arrives back from his conference in Moscow. His flight back had been delayed a day. 'I shouldn't have gone away', he whispers. 'She promised me she would never do this because of the children.'

'Do what?' I ask.

'Never mind, ducky, I'll explain it all one day.' He gives us presents of a Russian doll and a little painted box, and I cry myself to sleep.

. . . .

There's another day like that and then for three days my neat handwriting and the reassuring lists fall apart; I'd scrawled a few indecipherable words on each page. By the 12th the diary is back to how it was before, although the handwriting takes some time to recover its former composure. There are no other references to my mother's death.

. . . .

We aren't taken to the funeral and I never see my mother's body. This is the way it was done by my aunt's wartime generation, one that made little fuss over death, and where the important thing was to carry on and not let grief tear you apart. I don't really believe my mother is dead, anyway. I dream about her constantly, seeing her auburn hair and her pale gaunt face, hearing her speak to me. I try and touch her and then I wake up and want desperately to go back, back to sleep, back in time. Please, somebody, rewind the clock. I don't want the day to start, each one taking me further away from her. I long to be eight again. Nine is definitely not a good age.

My father copes by sticking to his routine with stoic determination. He writes a poem about my mother called 'Threnody':

> ... As if dissecting a corpse — he scans previous
> years more precious than they seemed: days
> in America with a wife who only by death would be
> unfaithful ... Sharing a lawn
> on sunny afternoons, which were a thinning
> out of time and moving towards the end ...

....

My sister and I adapt as children do, becoming ever more independent as well as expert at improvising dinner. We're soon adept at 'boil-in-the-bag' cooking, mashed potato, grilled fish fingers, lamb chops and sausages. I am praised by my friends' parents for being so helpful, and become a fast and thorough washer-upper. I choose what to wear, do my homework without help, and everyone says, 'Isn't she doing well!' I lap up the praise as if I can never get enough and become the perfect guest, inserting myself easily into other people's families, wondering in awe what it must be like to have a 'normal' home.

....

Years later I learn what really happened. My mother, an intelligent and dedicated schoolteacher, had in fact been suffering from manic depression, alternating between feverish, talkative phases and suicidal gloom. She used to say to me she was depressed, and I would ask 'What does depressed mean, Mummy?'

She suffered a breakdown while visiting her mother in America over Christmas. The doctors there treated her for 'disorganised thinking and bizarre behaviour ... aggravated by long-standing marital dissatisfactions ...' She was prescribed anti-psychotic drugs and sent for tests to the Neurological Institute in New York. She was discharged a few weeks later and came back to London, where the doctors reduced her prescriptions. By April she entered a deeply pessimistic phase, writing one of her last letters to her mother:

> This is by far the worst patch I've ever lived through and I don't see any end to it as I've lost interest in everything ... All I can do is somehow to keep going and hope that the cloud will lift ...

It didn't, and on that black day in June various fateful coincidences conspired to give her the opportunity she had been waiting for. My father was in Moscow, and his plane was delayed. Meanwhile my mother, who had been staying as a precautionary measure with her sister, had been allowed to go home as everyone expected that my father would be already there. In an empty flat, and with the imagined nightmare of the arrival of a new psychiatrist who would take her away, she threw herself out of the window of our living room. She was found dead on the pavement by a passer-by. It was decisive and final. She hadn't toyed with death; she had confronted it head-on.

....

Thirty-one years later I was covering Cardinal Hume's funeral for BBC News. His fellow monks from Ampleforth Abbey were commenting on how fearlessly the Archbishop had faced his death from cancer. As the mourners gathered, I looked up at the window opposite Westminster Cathedral where my mother had ended her life, and knew that she too in her own way had looked death in the face. I hoped my father's words which he wrote then about her were true:

> ... There is no requiem. The blue church windows
> the stained-glass hierarchy, are not for her
> When the choir sings *libera me, domine*
> she is already free, outside that paradise.

....

I finished telling Rana the whole story, and then quickly added nervously, 'At least you can say that I know what it's like to be abandoned by my mother ... that'll be something I'll have in common with my daughter.'

Rana raised her eyebrows and continued taking notes. Eventually, after what seemed like an eternity of writing, she put her pen down and said, 'Thank you for being so honest. Now, do you think you've come to terms with your mother's death?'

I didn't know what to say. I lived a normal enough life now, but that loss, that hole inside, never went away. It only compounded the grief of my miscarriages. I'd lost my mother, and now I couldn't have a child ... The whole concept of motherhood had become mysterious and unobtainable, and I yearned to experience it directly for myself. I wanted to live out that close bond between mother and child: otherwise I would always wonder what it was. I told Rana about the course of therapy I had done, when I had wept more or less non-stop for a week. I'd had to relive that moment of abandonment, and work out how it had ricocheted through my life, affecting my decisions and my relationships. It had been frightening but also powerfully cleansing. I wondered if all this counted in my favour, or was this yet another weakness that I had revealed?

I asked Rana tentatively, 'Are you going to fail us now? Are you going to write that I have too many unresolved issues about motherhood, just as my friends were turned down for having too many unresolved issues about religion?'

She was able to reassure us that if there was a problem she would let us know there and then and not wait until the end of the Home Study. If I had 'worked on' trying to understand the issues then I should be all right. I still regretted blurting out quite so much.

Any attempt at then putting on a sane and orderly face was undermined in the following session when we all watched a TV programme about Chinese adoption. It featured a couple in Brighton who had adopted four children, two of them Chinese girls. The mother had such a positive, pragmatic attitude: 'I may not be these girls' biological mother, I may not be Chinese, but at least I am a mother.' I found myself touched by what she said and tried to hide the tears from Rana, without much success. This whole process wasn't going well, I thought; she's going to think, quite rightly, that I'm a basket case.

. . . .

After four months of interviews, Rana was ready. She showed us her twenty-page report and asked if we had any comments.

We read the state's official view of our parenting potential with trepidation. But apart from some misprints and mis-understandings, such as saying that during World War II Gerald's father, who was a keen mountaineer and electrical engineer, had somehow managed to do his bomb disposal work high in the Alps, we couldn't find anything to disagree with. We had passed, and we were being recommended to 'Panel' who would be the ultimate arbiters. This time I cried with joy. 'You definitely charmed her!' I said to Gerald. 'It was your mother and all those fostered children that did it. She must have just given *me* the benefit of the doubt!'

A few months later we heard that Panel, the powerful body made up of social workers and adoption experts, had also passed us and we were through to the next stage. All we had to do now was get the Department of Health to process our application and forward our papers to China. It was again grindingly slow, but at least now there were no more difficult questions, no more probing into our past: just medicals and documents to gather. Once the bundle was sent off there was suddenly nothing more to do. After all the effort and the bureaucratic hurdles we were left with acres of time stretching out ahead of us. We were now in the hands of the Chinese authorities and they were predicting an eight or nine month wait before we would hear anything.

. . . .

Within weeks we went to China, for a holiday, a long-overdue visit to begin to discover something about the country that was to give birth to our first child.

- Chapter Three -

Chinese Revelations

Beijing was in metamorphosis. The stained concrete blocks adorned with red balloons and dusky orange lanterns rocking in the wind were from old China, while confident new glass and metal structures vaunted their capitalist paraphernalia: flags, film posters and endless giant advertisements for China Telecom.

I stared out of our taxi window at the slate-grey sky, dazed and deafened by the rush of traffic and impatient car horns. Permanent construction seemed to have replaced permanent revolution. Digging on one intersection quickly brought our wide new highway to gridlock; cyclists in their packed lanes ground to a halt next to us, tipping their perilous loads onto the ground. These new ring roads carved into land around the city: a kind of ever-expanding urban skeleton that was being fleshed out with gleaming new flats and offices. But the traffic was still solid; even high intensity, day and night building schedules couldn't accommodate the soaring demand for road space.

The taxi eventually dropped us at the calm, modern complex of the Asian Games Village. Our friends Nick and Xiaodi were taking a sabbatical in Beijing, and put us up in a flat next to theirs. Xiaodi once worked for the Chinese Foreign Ministry and took a dim view of Western journalists and their often-superior attitudes by and large, but she forgave me for being one of the breed, and she and her husband warmly made us feel at home.

....

I felt embarrassed at how little I knew about this giant country which, in spite of being home to 1.3 billion people, had deserved barely a mention during all my years at school. No one in my immediate family had been here, although a great-grandmother had visited Shanghai in 1900 and brought back beautiful silk robes covered in embroidered dragons – but these had been sold. My earliest images of China were from television, of children in plain blue jackets and trousers waving Mao's Little Red Book. The day my sister got hold of a copy, we brandished it as if it was the latest fashion statement. I had seen peasant women bending over fields with babies on their backs, in films like *The Inn of the Sixth Happiness*, and I thought of China's leaders as ageing, unsmiling men presiding over a vast, parading army. When I was seventeen, I had a mad crush on a French student activist who sounded so sophisticated and sexy when he whispered in my ear, '*Je suis un Maoïste!*'; I had no idea what it really meant and, I suspect, neither did he.

As China began its reforms and opened up to the foreign media, much more filtered through, and certainly I couldn't fail to be shocked at the events of 1989 in Tiananmen Square. Soon after, I read Jung Chang's *Wild Swans*, ready to be horrified at the strife and famine of the twentieth century, the senseless brutality of the Cultural Revolution, and in particular at the depth of suffering of millions of Chinese women.

....

Now, as a first-time foreign tourist, I knew I wouldn't see much outward sign of the horrors that China had inflicted on its own people. I would no doubt see what I was supposed to, but even that was going to be for me a vital step in trying to understand some fraction of the culture my child would be from.

Xiaodi took us to the opening ceremony of a new primary school of performing arts in Beijing. On a playing field of artificial grass, encircled by a pink running track at the feet of some concrete tower blocks, the pupils gathered in brilliant sunshine. Rows of girls in short red skirts, luminous white blouses and white tights, with smiles to match, played accordions in unison. I gazed at each of them, wondering whether my daughter would look like the one with a moon face, or the one with short pigtails, or that tiny one on the end who was struggling to hold her huge instrument. They belted out a chorus from *Carmen*, and then seamlessly changed to the quick, springy tunes of traditional folk songs. Three eight-year-old girls stood up, waved their red fans and sang piercingly high, without a hint of shyness:

Chuntian zai na li?
Chuntian zai na li?
Chuntian zai na xiao pengyou de yanjing li ...

Where is spring?
Where is spring?
Spring is in little friend's eyes ...

....

Underneath the blue sky, they grinned into the distance just like a propaganda film about the glories of the Revolution –

© Gerald Slocock

The Little Angel Art School, Beijing.

but this joy and optimism came from no government instruction. The children were genuinely proud to be showing off their impressive musical talents and the mood was festive. As foreigners, and friends of the headmaster, we were quickly turned into dignitaries and put in the front row as guests of honour, while Gerald was asked to cut a wide red ribbon to mark the official opening of the school.

We ate that night in a restaurant in which every table had a big hole in it to make way for a steaming casserole of boiling water and herbs. The waitresses brought round thin slices of beef, lamb and vegetables for us to dip into the broth for a few seconds before eating them. This was fast food at its best. Any suggestion that our cooking skills would be stretched any further evaporated when Gerald opened Xiaodi's oven to find it home to piles of clean tea towels.

. . . .

A couple of hours drive out of Beijing in the blistering May heat, we began our induction into Chinese history with the Western Qing Tombs. Just as we stepped through the main ceremonial gateway we had to make way for some paunchy officials in floor-length silk robes with red berets who marched past the ceremonial lions and knelt and kissed the ground in front of the throne on the far side. Most were in black, but the grandest wore a golden robe embroidered with dragons as he bowed his head to honour the ruthless eighteenth-century emperor Yongzheng. Yongzheng had usurped his father's throne, executed all his ministers, and slaughtered even his own brothers to eliminate any threat to his power. So, in a rare pang of imperial guilt, he had decided not to be buried with the rest of his family in the established royal tombs,

© Gerald Slocock

Western Qing Tomb.

but to build his burial place far away on the opposite side of Beijing.

Squeaky music blared out over loudspeakers and the guards' canopies, held aloft in orange, pink and yellow, swayed in the breeze. Then, as suddenly as it had begun, the daily ritual was over. The group of courtiers allowed their scarlet flags to flop over as they sauntered off for a break; the grace of imperialist China vanished instantly with their slothful, modern gait. Outside the tomb's white-hot central courtyard, a camel lazed, half-asleep under a tree, chewing her cud, overdressed and spoilt in her elaborate saddle and bridle.

Lunch was courtesy of the bespectacled local head of the provincial government. There was pork crackling so thick and dark it almost broke my teeth, bowls of spicy peanuts, deep green seaweed and hot soup. We made polite conversation and quickly learned the first rule of Chinese manners. Gerald found that each time he finished the food on his plate more would be piled onto it, stretching even his gargantuan appetite. We were told it was a sign of affluence and generosity if the table was still laden with food even after the guests had finished eating. This clashed with Gerald's firm north of England upbringing where waste was a sin, and he was horrified to see piles of food returned to the kitchen. We could barely move after this feast, and just managed to totter round the Hall of Enormous Grace, with its red walls cemented by gluey rice and pigs' blood, before driving back to Beijing.

On the way back we came across a deserted wooden town, as if emptied by war or plague. A few thatched roofs lay torn up on the ground and dust swirled in the courtyards. We wandered the streets imagining what disaster or spell had been cast over this place. Then we saw a woman in a black and grey striped gown, a red shawl swept over her shoulders and her hair pinned up with poppies posing seductively in front of an ox cart. She stroked the two jet-black ringlets in front of her ears, admiring in a hand mirror how they stood out on her face, whitened by chalky make-up. Men in grey tunics and tight black turbans with a bun of hair on top looked at her, smirking. Others sat around smoking.

It slowly dawned on us that we had fallen on a set for the latest historical television drama. The elegant lady was one of the stars having some publicity photos taken, while inside a courtyard film cameras whirred on the 'First Emperor' lounging on his throne and barking orders to his courtiers. Some of his attendants were getting restive waiting for their cue. Their wizened, country faces looked down from a balcony and soon became distracted by us, the 'big noses' (as Westerners are called) who had wandered in. They surrounded us, eagerly chatting and ogling in particular at Gerald's unusual height.

In Beijing, over the next few days, we packed in as much of the standard tourist itinerary as the early summer heat would allow – the languid lake of the Summer Palace, the massive squares of the Forbidden City, the mind-stretching statistics of the Great Wall and the brash commercialism of Silk Street Market. We managed one less well-trodden visit, and that was to the spartan offices of Bishop Joseph Liu Yuanren. He was the head of the government-approved branch of the Catholic Church, the one that did not defer to the authority of the Pope. It was perhaps no coincidence that our parish priest in London had recommended we see this old friend of his, saying, 'It might be unfashionable to say it, but the official "patriotic" church in China does a lot of good work.'

Bishop Joseph's small, scruffy office in a courtyard off a shady street was a welcome detour from the heat of the tourist sites. The walls inside were a dish-water green while the Bishop himself looked immaculate with his swept-back grey hair, white shirt buttoned to his neck and black waistcoat, more like a professor than a man of the cloth. He told us that he longed for unity with the unofficial church. His was a bit like a Protestant branch of the church where the state, Beijing in his case, appointed the bishops. The other, unofficial, church had to remain underground, secretly deferring its appointments to the Pope. Just like Henry VIII in England, the Chinese Communist Party would not tolerate the idea of the Vatican, a foreign institution, dictating who would become church leaders in their country.

Bishop Joseph was from Nanjing and had been banished to the countryside for fourteen years during the Cultural Revolution, but he was now fully rehabilitated and regaled us in true Communist style with a hail of numbers that would have been the envy of church leaders in Britain: 'There are now 5,000 churches, 5 million church-goers, an increase of 70,000 every year, as well as over 64 seminaries ...'

We talked through a translator who was word perfect until an uncomfortable moment when she said that our parish priest had posted a 'bullet' to the bishop. For a moment we thought we had touched on a new ecclesiastical rift, perhaps a veiled threat. After much consternation at her mistake our student realised that she'd meant to say 'bulletin'. In retaliation the Bishop simply gave us nothing more deadly than packets of green tea to deliver to his friend back in London.

After this religious bridge-building I was ready to face the mysterious and all-powerful China Centre of Adoption Affairs. This was the place where our adoption papers were now resting. I imagined our Home Study, medical reports and police checks lying at the bottom of a huge pile of other papers from 'prospective substitute parents' beginning their slow climb to the top before being matched with another set of papers representing an abandoned child: a kind of bureaucratic moment of conception. This was the office that would determine our future lives: the hub of the whole adoption process in China. It stood in a God-like position, organising the slow transfer of a slice of China's gene pool to the West. In spite of this momentous role, it was housed in a modest modern building behind simple iron gates.

We were greeted by a beaming representative from the Liaison and Service Department and ushered into the director's office. He was formal and polite but it was difficult to make much headway with our questions. We wanted to know whether there was a system for matching children with their new parents. He talked of how batches of abandoned children in one province would be matched with a batch of parents from one country. Then he said, 'We look at the face, we match the photograph of the child with the parents, often the father.'

Xiaodi turned to me and winked. 'Of course it's the father, what importance do women have?!'

The director seemed a little suspicious of our motives in coming to see him: 'You have to be patient; don't think because you are here that your application can move any faster, we have to give priority to domestic adoptions.'

'Of course,' we replied.

Domestic adoption was notoriously slow and expensive in China, although it had very recently become the state's policy to make it easier. In the past parents had to be over 35, perhaps the norm for adopters in the UK but in China viewed as being very old to start a family. Now the approved age had dropped to 30, but it was still a long and intrusive bureaucratic process which many Chinese people didn't want to undertake.

As we left, catching glimpses of an office piled high with files from all over the world, we chatted to the Liaison man. He was obviously used to quick repartee, and when I told him I thought we had about nine months to wait for our referral of a child, he said, 'Ah, so from today you are officially pregnant!' I liked that: 'officially pregnant'. It had all the solidity and reliability of the heavy Chinese state machine behind it. Once the cogs started turning here parents did end up with a baby. It seemed so much better than all my fragile biological attempts to have a child. I felt for a moment grateful to this centralised, all-powerful state; it had awesome, sometimes terrifying powers over its people and now over my life too.

. . . .

My early impressions of China had always been of a monolithic, even monochrome, country. As we flew south to China's official tourism province, Yunnan, I realised how totally wrong I had been. Yunnan alone is home to twenty-six ethnic minorities and as many cultures, costumes and languages. Kunming, the capital, is also known as 'Spring City' because of its mild climate. I wondered if this was a dangerous nickname, given that the other city to boast eternal spring is Medellin in Colombia; it too had a perfect climate, along with the mother of all drug cultures. Yunnan bordered the Golden Triangle countries of Thailand, Myanmar and Laos, and suffered from rising drug addiction. But none of that was mentioned in the colourful brochure, filled with photographs of floral displays and lines of ladies in ethnic dress advertising the Kunming International Tourism Festival.

This was a city, like Beijing, in the throes of change; it felt youthful and vibrant, but was still suffering from the apparently unstoppable march of the property developer. Crammed between the white-tiled modern blocks we found a few streets left of the old town that hadn't yet been bulldozed. Rough wooden houses bordered a market humming with trade. Stalls sold roots, herbs, mah-jong sets and baskets of eggs painted in rippled bright colours like Venetian glass. All forms of life were on sale: dogs and cats were squeezed into tiny cages, while luminous fish glowed in tanks piled so high they filled a whole shimmering wall of one shop. Street cooks threw sizzling fat into woks, not flinching as they burst into flame, and we watched an old man draw on a long thick wooden pipe making the cigarette he'd put into a small hole at the bottom glow.

I found wandering this market just as fascinating as the splendid but sometimes sterile tourist sights. We were jostled by men carrying baskets on long poles over their shoulders and admired the serene elegance of a woman in a flowing dress and straw hat riding sidesaddle on the back of a bicycle. And just as we felt weary, we found a group of blind masseurs in white coats on a street corner who pummelled and prodded us until we felt the energy return to our tired spines.

When it comes to the status of women, Yunnan has much to teach the rest of China. Its ethnic minorities are exempt from the One Child Policy, so here the preference for sons – or at least the need to reject daughters – is far lower than in other parts of the country, but even without that, the province is home to groups who honour women in a way unheard of elsewhere in the country. Near Lijiang there is a branch of the Naxi people, called the Moso, who make women the heads of households and shun the idea of marriage. The head 'mother' lives with her brother who does all the heavy labour on the land – which she owns. Each night a man from another household comes to visit her, while the brother goes to another house to sleep, perhaps with another female head of household. In the morning the lovers or '*a zhu*' return to their own homes. Any children who are the product of these relationships are brought up by the mother.

The Moso people appeared to follow the opposite pattern to China's patriarchal society. They are just as keen to give birth to a girl, to whom they can pass on their land and who will continue the family name, as the rest of China seems to eager to have a boy. They live in a beautiful valley beside a lake, but their Eve's paradise has recently been marred by the increasing incidence of sexually transmitted disease, including HIV.

Lijiang is the centre of the Naxi region and we walked the narrow canals, criss-crossed by little stone bridges, admiring the restored wooden buildings, the atmosphere of confidence and prosperity, even if it was slightly overrun by tourist groups.

The Naxi orchestra plays every night the late eighth-century ceremonial music of Taoism; ironically these descendants of Tibetan nomads were preserving part of Chinese history that the Chinese themselves had all but destroyed. The dedicated musicians had been forced to disperse during the Cultural Revolution, burying their instruments for safe keeping. Today many of them were in their eighties; their long beards gave the impression of deep wisdom while their shrunken faces stared into the distance, as if some part of the spirit of their music was still buried in the mists of time. They played, hypnotically, two-stringed fiddles, Persian lutes, bamboo flutes and a giant brass gong, recreating the sounds of ancient dynasties. It could have been so beautiful but the organisers had cast them all in a strange red light to prevent visitors making video recordings of the performance, so the rich colours of their clothes were lost and I had to shut my eyes to prevent a headache. The ageing players, too, clearly found the whole experience draining as they nodded off to sleep one by one; even though we all applauded enthusiastically, the old men remained expressionless, some still asleep. Later we saw them change quickly out of their ceremonial costumes into blue 'Mao' suits before hurrying inconspicuously down the street.

For a taste of the outdoors and the dramatic landscape around Lijiang, we took a cable car up a small peak to view the immense Jade Dragon Snow Mountain. We panted in the rarefied air, dazzled by the sunlight as locals slid down the snowy slopes on inflated cushions. Several nineteenth-century botanists, including the famous Joseph Rock, had explored these mountains and their foothills discovering exciting new plants, like camellias, chrysanthemums, rhododendrons and azaleas, which now adorn English gardens.

In the shadow of the mountain, the wide, slow flow of the Yangtze gathers speed and at one famous site, rages through a fifty-foot gap in the mountains. Legend has it that it's narrow enough for a tiger to flee a hunter, hence its name – 'Tiger Leaping Gorge'. The river here was a boiling thunderous torrent, as it crashed between boulders, trying to escape the narrow confines of the cliffs. The dramatic scene attracted a steady trickle of tourists, including large Chinese ladies who were carried down hundreds of stone steps on a *huagan*, a chair on poles carried by porters. An incongruous party of giggling office workers, complete with smart suits and high heels, posed at the railings as the water crashed behind them, while some bored-looking girls decked out in Moso traditional dress waited for the cameras to point at them before asking for money. Their mothers, eagle-eyed, watched nearby. There are plans to build a giant dam here to supply power and water to Kunming, and in a few years this place may have disappeared for good. This simple, dramatic beauty was under threat from the needs of millions of people, thirsty for the comforts of a modern life.

We had been inspired by reading Simon Winchester's book about his journey up the Yangtze, *The River at the Centre of the World*, so we couldn't fail to visit Cloud Mountain at Shigu. It was, he wrote, 'the axial point of China's very being', quite a claim for an apparently insignificant lump of carboniferous limestone. We drove to this modest green hill, in no way as dramatic as the sights we had just seen and tried to understand its legendary role in the creation of China. The Yangtze flows due south here, now less of a cauldron and more of a swirling soup bowl, but when it hits the base of Cloud Mountain it is forced to turn virtually back on itself and flow north-east – and ultimately on for 2,000 miles to become the third longest river in the world, irrigating land for a twelfth of the world's population before reaching the Pacific. Without Cloud Mountain the Yangtze would have carried on south into Vietnam, and China might never have been able to sustain its massive population. Although there must have been other mountains keeping the river from flowing south, the Chinese have credited Yu the Great with the brilliance of having planted Cloud Mountain in this particular place, at around 2200 BC, as part of a general flood control programme demanded by the emperor at the time.

After taking in the enormity of this idea and wondering what the history of the world would have been like if Yu the Great had failed to put Cloud Mountain in the right place, we decided to steady our thoughts in the little town of Shigu nearby. We rested beside a 300-year-old wooden slatted bridge, suspended by iron chains between two ornamental gates from the Qing dynasty. Men tottered across carrying huge piles of hay; a woman with a dark blue apron staggered as she too carried a heavy basket on her back. Little seemed to have changed here since the bronze statue nearby was erected, a statue of a young revolutionary officer shaking hands with a grateful-looking peasant to commemorate the People's Army crossing the river in 1936 during the Long March. In the

© Gerald Slocock

Wooden bridge at Shigu.

fields, the women were cutting sheaves of corn, and tying them up with string before loading them onto an ox cart.

The Upper Yangtze valley was filled with Naxi villages perched above neat rows of terraces and then, as we climbed higher, we hit rolling plains bordered by snow-capped mountains. Once on the high plateau the architecture changed from curvy Chinese roofs to the straighter Tibetan style, over houses made of compressed earth and timber. Their whitewashed walls and heavily decorated high windows overlooked fields dotted with giant spiked wooden stoops for drying straw.

Our destination, Zhongdian, is a special Tibetan autonomous area within China. Tibetans here have strong links to the Naxi and Han Chinese and the Chinese army is said to have protected them from Tibetan robber bands descending from the rugged mountains further north. Like every other town we visited Zhongdian was enjoying a boom time. New buildings, and a long and bustling new high street, overshadowed an old quarter where ancient wooden buildings were slipping precariously into the dusty earth.

Our home was the Yongsheng Hotel with its graceful courtyard, ornately carved windows and a reception area so beautifully painted it kept us transfixed while we waited for anyone to notice our arrival. Floor to ceiling were golden carvings of dragons and monsters. 'Welcome to a bright pearl on the crown of "shagrila",' [sic] said the hotel brochure, promoting the city's nickname of Shangri-La, after the mythical Himalayan kingdom of peace and harmony. And certainly the hotel staff displayed few worries. The place was light-hearted and echoed with laughter; in fact it had all the atmosphere of St Trinian's without Joyce Grenfell to keep order.

The hotel appeared to be run by 17-year-old girls wearing the Tibetan traditional costume: a long tunic with a white apron in front and pleated half skirt at the back. They would giggle and run after one another round the courtyard, waving their yak-tail dusters before taking a hose and spraying each other with water, stopping suddenly when they remembered, with more snorts of mirth, that they were supposed to be looking after the guests. The smiling, miniskirted yuppie manageress Tsao Ye was all of 22. She would carry a skipping rope across the yard, and then impishly take a few skips, or we'd see her casually throwing a ping-pong ball against a window and playing catch. The only shadow on the jollity was the mauve lighting in our bathroom which we were told was there to make it difficult for drug addicts to find their veins: a strangely incongruous precaution in this land of laughter and sunlight.

We hired a driver to take us further up the Yangtze valley as it wound up towards Tibet. We could see the yellow silted river twisting and turning far below as we rattled over the rough road. In a small mountain village, perched on the edge of a steep valley, we watched girls in tutus prance about the street. Older women were sitting out doing embroidery while a farmer ran behind a plough trying to keep up with his two oxen pulling it through the muddy earth. It seemed unlikely that our daughter would come from a place like this but just across the river, a short ferry ride away, was Sichuan, a place where girls were being abandoned in far greater numbers.

This little village was full of strange contradictions. The one guest house reserved for 'aliens' was adorned with solar panels on the roof and televisions in each room, yet the only toilet for guests was outside, right next to the pigsty, and given the stench it might just as well have been in it. In spite of the lack of modern plumbing, the restaurant over the road produced one of the best meals we had yet eaten: sliced marrow, yak with pepper and sesame sauce, and pork with green peppers, all locally produced and delicious.

During our entire journey our driver appeared paralysed with fear that he was heading too far from base, and he kept ringing his female boss and his wife for reassurance. We were amazed, then, when he agreed to take us the next day to the Dongzhulin monastery, an hour's drive further towards Tibet. Dongzhulin was more like a village than a temple, perched on a spectacular rocky promontory. Money was pouring into monasteries after the dark days of the Cultural Revolution, and here there was yet another mini building boom; monks in crimson robes sat astride the slate roofs doing repairs, while others rolled huge logs down a hill to a mechanical saw. Overseeing this were older monks pruning rose bushes in their garden; their red tunics and the red roses radiant against the whitewashed walls behind them. Younger monks peered at us out of their high windows, coy and curious. Inside the central temple every inch of the walls was covered with frescoes: pale-faced, long-eared, laughing Buddhas and blue-faced, scowling ones with bulbous black eyes. The red pillars, silk hangings and lacquer chests were lit by a stream of white light pouring in from the upper windows. Monks came forward to pray, beside them an official photograph of the Government-approved Tibetan religious leader, the Panchen Lama.

. . . .

We didn't want to push any further away from Zhongdian because of the lure of its celebrated Minorities Festival. Back in town we made several inquiries but were none the wiser. Being on the fifth day of the fifth lunar month the date changed each year, and no one in the Western-style 'Tibet Café' in town nor at the travel agents nor at the hotel knew when it started. Then suddenly one morning Tsao Ye told us it had begun and that we were already late. She was wearing her well-cut, western-style jacket, miniskirt and a delicate straw hat with black netting at the front. She grabbed her sister and rushed us all to a bus packed with excited spectators.

The opening ceremony was already over and the valley filled with milling crowds. At the centre was a vast stadium encircling a racetrack, with great red helium-filled balloons floating high above. Dozens of rectangular white Tibetan tents with black animal designs sewn on the top stretched away up

© Gerald Slocock

Minorities Festival, Zhongdian.

the mountainside; below them were row after row of stalls and games.

Traders were selling sizzling hot roast potatoes from their woks, and water melons from the backs of lorries. A hoopla was set up, but here the idea was to throw the ring over a sitting chicken, its legs tied together so it couldn't move. The poor birds would duck their heads every time a ring went flying over them. Every ethnic headdress was on display; women in shocking pink and white bonnets, with tassels and twists of flowered garlands in their hair, and men with weathered faces wearing tall, thick fur hats.

We sat in one tent with Tsao Ye and her family, and were offered a grey jelly-like substance with sesame and chilli sauce, dumplings, white goat's cheese, small cakes and a very greasy Tibetan butter tea. We watched a game of mah-jong, the women and men at separate tables, lining up their rectangular pieces with intense concentration before slapping them down on the chequered board with shrieks of laughter.

Horse racing was the star attraction but there were no sleek thoroughbreds here; the scraggy wild ponies brought in for the occasion had brightly coloured ribbons tied to their bridles and knotted into their tails. The jockeys, in pink shirts, were given crude racing numbers, hand-painted on pieces of square cotton; anxious punters puffed on cigarettes nearby, before placing their bets. Some jockeys rode bareback, their legs dangling almost to the ground; others had rough saddles made from blankets.

At the starting point, the ponies pranced and bucked, but once the red flag went down they clattered off into the distance, quickly disappearing in a cloud of dust. The crowd cheered as they swept round the circuit, past the seats where the mayor and Party dignitaries were sitting. Before long the ponies' short legs grew tired and some lagged well behind the others, impervious to their riders lashing them with a piece of rope. Occasionally one of them became so obviously sick of this treatment that it headed for the exit, only to be whipped back into the race. The crowd loved these moments; lines of women in their plaited woollen head bands screamed with delight and men clinging to the fence waved and jeered. Sometimes a disconsolate jockey, whose pony had become just too tired to go on, dismounted and thwacked his mount angrily before leading it out.

As soon as the races had finished, the crowds started to leave. Buses and taxis jostled for position on the road as columns of spectators crowded the paths, walking slowly across the

© Gerald Slocock

The spectators.

....

fields back to town, balloons and mobiles still fluttering in the late afternoon sunlight.

....

The next day we said goodbye to this happy land, and continued our journey. We managed a brief stay in Yangshuo near Guilin, where we admired the swirling river and the vertiginous peaks that rose out of the valley. It was beautiful, but the rain never stopped, and I missed the spontaneous good humour of Zhongdian. We found ourselves heading to an underground cave to escape the downpour only to get more drenched and coated with mud in the subterranean passages.

On one very rainy day we sheltered for a coffee, watched a pirated video of *Seven Years in Tibet*, and found ourselves talking to a Scottish girl who was living in Yangshuo and studying Mandarin. She pointed to a sign in the street and translated it for us: 'Girls grow up to be adults too, girls are equal to boys', it said. Travelling without the language we were blind to such messages. After our carefree journey this was a salutary reminder of why we were there, and the harsh reality of a mundane, day-to-day prejudice against girls which was eventually to deliver us our daughter.

....

After the trip, the prospect of going to China for the adoption seemed less daunting. We'd seen the colour and the vibrancy, the warmth and generosity of the people, all so diametrically opposed to the stern official face of the country. We were in a hurry to go back, but 'hurry' is not a word to be used in the same sentence as 'adoption'. We still needed the patience of those Buddhist monks.

It was hardly a coincidence then that back in my job covering Religious Affairs, I felt an extra drive to put a story about the rise in the popularity of Buddhism onto the news. The Shaolin monks and their superhuman body-bending feats were in London, having come over from Henan Province, the same region where my niece Octavia was born. I could almost see her oval face in the little boys who stood motionless on one leg while they nonchalantly tucked the other behind their ear. These athletic, extraordinary people were descended in a continuous tradition from the mystical founders of kung fu.

I contrasted them with the kind of Buddhism we were more used to seeing in the West, visiting a retreat centre in Devon, called Gaia House. It had once been a convent but now, instead of housing contemplative nuns, people suffering from the noisy, fast pace of modern living would spend weekends there in total silence, breathing deeply and walking in snail-like slow motion across the lawns. For 'socially engaged' Buddhism, I tracked down the Buddhist chaplain of Grendon High Security Prison. Dressed in orange robes and sandals, this former actor sat and meditated in front of rows of muscular, battle-scarred criminals. As they chanted calmly in the shadow of a life-size bronze Buddha I could well believe that their violent lives were being transformed for the better. It may be no coincidence that Grendon had one of the lowest reoffending rates in the country.

. . . .

Although it was still many months before we would bring our child home, I started making enquiries about local nurseries and primary schools, aware that in our area people often put their children down for them at birth if not before. I didn't know when my daughter had been born, but supposed she must by now exist somewhere in China, a crying little speck in a sea of 1.3 billion people. It was my first time as a 'prospective substitute parent' ringing schools that dealt mainly with 'parents'.

I phoned one private primary school near Notting Hill. 'Excuse me, could I register my child at your school?'

'Yes, madam. How old is she?'

'I don't know.'

'When is her birthday?'

'I don't know.'

'Has she been born or hasn't she?' came the slightly irritated voice.

'Yes, she has been born, at least I think so, somewhere in China, and we are going to adopt her. She's probably a few months old by now.'

'I see. well, it is very late, there probably isn't much point registering her.'

'Why?'

'We have mothers putting their children down on our list at birth. For each month of the year we give five confirmed places to children born in that month, and we put five more on the waiting list.'

'What about adopted children? Aren't they then always at a disadvantage?'

'We have to be fair, and act purely on a first come, first served basis.'

I could feel the cold logic of her argument was going to be impenetrable. 'So what do you do about adopted children?' I asked.

'We don't have any adopted children here,' came the unforgiving voice.

First come, first served. I went over and over that in my mind. It sounded so innocuous, so fair-minded, but it put an insurmountable barrier in front of any adopted child, and I'm sure the people in charge of admissions never lost a moment's sleep over it. I was incensed at the narrow-minded, rigid attitude; I would never want to send my daughter to such a school anyway, so there was no point arguing further.

A few other schools were more welcoming and I was able to put my daughter down for them in the abstract, but most were simply apologetic and full up. One stood out above the others, a nursery school called Mrs Mynor's. In spite of its huge waiting lists, the response was quite different when I rang up. 'Ah, how interesting, a little girl from China. That sounds fine, we have a policy of reserving two places every year for adopted children, and I am due to go soon on a study tour of early learning centres in China to find out more about education there,' said the breezy headmistress without drawing breath. 'I'll send you a form and you can fill it in and there shouldn't be a problem.'

'Thank you so much,' I said, ready to cry with gratitude. It was hard enough wondering if I was actually going to be a mother at all, without the overly precious private schools in our area confirming that, in their eyes, we were low priority. I couldn't bare the thought of my daughter playing second fiddle to children of privileged families just because she had been abandoned at birth. I was determined that she was going to be the equal of any of them.

Seven months into my 'official' gestation period, I went to visit one of our local state schools, which the headmaster, who was once an artist, had filled with African and Far Eastern sculptures. The children flocked up to him in the playground eager to talk, an array of nationalities, including an adorable Ethiopian boy who showed me a piece he'd written about himself: 'My grandfather was imprisoned by President Mengistu and my father fled to Britain ...' The son of an asylum seeker: I thought I would be proud for my daughter to be educated alongside people like him. Anyway she will be a kind of asylum seeker, but starting from babyhood, and growing up as my daughter.

....

I had a vague idea of life after adoption. I thought I could probably just about cope if everything went well, but still felt desperately underprepared if things went badly. What if our daughter came to us traumatised and unhappy? How would we teach her to trust us? Our Home Study had been more directed at assessing our abilities at parenting, rather than teaching us how to deal with the reality of a child who had been wrenched out of her familiar environment.

We were friends with an excellent adoption psychologist, Franca Brenninckmeyer from the Post-Adoption Centre, but strangely I found myself avoiding talking to her about adoption, afraid that what she might say would make me falter, or fill me with fears about my child. She dealt day to day with children scarred by separation and trauma who took years to settle with their new families. She saw the problem cases, and helped couples become 'therapeutic parents' and learn how to heal their child's wounds. I didn't really want to hear about them, preferring to live in a bubble of not knowing, of hoping that everything would just work out. It was a short-sighted approach, but on the other hand I had to believe in adoption as something that was going to be positive and happy, otherwise I didn't think I would have the energy to pursue it.

Luckily Franca took the initiative in her own hands and plied me with books to read. I learnt about parenting 'the child who hurts', about the symptoms that would show if there was trauma: lack of eye contact, unstoppable tantrums, aversion to touch, being fearful, too independent or excessively clingy. But as I knew absolutely nothing about how to parent an untraumatised child, I could barely imagine trying to deal with these extra layers.

I also needed my rose-tinted view to counteract the negativity in the press about overseas adoption. The news was full of a British couple who had adopted – although the press was saying they'd allegedly 'bought' – a pair of twins in the US state of Arkansas after finding them through the internet. These people were now in a battle with an American couple who had also been allocated the same children. The next day my boss came up to me in the office. 'Is this story of the internet twins upsetting you?'

'Well, it's a lesson in what happens when you step outside the very rigorous procedures in this country. What does upset me is that people get the idea that you can "buy" a child over the internet and that just isn't possible to do with all the social service checks we had to go through.'

'You're our resident expert on adoption; can you go to the US tonight to cover it?'

Within a few hours I was heading for Arkansas via Chicago to examine the strange workings of the adoption system there. Apparently the birth mother of the twins had given them first to a couple in California, but after two months had changed her mind and decided to give them to the British couple. They had then driven 2,000 miles with her from the West Coast to Arkansas to get a quickie adoption from a compliant judge.

Just after we landed in Chicago, the newsroom decided to divert us to Los Angeles at the last minute with the brief to try and interview the American family there. We drove straight to the suburb of San Bernadino, and knocked on the door of a large suburban house. Inside, behind the curved, regal staircase and highly polished floor, we found a family bereft. They had nothing, except a brief memory of parenthood and a mortifying sense of having been duped. They felt powerless in the face of a system that gave them absolutely no rights until the children had been with them for three months. They showed us the little bedroom where the twins had slept for a few weeks, the rows of clothes they had prepared for them, even the little white baptism dress.

Adopting in the US, where the birth mother chooses the family she wants to parent her child, is a very open affair. There is a lot of contact between the adopters and the natural mother, but this case showed up the weakness in the system. Take a poor, impressionable young mother, a corrupt adoption 'broker' who wants her to give her children to the highest bidder, a couple who will bypass all the regulations, and a state like Arkansas where adoptions are relatively easy to arrange and it was all too easy to see how things can go so wrong.

. . . .

The trouble with a bureaucratic pregnancy is that there's no maximum time limit. Our nine months gestation began to extend until the baby became alarmingly overdue. First, Chinese New Year added a couple of weeks, and then a backlog of applications pushed things further back. Everyone around us was eager for a date and it became increasingly awkward trying to explain why we didn't have one. We had recruited a translator in China who told us we could expect to hear in another month. The Department of Health backed this up; it looked like March or April. Still it was hard to feel confident. It was ten months since our papers set off for China and we had heard absolutely nothing since − not a letter or a message to say that everything was fine. They could have got lost, we could have been refused a baby without knowing: the possibilities were endless. The Chinese might have seen that I worked for the BBC and in a fit of pique after a critical story just decided to slip our papers in the bin. I began to doubt again that the journey would ever end.

I found myself both yearning to know what child would be picked out for us, yet terrified too. I longed to be a mother, but found myself secretly enjoying the freedom of not yet having entered that world of selfless devotion. I knew, deep down, I wasn't really the selfless devoted type, never having thought of myself as a great earth mother. After all, I'd started to want children late in life and certainly hadn't had an earth-mother role model. My mother used to find cooking a chore and once, my aunt told me, when she was frying an egg and it somehow flipped out of the frying pan onto the floor, she simply flicked it up and threw it back in, without pausing in her diatribe about nineteenth-century French literature. Domesticity was not her strong point.

So I had no maternal reference point and on top of that it was very unreal; after all, I was effectively nine months pregnant but without any physical sign of a baby. Mentally I tried to prepare myself, but emotionally I felt strangely detached, as if a new baby was something that was going to happen to someone else.

What we weren't short of was helpful, if sometimes contradictory advice from other adopters: 'Make sure you take nappies, milk formula, a pushchair ...' Others said, 'Don't take nappies as you can buy them there, use the local milk formula because it will be more familiar to her, and don't take a pushchair, take a sling, body contact is so important, and don't forget the scabies ointment.' We heard how one baby was infested with scabies which her parents didn't initially recognise; they ended up back in London having to wash every item of clothing and bed linen to get rid of the parasite ...

Then a month later this strange limbo came to a head. One Saturday in April, the postman left a card to say there was a letter or packet to collect from the sorting office. It could have been our long-awaited referral from the Department of Health, a supply of contact lenses or a new credit card.

....

I also noticed that I was feeling distinctly peculiar and queasy, and discovered, to my amazement and shock, that I was pregnant: an accident if ever there was one, but what fateful timing, two potential babies in one day and either − or both − could be a phantom that might evaporate. It was April Fool's Day and someone had to be playing an enormous joke. On the same day an American spy plane collided with a Chinese fighter jet off Hainan Island, sending it spinning into the sea south of the Chinese mainland. The next few days would be a whirl of hopes and confusion, just as a diplomatic crisis went into overdrive.

....

On the Monday Gerald went to the post office. In his hand, as he charged back through the front door, was a large brown envelope stamped with the immortal words 'Guaranteed Delivery'. He handed it to me and we looked at each other. This was it. I tore it open and pulled out a letter from the Department of Health: 'We are pleased to tell you that you have been matched with a little girl called Lin Na from Shaanxi Province.' It went on. 'She was born on 21 June 2000 and is now in the care of the Yulin Child Welfare Institute.'

Attached to the letter was a photograph taken when she was five months old: it showed a pale, chubby baby, with brown eyes, a slight red rash around her mouth and a glum expression. She was sitting in split trousers with no nappy, looking as if she had just wet herself. 'Poor little mite', I said to myself. Her eyebrows were a little wrinkled, her eyes questioning. Was this really our daughter? She looked solid and real enough, but I couldn't feel her presence from the photograph. I wanted to hug her, but the motionless picture just stared back. 'She looks a bit like you!' I said to Gerald. There was something about the breadth of her face which gave her a passing resemblance to him and to what his dentist called his 'eccentric jaw'. I searched to feel a link with her. This was now our child, but at the same time I felt she was a stranger.

We reached for our map of China and looked up Yulin. It turned out to be a town on the fringe of Inner Mongolia's Mu Us desert, about 300 miles north of Shaanxi's provincial capital, Xi'an. We could see the black dot, right on the line that wiggled across the length of northern China marking the path of the Great Wall. It was described as a 'garrison town' and patrol post serving the Wall. We had always loved remote regions and the people in them so to find our own daughter was from one of the less accessible parts of China seemed to augur well.

I drove immediately to Xiaodi's house, thrusting into her hand the medical report in Chinese for her to translate. She told me Lin Na meant 'girl of the forest' and she read out her head and chest sizes and showed me the list of tests that she had undergone. Everything was listed as 'normal' and then there were a few paragraphs outlining her monthly development. When she was a week old she had been left on the steps of Yulin's Child Welfare Institute. The staff there brought her in and she was soon having seven feeds a day, including two at night. When she was three months old she started smiling and moving her hands and feet, holding toys and not letting them go. By six months she was starting to eat rice porridge, eggs and bread, and showing more interest in the outside world. I searched in vain for some evidence of her character. Did she smile? Did she like to play? There was nothing like that. This brief sketch was all there was.

I emailed our translator and begged him to find out more. We called our daughter Jade Lin to keep some of her given Chinese name. She looked so forlorn that I wanted to get her home, to smooth out those wrinkled eyebrows and squeeze those round cheeks.

That night, a couple who were about to adopt twins from Sichuan Province came to supper. While we revelled in having our referrals at last, hanging over us was the shadow of a diplomatic battle raging in the Far East. American warships had been ordered to steam towards Chinese territory as the row over the downed American spy plane deteriorated. It was a stand-off reminiscent of the Cold War. The American patrol plane was forced to land on Hainan Island, while the Chinese plane crashed with the loss of the pilot. The rhetoric was becoming increasingly heated on both sides. We knew that overseas adoptions from China had been suspended once before, when the US bombed the Chinese Embassy in Serbia, and we couldn't bear the thought of global politics getting in the way now.

We wrote to the Department of Health to say we accepted Lin Na, completely hooked by her photograph, and didn't wait for any update on her medical state. Perhaps we were foolish, but then emotion was taking over from reason. I kept looking at her picture. It was a strange feeling, but was I falling in love? After thinking at first that she didn't look particularly like our child, I now just couldn't take my eyes off her. It was as if something deep and hormonal was kicking in just from staring at her picture. The signal between eyes and brain was already creating a bond. We now just had to wait for our 'Invitation to Travel', a vital document that would enable us to get the right visa.

The stand-off between America and China over the crashed spy plane dragged on and now former President Clinton was on a visit to Beijing. To see him striding along the Great Wall was an odd coincidence. Just to think, little Lin Na was sitting in her dusty 'garrison town' a few hundred miles west, along that same Wall — like an ancient stone thread linking that TV image to our child. I wondered what she was doing now, eating, sleeping or crawling? I didn't even know if she could crawl, and what about the rash around her mouth? She could have no idea of the momentous change that was about to hit her.

Gerald rang the Department of Health, to find out when we should book our flights to travel to China. It was unclear how many weeks it took for the 'Invitation to Travel' to arrive. He managed to get through by devious means, contacting a neighbouring department and getting them to leave a message for our contact there. They told us it would be another six weeks. The DoH did its job in processing adoption applications but didn't apparently relish personal contact with prospective adopters, whether from underfunding or lack of motivation, it was hard to tell. Overseas adoption was understandably a low priority, but on the other hand I could imagine worse jobs than putting abandoned babies in touch with eager new parents.

We received an email from our translator in Beijing saying that he'd phoned Yulin and discovered that Jade was a very big baby with enormous feet, and apparently healthy. She was living not at the orphanage, but with foster parents. That was great news as it meant she would be getting more attention, learning to attach to her foster mother and would not be nearly so deprived. Overseas adoption had only recently begun from this remote region, and it was impressive that they had already begun to foster out the children. Or perhaps they just couldn't look after all the children in the children's home.

We also heard from our parish priest, Father Oliver McTernan, who was away studying religious conflict at Harvard. It turned out that one of his close colleagues there was a colonel in the People's Liberation Army who was 'very pleased' to hear of our adoption. It was strangely reassuring to think we had the PLA behind us if anything went wrong: clutching at straws perhaps, but the paranoia that all this would fail would not go away. After all, the US – Chinese stand-off was in deadlock, with the Chinese still holding the US flight crew, and still furious that American spy planes had been nosing so close to their coastline. China, by this time, had elevated its lost fighter pilot into a martyr; there was even a memorial website for Pilot Wang where visitors could offer online versions of traditional funerary gifts of wine, flowers or songs. President Jiang Zemin had given him the official posthumous title of 'The Guardian of the Air and Sea'. Then, eleven days into the row, the Chinese suddenly decided to release the American pilot.

Tension eased a little, although the bickering continued with George Bush flexing his muscles and insisting America had the right to resume its spy flights at any time. Father Oliver had also spoken to one Chinese military man who was amazed that the American plane had not been shot down by the second Chinese pilot; the normal instructions were to shoot if there was any incident whatsoever. That pilot had decided to return to his base. He would have known that he had saved the world from a deeper international crisis, but what he couldn't have realised was that he saved our adoption as well. I shall always be grateful to him.

....

Amidst all this turbulence, I had been trying not to think about the activity inside my own body. When I went to my gynaecologist for a scan, I held no hope that the pregnancy would still be viable. I just wanted to get the appointment over with. As he did the scan, he said casually, 'Oh yes, everything looks fine, I can see a little heartbeat.'

'What?' I strained round to the screen and saw the flickering heart beating fast and definitely. Could this be true? After all the black holes that I'd seen, did my biological system work after all?

I thought about all those times I'd been told that when you adopt your chances of becoming pregnant are greater – 'Don't worry, you'll have a "real" child soon after' – but I had dismissed it as folklore, part of the irritating attitude some people have of assuming that when you adopt you really still want a biological child. It was supposed to cheer me up in some way, as if I needed it – but actually it was so patronising and loaded with prejudice against the adopted child. I began to see how deeply adoptees were viewed as second-class children even among liberal-minded people. I heard that some adopters used the phrase, 'second choice but not second best'; second choice only because adoption is so hard to do, but it was vital the child itself must never feel less valuable as a human being. I could already sense that adoptive parents had a lot of work to do to change public attitudes.

But back to my little 'heartbeat'. I had never got as far as this before, and now was in a quandary. The social services were very strict about not getting pregnant while you are about to adopt. They insist they be told and it can completely negate your right to proceed. I agonised over whether I should tell them. If I did and they took away my precious Jade Lin, what would happen if I subsequently lost this baby? I'd end up back at square one. That was an unthinkable prospect. If I didn't tell them and this pregnancy continued, perhaps they would take Jade away when we got her back to England. Why was life so complicated? I must be doing something wrong. Other people, I was sure, had simpler, easier paths to motherhood.

Three weeks later on a hot, sultry day, I was watching Gerald play cricket feeling washed out with a profusion of different emotions. Something, no one could tell us what, had suddenly stopped our little 'heartbeat'. The next scan had shown that the baby had died. My sister said wisely, 'It's better to deal with one baby at a time,' which, of course, was true. It had been an odd twist of fate that could have entangled us into all kinds of problems. So it was better this way, I told myself firmly, although my body didn't always listen to this rational approach at all. And it was a lot less complicated. True, I thought, but the tears still flowed.

It was such a relief to focus on Jade's picture, her sturdy-looking body and the lists of baby things I needed to take to China. We were inundated with gifts, boxes of clothes and toys, while colleagues at work contributed to a Mothercare voucher which I spent on new blankets and sheets for a cot. The office had been incredibly patient, as my January departure had been extended by another four months. At my leaving party I joked about the longest pregnancy ever. 'The same as an elephant,' someone said, and we all laughed. It had been a mammoth task to get this far. For me it felt like this was the end of a career-driven era and the beginning of a new, mysterious experience: being a mother to a Chinese child.

- Chapter Four -

Journey to Jade

The monks in their red, mauve and black robes, their heads bowed, walked past chanting rhythmically. We were at the door of Puji Temple on the Buddhist Island of Putuoshan. They looked so serene in the low light, in contrast to the agitated Buddha statues, some angry, some smiling, which stared down at them. We had hoped this visit would give us a much-needed moment of spiritual tranquillity: an antidote to the nerve-straining anticipation of meeting our daughter.

It had been a frantic week getting ready to travel, working out what to take, as well as trying to discover where we were and weren't allowed to go. Although we were about to become Lin Na's parents and her roots were vitally important to us, the Chinese authorities had decided we would not be going near them. 'All the paperwork will be done in Xi'an, and you will pick up your baby from there,' our translator told us by email. We phoned him up and asked how hard it would be to go to Yulin, the town that played a vital role in Lin Na's short life. 'You can't go to Yulin, it's too difficult,' came the reply.

'What about going to the orphanage or meeting Lin Na's foster parents, is there any way we can do that?'

'No, the government doesn't permit this.'

'Why not?'

'Once a foster mother asked some Western parents for money, so now the government doesn't allow it.'

There seemed no way round this. It was frustrating, especially as we knew that some families adopting from elsewhere in China had been able to visit their child's orphanage and meet the foster parents. It seemed that in our case the veil of secrecy about Jade's origins was being well and truly held down. This Chinese version of the post-code lottery had delivered its verdict. In a few years, no doubt, it would all be different, but we were adopting from northern Shaanxi province, an area with a deeply entrenched communist culture that had only just begun overseas adoptions and was not used to foreign visitors. Ordinary tourists were encouraged in huge numbers to the provincial capital, Xi'an, but Yulin was in a sensitive area, with military bases nearby. It had originally been built as part of defensive fortifications protecting China from the Mongol hordes to the north and was still guarding itself against an invasion of nosy adoptive parents.

Normally, as a journalist, I would have challenged official obfuscation but I felt my hands were tied and I was nervous of alienating anyone in authority at this crucial stage. It might not matter if we became troublemakers, but then it might, and I would never forgive myself if anything went wrong.

We did manage to assert our independence a little by arriving in China a few days earlier than we were asked to, so we didn't actually receive our child on the same day as a long flight. Friends had told us this was the normal procedure and it had been very tough on them when they were exhausted, jet-lagged and drained from all the preparations. So we had decided to try and find a restful spot for a few days and we'd picked on a small island off the coast of Shanghai, one of the main spiritual destinations for Chinese Buddhists.

We had wanted to arrive by ferry and catch a glimpse of Shanghai's famous harbour, but the express boat had broken down. The only way to get there was to fly. Any irritation we might have harboured over this change of plan couldn't survive the serenity of Shanghai's modern airport at Pudong. The roof of the departure lounge was a giant blue canopy criss-crossed with hundreds of white struts and black cables stretching the full length of the building. It was a work of art, and as we waited for our flight we were showered too with audio Valium. The slow, sing-song tones of the tannoy announcer echoed through the cavernous hall like a voice from a distant planet: 'The flight to Zhujiajian is delayed [pause] because the plane is delayed, [pause] please wait.' There was nothing to do except give in to this brave new world. We did what we were told. We had truly arrived in China, and we felt all control over our destiny draining away.

Once we had landed at Zhujiajian we found the boat heading for Putuoshan, and watched with relief as the lush green oasis in the ocean hovered closer and closer. We stayed in a privatised state hotel, complete with red lanterns and beds that were rock hard even by Chinese standards. There were no cars on the island, only a few mini-buses − although their drivers were strangely aggressive given that they only had to compete for space with a handful of bicycles.

Inside the courtyard of Puji Temple I stood behind a crowd of pilgrims in neatly pressed shirts watching them hold their sticks of incense, kneel down and prostrate themselves in front of the giant Golden Buddha. They would turn round and then throw fake bank notes into a large iron pyre. The flames curled round them and I couldn't help thinking of all the piles of paper we too had generated to get this far. I stared at the billowing smoke, imagining throwing all those forms, those pages and pages of our Home Study into the fire. If I closed my eyes a little, I could almost see a baby girl grinning triumphantly as she rose from the ashes, clutching our report in her fist.

The temple was brand new. The original, along with its statues, was destroyed during the Cultural Revolution when all its monks and nuns had fled. In 1979 the government allowed the island to be opened up again, and guidebooks showed pages of official visits by leading members of the Communist Party. Now, about 1.5 million tourists and pilgrims came every year, drawn by what was described as 'the Buddhist Kingdom between the Sea and the Sky' or 'Fairyland in the South China Sea'. The tourist touts selling 'name stones', incense and other Buddhist bric-a-brac were so laid-back they barely murmured as potential sales opportunities walked past them.

Perhaps they were drugged by the magic of the island and the legend of its Bodhisattva, Guanyin. She was the Goddess of Mercy who, so the story goes, arrived in statue form 1,000 years ago, brought by a Japanese monk from a sacred mountain in Shaanxi Province. His intention was to introduce Buddhism to Japan but, passing in his boat by Putuoshan, he was stopped by a strong wind. He took this to mean that Guanyin was reluctant to leave China, so he decided to let her stay and consecrated her statue in a local resident's house, which later became the 'unwilling-to-leave' Guanyin shrine. In its heyday, Putuoshan was home to a trio of Grand Temples, 128 shrines and 88 nunneries, as well as 3,000 monks and nuns.

Although the island did help us feel calmer, because the weather was so sultry, the air murky and humid, we found it difficult to get the energy to do anything. Gerald couldn't sleep in his bone-bruising bed, and the heavy atmosphere was sapping our fire and enthusiasm. Perhaps it hadn't been such a good idea coming here, but it was too late to change our plans. Anyway, we no longer had the willpower to do anything except wander around in a daze.

We sat down exhausted one afternoon in a park by the 'Thousand Pace Sandy Beach' and watched a flock of white doves circle around groups of excited Chinese tourists. Each person wore a uniform of a red baseball cap and a white cotton suit. The sign on the beach was inviting and lyrical:

> In summer or autumn you may enjoy yourself by barefoot, accompanied by blasts of billows ... the beach is in easy flight and facing wide sea front as there is not rock or stone in the water ... The beach park covers an area of 10 hectares, pavilions, terraces and pagodas, bridges and waters, green grass, birds and flowers, thousands of pigeons ... You may watch sunrise and sunset at the park ... In moon nights, sounds of billows accompanied with quiet scenery makes the park rich in poetic flavour.

. . . .

This was an island where the romantic image never quite matched reality. We hoped to take the boat back to Shanghai, but our desire to see the great harbour was again sabotaged, this time by an impenetrable fog. It descended onto Putuoshan like a heavy blanket and no amount of wishful thinking was going to budge it. We waited at the ferry terminal along with several hundred others, and after fierce arguments broke out between passengers and officials at the barrier it became clear that the 'fast boat' to Shanghai was delayed indefinitely. I felt stabs of panic. We wanted a few days here, but not to be delayed so much we'd miss our flight to Xi'an and our precious rendezvous with Jade. That would be ridiculous. What were we doing here? Perhaps Bodhisattva Guanyin was having her last laugh. She wasn't the only one to find it difficult to leave Putuoshan.

We eventually worked out that the best option was to get a boat to a port on the mainland. We should actually have got the one to Ningbo, where there were trains which could have taken us straight to Shanghai, but our island-dulled brains didn't think quickly enough and we watched that boat chug off without us. We managed to team up with a couple of German students who spoke Mandarin so when the ferry finally took us over the water to another town, they helped us get on the right bus for Ningbo. Our quick little trip to Putuoshan was descending into something of a drawn-out ordeal. I wondered why I seemed to have become expert at starting long journeys that refused to end.

On the packed, three-hour bus ride, I sat next to a young man who worked for Nestlé — that great capitalist multinational well established in the People's Republic. I pointed to a phrase in my guidebook which asked which of China's leaders he admired the most. He replied without hesitation, 'Mao Tse Tung'. I was to be constantly amazed at the loyalty to Mao, even amongst people who had suffered hugely under his leadership, or who no longer believed in his policies.

There was an eight-year-old girl in front of us with two little pigtails surrounded by her adoring mother and grandparents. She chattered away for much of the journey, enjoying their undivided attention. This was just the kind of happiness Jade would be denied here, unless of course she was adopted by a Chinese family. But we had, after all, been told that domestic adoption was expensive and difficult, so not enough couples embarked on it. I began to wonder if Jade would berate us in future for taking us away from a culture that obviously adored as well as abandoned its girls.

At Ningbo, we sat in the vast waiting hall at the railway station where hundreds of passengers were arranged on row after row of pale green plastic seats. We boarded our modern diesel train to Shanghai just as a great black steam engine rolled into the station, hooting and belching smoke.

It was now nearly eleven in the evening and the rocking motion of the train had already sent some passengers to sleep; we had to squeeze past them while their heads slumped onto the tables in front. Others were talking in low voices, sipping their jars of tea and playing cards. By a strange coincidence the train was going all the way to Baotou in Inner Mongolia, via Yulin, Jade's home town. I thought that maybe if we just stayed on it we could go there now instead of waiting until Jade was grown up. I wondered what she was doing now. Fast asleep, I hoped, unaware of the huge change that was about to hit her. At least we were now one day nearer to meeting her.

We still had a little time to spare and spent it exploring Shanghai, China's dynamic commercial capital. The newly rebuilt central square had obliterated the old narrow *hutongs* to leave a huge expanse of grass and asphalt encircled by municipal buildings. One was the showcase for Shanghai's spectacular urban growth – a museum dedicated to town planning. Inside we admired a scale model of the city, lit by almost as many lights as we'd seen in the real one. Groups of workers on an outing wearing yellow baseball hats were being ushered round by a young, slightly impatient female guide. These same elderly men would probably have once lived in cramped buildings with neither running water nor electricity until a few years ago, and they nodded approvingly at the futuristic plans for their city.

Next door was the dome-roofed national museum. It was filled with fascinating objects: three-legged bronze vessels, porcelain and great parchments depicting the history of calligraphy. There was a special exhibition of artefacts from Tibet, attracting bevies of Buddhist monks who gathered outside posing for photographs. As they wandered inside looking at the intricately embroidered silk gowns, the copper vases with dragons clambering up the sides and the long carved horns, they must have inwardly cried at how much of their culture had been destroyed back home. Now China was showing it off, and a sign at the exhibition spoke only of how Tibet had always been part of China and now enjoyed positive relations with Beijing.

We ate in a vast restaurant in the French Concession area where there were two weddings going on simultaneously. We wandered down to the famous waterfront, the Bund, which at night was spectacular: green and blue laser beams searched the night sky, the colonial buildings were a blaze of fluorescent light, while on the other, futuristic side Pudong's skyscrapers looked as if they'd descended from space and were aching to return, reaching upward, one competing with the other. Giant cranes were silhouetted against the floodlit buildings. The water was a hive of activity with workers unloading cargo boats and tugs churning up the water between heavy grey ships.

We went for a drink at the Peace Hotel and found its famous jazz band half asleep, oblivious to all this energy. The crusty old players stared into the middle distance, although the trumpeter did show signs of life. Gerald requested 'A Night in Tunisia', but they played it so slowly and ponderously that it was barely recognisable. In fact there wasn't much jazz here; it felt more like Hyde Park on a Sunday afternoon.

. . . .

Then, at last, it was time for our flight to Xi'an.

I could only imagine this was a bit like going into labour without the physical pain. Everything around was serene — huge banks of cloud beneath us and the first glimpse of blue sky since we'd arrived in the country. But internally I was a mess. I might have been able to face up to muggers in Colombia or slippery lawyers in Paraguay, but the thought of meeting my child for the first time felt far more terrifying. My thoughts were really a jumble of unanswered questions. Would she like us? What if she didn't, and couldn't attach to us? Even worse, what if I didn't like her and couldn't find a maternal bond? No, don't go there — that was the biggest fear and I mustn't imagine that. Could I bring up a child I didn't like? How could I love her as my own? What kind of a mother was I going to be? No amount of Home Study sessions, reading or thinking about adoption could bring my emotions under control.

We began our descent through the dusky yellow light. I could see flat, dry arable land, neat rectangular fields and straight roads. I peered out of the window and thought 'our new life starts down there'.

We met a friend of our Beijing translator at the airport. Her name was Cici and she met us, full of bouncing smiles, at the arrivals gate. She immediately said, 'You are going to meet your baby this evening.' We had been expecting to see her the following day, but apparently the people who had brought her down from Yulin were eager to unload her.

My imaginary pregnancy was about to end. This interminable journey to motherhood was reaching its climax. I was soon to be no longer a 'prospective substitute parent', but a real mother. Time, which had passed so slowly for the two years since I had made that first phone call to our social services department, suddenly began to race by. How was it possible to feel so unprepared after all that preparation? Then the hurried minutes seemed to grind to a halt. We were in our hotel room, everything was suddenly calm. Gerald and I held hands. We couldn't speak. We heard voices down the corridor, and then the knock at the door.

. . . .

I rushed up and opened it. I scarcely noticed the four people from the Yulin Social Welfare Institute standing in the doorway. All I could see was our daughter, Lin Na. She was being held up by one young woman, who was chattering to her in Chinese. '*Zhe shi ni mama, zhe shi ni baba*' – this is your Mummy and your Daddy.

Lin Na smiled, not sure at first if she wanted to be handed over, but gradually letting go and allowing herself to be put in my arms. She looked confident, and examined me with her piercing brown eyes. That moment seemed to last an eternity. I don't think I had ever been looked at so hard. She gazed at Gerald and he described it as being like a 'laser beam of love' passing between them. She went to him without protest. It was instantly obvious that she had been well looked after. She was much healthier, and much happier looking, than in her photograph and was far more outgoing than we had expected.

I thought she would be terrified of us as complete strangers and that she would be a traumatised little girl, but instead she seemed robust, confident and certainly well fed.

'Lin Na, Jade, Lin Na, Jade,' I hugged her and squeezed her, feeling her warm, solid body in my arms. She was so real, so present. It was hard to take in the realisation that this little human being was now finally ours.

....

Everyone seemed to be in a hurry but this group was our only link to her past. I had a list of questions already translated to try and find out more about her. Zhe Ming was the smiling young woman with long black hair who'd been in charge of her at the orphanage. With her was a young man, Bai Shi Fung, who helped her. I didn't catch the names of the others, but learnt that the orphanage director was called Mr Huang Yu Lin. The 'Lin' part of his name was given to all the babies he looked after, hence the name Lin Na. They told us her nickname was '*er mao*', meaning second little baby as her foster parents had already looked after one child.

They explained that when she was found on the steps of the Social Welfare Institute at a week old there was a note pinned to her giving her birthday. I imagined this forlorn bundle, wrapped up like a parcel with a piece of paper attached; at least her parents must have wanted her to live, leaving her in a place where she was bound to be found. We noticed a jagged scar on her left thigh that looked a bit like a dog bite, but no one could tell us what it was or how it had got there.

After the flurry of people and chatter, we were suddenly left alone. I struggled to put some formula into a bottle, unsure in the fading light how much to put in, but Jade Lin didn't seem to mind and drank it non-stop. Then she fell asleep in Gerald's arms, exhausted by her eighteen-hour bus ride from Yulin and the shock no doubt of meeting the fourth set of carers she'd had in her short life: there had been her birth parents, the carers at the orphanage, her foster parents and now us. He put her into the hotel cot. As she slept, snoring gently, she could have been on a bed of lilies, without a care in the world. The cot had a built-in rocking mechanism, and Gerald let her sway back and forth, singing quietly a favourite melancholic Irish ballad:

> Oh Mary this London's a wonderful sight
> With people here working by day and by night
> They don't grow potatoes, nor barley nor wheat
> But there's gangs of them digging for gold in the street
> At least when I asked them that's what I was told
> So I took a hand at this digging for gold.
> But for all that I found there, sure I might as well be
> Where the Mountains of Mourne sweep down to the sea ...

....

She looked beautiful, peaceful and at home. Watching her gentle breathing, I couldn't take my eyes off her. I realised I was falling head over heels in love. 'So *this* is what it feels like to be a mother,' I said to myself. No one had told me that it's like a romance, where you become madly besotted with this defenceless little creature. This was the closest I could imagine to the joy of giving birth. I felt suddenly thrilled and so lucky that this long, tortuous path had given us such a beautiful baby. My mind raced to all the things we were going to do together: the trips to the park, teaching her to walk, piling up bricks ... I'd been worried that I wouldn't feel maternal, even that I might not like her, but in that moment, all the anxiety, the struggle to be a mother began to fade. I knew now she was the ultimate cure.

....

I went out on the balcony and breathed the night air – still choked with car fumes. The Bell Tower, with its graceful sloping roof, was lit up, an island of stillness in a sea of surging traffic. I could just hear its sonorous bell tolling above the cacophony of car horns. Behind it were the blazing neon signs advertising China Telecom and Xi'an's new golf courses. So here we were, in the capital of a province that was only slightly smaller than Britain, a place that once rivalled Rome and Constantinople as a centre of civilisation: it had been the start of the Silk Road at the crossroads of trading routes from eastern China to Central Asia, and the capital of many dynasties. This was a province whose political fortunes had declined over 700 years but which had risen in importance again when it became a Communist stronghold in the 1930s. Mao Zedong's Long March ended in the town of Yan'an, further north. Compared with his 6,000-mile endurance feat, my emotional journey was of course nothing, but even so it was strange to think of it too ending in the same region.

Xi'an was at the centre of a huge fertile plain that grew wheat, rice, corn, potatoes, peanuts, sesame, cotton, dates, palm and pomegranates but at the other end of that eighteen-hour bus ride it was a different picture. Jade's town was 300 miles north where the fertile valley gave way to the moonscape of the loess plateau, made up of yellow earth etched and eroded by wind and water. Where once there were lush green prairies and elm forests there were now sand dunes and dry hillsides. As we'd discovered, Yulin originally grew up as a garrison town along the Great Wall to keep out the Mongol invaders, and was home to the largest stone tower along the Wall called Zhenbeitai, or 'Pacify the North Tower'. Today it guards only against encroaching desert.

It is a place where poverty and rebellion have often gone hand in hand. I had read about one extraordinary man who made the region famous. Apparently in the early decades of the seventeenth century the Ming Court in Peking was undergoing an economy drive and laid off one of its junior officials, called Li Zicheng who lived in these wilds of north-west China. It turned out to have been a bad decision. Li desperately needed a job and enrolled in a military unit but was once again let down by the government. Without promised supplies, Li and other soldiers then mutinied and over the next few years he emerged as a natural leader among a group of rootless men looking for action. He and his rag-tag army roamed northern China competing for land with other rebel groups and clashing with the Ming army before finally, in 1644, he decided to mount an ambitious attack on Peking. He moved across the north of China with hundreds of thousands of troops, sacking the towns that resisted him and incorporating the forces of those that surrendered into his own army. Li succeeded in entering the capital without a fight after the gates were mysteriously opened for him.

Meanwhile, the Emperor Chongzhen, hearing that the rebels had entered the capital and his own ministers and courtiers had deserted him, mounted a hill behind the Forbidden City and hanged himself, ending the dynasty that had ruled China for almost 300 years. Li Zicheng himself didn't last long in power and was within a few months driven out by stronger Manchu forces from the north-east. Even so, it had been quite an achievement; I could only wonder whether this kind of strength and audacity would be part of Jade's nature too. From Beijing's point of view this province was aptly named 'Thieves Mountain West', although standing here in Xi'an everything seemed so affluent and peaceful.

．．．．．．．．．．．．．．．．

I came inside and looked at our little Shaanxi baby. Was she going to inherit the rebellious nature of her compatriots? What was she going to become? How had her parents managed to survive all the hardship and famine? Why was she here with us, sleeping so peacefully? And why was the back of her head so flat, was that something she'd inherited? Why had I never noticed other Chinese babies having heads shaped like that? She was a mystery: her roots, her genetic make up − everything was hidden from us. It was a case of what we saw was what we got.

Our first night as parents was anything but restful. 'She likes a feed at 5 a.m.,' we were told. But long before, probably about 3 a.m., we were awake, whispering about her, wondering when she would stir. She made a few squeaks and we both leapt out of bed to see her. She just wriggled around and went straight back to sleep. But we couldn't. A few more cries later, and eventually she did wake up. I fumbled around yet again with the milk bottle, not sure if I had the right dilution. I couldn't remember learning anything about this in all those months of Home Study; funny how we'd never actually been taught how to look after a baby, amidst all that examination into our suitability to be parents. Luckily she was too hungry to notice if the dilution was correct, and as the dawn light

© Gerald Slocock

First days of motherhood in Xi'an.

began to break through we could see her eyes swivel to each of us, sizing us up as she drank.

At eight the next morning Cici arrived to take us to have an official photograph for the adoption certificate. We'd managed to dress Jade and put her nappy on, although nappies were obviously a new experience for her as well as for us. She'd been used to being just held over the toilet and patted on the bottom to encourage her to perform; we'd seen her carers do it in the hotel bath-room. Now she was to be coddled in Pampers' best, and forget all her skill in that department for another year.

She was quite heavy and hadn't yet learnt to crawl, so it was clear she had been loved but not allowed to move around much. We were told that often crawling is not encouraged in houses where there isn't a suitable floor. Gerald instantly took it on himself to teach her and began crawling around the hotel room on all fours. Jade looked at him and laughed but couldn't get her chubby but weak arms and legs to support her weight. She just collapsed on her tummy and rolled on her back.

We crossed the traffic-choked, six-lane avenue in front of our hotel and through the thick haze we could see at the very end the crouching silhouette of one of the towers of Xi'an's City Wall. We stepped into a small photographic shop while Jade dreamily sat in her pushchair as if this was all just another day. She laughed and creased up her face as we held her up for the camera, apparently at home with us and happy, but I couldn't quite believe it. What about her foster parents? Surely that loss would hit her soon and she would dissolve into misery?

The Shaanxi branch of the Civil Affairs Ministry had a grim exterior, but was light and modern inside. A young man in a smart blue shirt and spectacles welcomed us and we sat in front of the vast acreage of his desk. This was Chinese officialdom with a human face. There were no obstacles being put in our way, no desire to score points over these foreigners who'd come to take away one of the daughters of China. He simply asked us whether we would educate Jade and tell her about her Chinese origins, and we must promise not to abandon her. Compared with the bureaucratic hurdles we'd been through this felt like a mere formality. I could see what Chinese priorities were and they were sensible; education was what they really valued and we could offer her that. 'We appreciate you coming with so much love to give families to children who haven't any,' he told us with a smile. Suddenly it all seemed so simple and uncomplicated.

He then put Jade's foot onto a pad of red ink and squashed it down onto a rectangular space on a form. Jade was a big baby and we all laughed as her footprint spilled over the edges. She was clearly not one to be boxed in. We were told to put our thumbprints on the same form. Zhe Ming and Bai Shi Fung were there with us, looking happy and tearful, kissing Jade on the palms of her hands and passing her round to the others in the office. One middle-aged woman administrator whisked Jade off down the corridor to show her friends, and Jade grinned, seeming to soak up all the attention. She didn't seem to mind being passed around. I wondered if that meant she was too independent. Had she become so used to being shared that she wouldn't attach to us? Or was she just naturally sociable?

There were more forms to fill in later, but Cici said it was time now for a visit to the City Wall, one of Xi'an's great historical features. We squashed into a tiny taxi and rattled down the crowded main avenue. We climbed the steps up to the City Wall and in the murky white light, we watched as a painter added bright curly decorations to one of the towers. Cici began her explanation. 'The City Wall was built in the reign of Zhu Yuanzhang, the first emperor of the Ming dynasty in the fourteenth century, the government then felt it important to build a wall to keep ethnic minority people out. It's made out of one layer of clay and one layer of sticky rice ...' I started to think of lunch, sitting down and cuddling Jade. I couldn't take much in. After all, a mother isn't expected to absorb the finer points of Chinese history immediately after giving birth. I couldn't imagine post-natal wards in Britain being visited by a local librarian offering mind-broadening books on medieval fortifications. This ancient city was our post-natal ward, but bliss had blurred our brains. And with the heat on top of it all, our motivation had gone. We were exhausted. 'The Wall is twelve metres high and twelve to fifteen metres wide, over there you can see Confucius House ... there are watch towers at each of the four corners of the Wall ...'

My eyes went constantly to Jade, looking for that endearing grin: the times when she'd screw up her face, her nose would wrinkle and she'd flap her arms with glee. I looked at her, feeling a growing bond as if an imaginary umbilical cord was forming between us. 'This is my baby,' I muttered to myself over and over again. 'She may have been born to another woman, to have come from a remote corner of this country that I am just beginning to discover, she may be genetically poles apart from me and Gerald, yet fate has thrown us together.' It was a bit like an arranged marriage where two people who don't know each other beforehand fall in love after their wedding. We were now stuck to each other like the bricks of this Wall, with an emotional clay and sticky rice that was beginning to set firm.

Later, as we gazed at some ancient inscriptions on a black stone stele, Jade's pushchair was surrounded by admiring women. I couldn't imagine her getting this kind of attention in London and felt a pang of sadness again that we were taking her out of her culture. Would she berate us for it later? Would she understand that without a family in China, many girls didn't have much hope of survival?

As we walked down one of Xi'an's wide avenues, we became transfixed outside a branch of Kentucky Fried Chicken; members of staff in green-striped shirts and red caps were engaged in a morale-boosting dance routine on the pavement. Somehow they managed to keep straight faces and showed no hint of embarrassment.

In a department store we were mobbed by shop assistants. They pulled Jade's yellow sun hat on and off, cooed at her, and held up an array of different dresses for her to try for size. They were the kind of clothes that would be ten times the price in British shops, and it made sense to buy several. One young woman hugged her and nuzzled her tummy, sending Jade into fits of giggles. This was more than just a sales pitch from a management handbook. Either they were so bored by the lack of customers or, as seemed more likely, they were genuinely entranced by the sight of a baby, especially one belonging to a Western couple.

We went to the bank to change money for a payment to the authorities. Every couple has to pay $3000 to the Civil Affairs Office, and a proportion of that goes towards funding the orphanage and fostering programme. On top of that there were some legal and translation fees. While we waited at the counter, I was amazed when the uniformed security guard suddenly scooped Jade up in his arms and began chatting to her and squeezing her nose. Barely out of the cloak of rigid communism, yet this guard needed no lessons in customer service. While waiting at one of the counters we met another British adoptive parent who had just spent a week in hospital with her daughter who was suffering from pneumonia. She was now getting better, but it was a reminder of how fragile some of the girls were, and how lucky Jade had been to have become so strong and been well cared for.

Down a small side street, Cici took us to a day-care centre. Its simple courtyard was equipped with a plastic slide and bright green tunnel. As we wheeled Jade in, we were greeted by shrieks from dozens of larky children who clustered round, poking at her and shouting excitedly. Their teacher brought them to order with a strident voice that cut through their piercing decibels, before they began to sing a Chinese version of 'Frère Jacques'.

I have two hands, I have two hands
There they are, there they are
Do you see my two hands?
Do you see my two hands?
One and two
One and two.

....

Jade sat with her thumb in her mouth, occasionally rubbing her eyes. We were told that until recently the same tune used to carry the words in Chinese of:

Down with the landlords,
Down with the landlords
Every day is getting better
Every day is getting better

Share the land among yourselves
Share the land among yourselves
We want to be the masters
We want to be the masters.

....

The song shifted to something that sounded like 'Ball on the table, yes, yes, yes, ball on the table, yes, yes, yes'. The girls then skipped to the centre of the courtyard to begin their dance class, set to disco music from the 1970s. These six- and seven-year-olds easily jumped and stretched in time to the music, their flexible, nimble limbs appearing to us more coordinated than those of their Western counterparts. This was just a simple local crèche yet the standards were impressive and the teachers clearly dedicated. I stared at the girls' faces one after the other and wondered again which one Jade would grow up to resemble. The following day we brought them a cake decorated with an icing-sugar ship and the message 'Love from England'. We were shown into one of the minute classrooms with its miniature tables and chairs that somehow crammed in twenty children. One girl came to the front and confidently led a singalong about learning the alphabet in English. A teacher then cut the creamy cake and they all devoured it.

Our days in Xi'an blurred together into a hot, wearing but happy mix of sightseeing and doting on our new daughter. On National Children's Day the city's streets became a party. Children were everywhere, girls dressed in white frilly dresses and hairbands, and the sky was full of green and red balloons carrying banners pronouncing that it was time to celebrate. It was bizarre to be out in the street smiling and exchanging balloons with families who obviously adored their children, while we were displaying for all to see our daughter, the very symbol of China's ancient tradition of abandoning baby girls. The couples who gave us the thumbs up and smiled approvingly must have seen the contradiction.

....

We were impressed by Jade's calm nature, and her acceptance of us as parents. Considering that she came from a desert town where water was scarce, she held no fear of it and loved splashing in the hotel bath. She also seemed keen to communicate in her international baby language, burbling back to a burbling Gerald. She grinned at the waiters in our hotel restaurant and we realised we'd become real parents when we decided that everything she did was extraordinary and special. We felt proud and proprietorial and talked about her endlessly.

I was discovering, too, how physical a relationship with a child is. I couldn't take my hands off her body, and wanted all the time to squeeze her gorgeous podgy limbs, stroke her soft head that was so improbably flat at the back and hold her close to drink in her delicious milky-baby smell. Of course at the time of a nappy change, it was a different matter; but even that was less repellent than I had expected. I learnt that by distracting her with the packet of wet-wipes she would be less inclined to roll over the bed and spread the mess around. Once she was clean I would wave my hair into her face as she lay on her back and she would sigh, giggle and squirm with pleasure, unfazed by the fact that this would have been the first time in her life she'd encountered hair that was anything but black or dark brown.

Although it was hard to tear ourselves away and focus on the fact that we were in the cradle of Chinese civilisation, we couldn't fail to visit the 2,000-year-old Terracotta Army. The main part of the archaeological dig was twenty-five miles east of Xi'an, along a road packed with trucks and farm vehicles, past fields of corn and vegetables. Pit No. 1 was now protected by a vast hangar that opened onto a concrete square, already baking hot in the morning sun. It was all on a military scale, and looked as if the museum architects were allowing plenty of space in case their treasured army might one day come to life and need a new parade ground.

Inside the hangar we could see down into the pit where line after line of clay warriors stood, gazing without expression ahead of them, condemned to stand to attention for eternity as they guarded their imperial necropolis. We heard that more than 700,000 conscripts from all over China had laboured here, building this resting place for China's 'First Emperor', Qin Shi Huang. He hadn't wanted to take any chances, making sure he was accompanied into the afterlife by a whole infantry regiment of thousands of soldiers, each with a different face modelled on men from different parts of China. Then there were bowmen and crossbowmen, chariots and life-size horses, as well as precious stones, models of palaces and even the great Yellow and Yangtze Rivers were included, represented by mercury. After Qin Shi Huang died and was placed in the burial chamber, his son decided that not only would his father's childless concubines be buried alongside him, but the artisans responsible for the carvings should also be trapped inside as they knew too much. He had the treasures sealed up, the middle and outer gates shut and no one was allowed to leave. After all, what were mere individuals compared to this imperial project? The tomb was a phenomenon, impressive and at the same time so redolent of the Chinese ability to put the big task ahead of any individual rights.

I wondered when Jade would become interested in her ancestors' powerful creative ability. I looked at her gurgling as her pushchair juddered down a bumpy slope between one rank of stony-faced soldiers and another. She was not taken with these remnants of past armies but did become extremely animated when we retreated to a nearby restaurant and watched a noodle-maker stretching and swinging his length of pasta, sending it splitting into dozens of strands like a skein of wool. Later, as we walked past the trinket salesmen, she wanted to stop and watch an old man sitting on a bench rocking a wooden pushchair – at least, it was really a handmade double buggy, though the two girls in it weren't side to side but facing each other, both fast asleep and slumped onto a small table perched between them.

On another day Cici took us to the National Museum where my lasting memory is of a map of the world showing several arrows pointing out of China in a westerly direction. The message was clear: China had pioneered most of the building blocks of our lives – paper, glass, gunpowder, the crossbow, noodles and many other things – and had exported them all to the West. We learnt that when this city was at the centre of Chinese power, the rich were eating and drinking from fine, decorated porcelain and engraved silver goblets, they were clothed in colourful embroidered silks adorned with jade and gold jewellery, and all this while early Britons were wearing rags. What's more, Chinese exploration, science and technology were centuries ahead of the rest of the world. I was proud that our daughter was from this cradle of new ideas: even though, at that moment the main thought in her round, bald head was how to attract the attention of a passing tourist carrying an ice cream.

. . . .

The Public Security Bureau was our final bureaucratic step in Xi'an. They were to issue Jade with a Chinese passport so that she would be allowed to leave the country. We had heard that one couple had suffered long delays as their translator had somehow alienated the officials. The PSB is one of the most-feared branches of government, so we entered with some trepidation. But to her lasting credit, Jade targeted her charm to perfection. I sat her up on the counter and she patted the security glass, sending the normally stern staff into fits of raucous laughter.

In a few moments they held up her passport, complete with the tiny photo which had captured her surprised, gormless look, created by her mouth falling open. Her Chinese name, Lin Na, was printed inside. She grinned at her own picture and got very excited without realising that this was her passport to a new life. It felt both momentous and sad to think that when she next returned to China she would be like a little English girl and these same people would see her as a foreigner.

Before leaving Xi'an we took Jade to the market and amongst the lacquer chests, stone tortoises and flutes, we found her a little green jade dragon. It seemed the perfect present as she had been born in the Year of the Dragon. We took her to the Bell Tower and rang the giant bell, we ate in a Mongolian restaurant where she fell asleep on the bench next to us — and then there was just one day left.

For that we visited a nearby mountain which we scaled in a cable car, before walking up to one part of the peak to find that, for a fee, Gerald could dress up in the uniform of the Red Army and pose for photos. It was kitsch, tasteless and irresistible, especially as the clothes were far too small for him. Some Chinese tourists chortled as he adopted the revolutionary-looking-in-the-distance pose. We had left Jade in the attentive care of Cici and about twenty-five eager onlookers, and as we came down the slope we could see Jade's eyes firmly fixed on where she had last seen us. She was lapping up the attention from her audience but was now very attached to us and didn't like it if we were out of sight.

Then it was time to leave this city that would always carry memories for us of this magical time, and we flew to Beijing. We were on the home stretch now; there was only one last bit of bureaucracy to attend to, going to the British Embassy to get her visa. There we found dozens of people waiting for permission to come to the UK and we were allowed to jump the queue. They looked at Jade curiously, as if they were thinking, 'Who is this girl that's being given preferential treatment? Why should she get into the UK when so many others are trying so hard?' Outside some students joked with us. They wanted to go to Britain and when they saw Jade they giggled, 'Will you adopt us too?'

We spent the evening watching Chinese acrobats with their improbable feats involving twirling plates and flaming hoops. We visited a busy shopping centre where the assistants raced up and down on roller skates; we took Jade swimming for the first time and she laughed so much she kept swallowing water. And then suddenly it was all over and it was time to leave. We had a last-minute bureaucratic hurdle as our exit form had mysteriously disappeared from Jade's passport, and strictly speaking she should have gone back to Xi'an to get another one. Luckily her charm worked wonders again and the female emigration official waved us by.

As we boarded the plane, I couldn't help thinking that this was China's loss and Britain's gain. It felt wrong that a country was allowing its girls to leave, but it was wrong too that they were abandoned. This solution suited everyone at the moment, and there seemed no hint of regret from the Chinese officials. To them we were just taking a problem off their hands.

Just at that moment, I realised that it was the thirty-third anniversary of my mother's death. What would she have thought of having a Chinese granddaughter? I will never know. Jade was asleep in her stroller, unaware of how she had now inherited a brand new family with many long-deceased relatives who could have adored her, unaware too that she was about to work her magic on the living ones.

Chapter Five

Practice Makes Parent

On our plane home were several Danish families; some had just adopted their second Chinese daughters. Their older girls, now confident children three or four years old, were running up and down the aisle, chattering naturally in Danish. They poked at Jade and laughed at her as she sat cradled in BA's regulation bassinette. Just a few years ago they too would have been totally Chinese and totally unfamiliar with Western people or their language. Today they were a reminder of how Chinese adopted children were becoming a distinctive international set, about 60,000 of them scattered all over the world and speaking dozens of languages, yet forever linked by this common heritage.

Mercifully Jade was in a good mood for most of the flight, and particularly liked my putting pieces of ham between her toes, which she carefully removed and ate: not the kind of manners to be encouraged, but who cared? We were demob happy, proud parents, and the further the plane took us from China, the more we felt Jade was truly ours. All the way through the adoption there'd been a niggling doubt that something could go wrong, some insurmountable bureaucratic impediment

© Gerald Slocock

Jade's last moments in China.

which would pop up to say that we were unfit to adopt a child. Now, no one could take her away. We stared at her pale, pliable little face and stroked her endlessly, finding every soft, podgy, dimpled curve more and more fascinating.

The triumph of overcoming all the bureaucratic hurdles, the glamour of travelling to China and the bliss of new motherhood lasted through the flight, through immigration control at Heathrow airport and through the joy of being met by Gerald's sister and a friend. We held Jade and took photos of her first moments on British soil, then we arrived home and carried her over the threshold of our flat like a new bride before collapsing into bed happy and exhausted.

....

Things were not quite so euphoric on the Monday morning after the front door clunked shut as Gerald left for work. From our fascinating adventure in an exotic country, I was now simply a mum alone at home with a new baby. It was a reality I hadn't fully anticipated. Life went from top gear to neutral. The glorious sense of achievement began to retreat in the face of jet lag and a gnawing fear of my own incompetence.

Jade and I were both disorientated, and she was constipated and fractious as well. I had no energy, yet she wanted my attention at every moment. I was now the only human distraction for her after two weeks of adoring audiences in China and, on top of that, she had to get used to yet another entirely new environment. She wanted me in the same room with her all the time as she couldn't crawl to follow me. I tried putting her in a sling on my hip but it was awkward; she was already too heavy for that, so I would sit her on the kitchen mat from where she watched my every movement like a hawk.

When I went to the bedroom she screamed, and then I almost forgot what I'd gone there for. Oh yes, I'd come to fetch her bottle to wash. I came back and started to wash up and the cries started again, so I picked her up and comforted her. While I was rocking her in my arms and feeling the tension in her warm body ease, I looked at the sea of devastation – the half-unpacked bags, the laundry, the sink full of dishes we'd been too tired to wash the previous night – and realised I had to put her down. I gave her a pile of bricks to play with and rushed to the sink. After a few seconds of washing up she started to cry again, sending the bricks scattering all over the floor with an impatient wave of her arm. I checked her nappy and she needed a change. Five minutes later I'd cleaned her, put on a new nappy, and placed her on the floor, while I went back to the sink for a few more seconds of washing up.

Then the phone went. It was my cousin ringing to congratulate us – at least, that's what I think she was saying as Jade wailed so loudly when I answered the call that I couldn't hear a thing. I put the phone down and comforted her, bouncing her on my knee while we played hide-and-seek behind a tea towel. After a few joyful minutes, I turned round and realised the washing-up was still there, the suitcases were still unpacked and we had no food in for lunch.

So I put Jade down again and rushed at the sink, determined this time to get more done. I did manage to finish, and decided to tidy up. But I'd never realised before how tidying implies one essential ergonomic component: free movement by the tidier to put things away. How could I put my clothes in the cupboard or take them to the washing machine yet stay within the non-crying orbit of Jade? And I couldn't carry her everywhere with me as I would have no hands free to tidy things. As soon as I left the room to take a pile of shirts and socks to the machine, grimy from our sweaty outing to Silk Street Market in Beijing, there were piercing cries. I still took them and tried to ignore Jade, but felt tense and worried and overcome with such a sense of urgency that I didn't actually put them in the wash but just dumped them on the floor: another half-completed task, that I could finish later after she'd gone to bed.

By the end of the first morning I was beginning to get my first taste of why mothers complain about losing their minds. I hadn't been able to do one task, have one train of thought that wasn't interrupted. Jade was like a little expertly programmed computer, hard-wired to get my attention, and her 'motherboard' was going to make sure she got what she needed. On the other hand, I had been programmed as a foreign correspondent with adrenaline-induced drive and purpose, always pushing to get things done before the next deadline. The idea of passing a whole day just mellowing out and ignoring the chaos around me didn't seem conceivable. I had heard that mothers were supposed to be good at 'parallel processing', doing several tasks at once, but I was beginning to realise that I was the exception to this happy rule. I much preferred doing one thing at a time. Perhaps it was just as well I hadn't decided to do all this when I was 25. That career I'd had, those unsuitable boyfriends: maybe subconsciously I had been trying to avoid this whole business of being a mother, knowing I was not really cut out to be one.

I suppose I should have read up more on how to be a good mother, but I'd been averse to relying on too many experts, preferring the philosophy of common sense espoused in Frank

Furedi's *Paranoid Parenting*, which basically said that you should trust your own instincts as a parent and not be made less confident by constantly deferring to people who claim to know better.

Still, the gear change to my life was much more dramatic than I'd anticipated. I needed to hear from other mothers how they coped so I decided to 'phone a friend' who had two lovely little girls: 'Do I have to give Jade attention and play with her *all* the time?'

'That's an incredible question for a new mum. Of course, normally you would have a tiny baby that sleeps most of the time, you've really hit the ground running, haven't you? You can't possibly be glued to her all day. She'll have to learn to do other things. But my advice is don't even think of getting all the washing-up done.'

'Yes, but I just feel wretched and hopeless, as if I can't do anything properly.'

'That doesn't matter either; as long as she's got you she'll be happy, she's your priority now. And without realising it you will be giving her so much just by being with her.'

I nearly said, 'But what about me?' and then felt too embarrassed that I'd even thought this at the moment when I had finally got my darling, longed-for child. I knew I shouldn't matter; the important thing was that Jade was settling in, and yet I still felt guilty as inner wellsprings of irritation and annoyance would come bubbling up at the end of hours of patience and cooing smiles. After a few days I found I would, without provocation, hurl a cushion at the wall and have to pace up and down to let off steam.

. . . .

The fact that Jade was adopted and might be traumatised made it all the more difficult to know what cries I could safely ignore and what represented her deepest insecurities and fears. Although she had been very good at attaching to me and Gerald — she had no problem about looking steadily into our eyes and being cuddled — I knew she must have deep anxiety about being abandoned again. If I left the room was I going to reactivate some inner trauma? How would she know that I was ever going to return?

I decided to talk to my friend and adoption psychologist Franca Brenninkmeyer, whom I had been trying to avoid before, and asked her how much attention was enough, as nothing seemed to be. 'As long as you are meeting her needs most of the time you will be building up valuable bonds of trust, that's what she must have now,' she said. 'Just the fact that she cries when she wants something and that need is usually met is fundamental in her early development. Children who don't get that are the ones that have more problems later on, as they learn to be too independent. But she has to get used to you going out of the room and reappearing, so don't get hung up on that!'

'Just from what I've told you, about Jade being highly gregarious and easily letting herself be picked up by other people, how much damage do you think there has been?'

'The fact that she showed no sign of distress when you collected her in China may not be a good sign. Perhaps she was used to being looked after by a lot of people, even though she was fostered. Some children who've had a lot of carers find it really difficult to have deep relationships, they much prefer superficial ones.'

I wondered if I was now doing enough to 'bond' with Jade, and create a deep relationship. 'I've read that some adoptive parents are advised to "hold" their children when they get upset, sometimes for long periods ... is that something you advise?'

On this Franca was reassuring. 'That's really only later on and for children who get into a rage or a tantrum and just can't calm themselves down, and especially if they are in the habit of pushing their mothers away. It's not advisable for children who respond pretty normally, and get angry about things, as long as they can become quiet on their own. Holding has its own dangers; it can be pretty suffocating for the child if not done properly.'

. . . .

A couple of days after our return from China, I took Jade to our local park. It was taking me a long time to get used to the fact that babies travel with an array of bits and pieces subject to what I have defined as Mrs Murphy's Law – whichever item is forgotten is the one most needed, and is also the one another mother is bound to tell you she always has: 'Now, I always bring several spare nappies/T-shirts/bibs just in case ...'

I found even getting out of our flat required more mental alertness than I possessed and I nearly always forgot at least one of the following: spare nappies, wet-wipes, nappy sacks, drinking bottle, milk, bib, snack and/or spare clothes. It wasn't even a question of parallel processing; it was any processing at all that I seemed to lack, and I couldn't even blame pregnancy for the impact on my grey cells.

As we walked past the fashionable cafés in Westbourne Grove where slender women draped themselves over frothy cups of decaf discussing their next modelling assignment, I felt self-conscious at being a harassed mother with a hungry baby and felt they were looking at me with that distant superiority

© Emily Buchanan

Ready to go shopping!

reserved for lesser breeds of street life. Our nearest grocery was a big health-food shop, but its design, with several flights of stairs, was more appropriate for the post-Pilates set than for mothers with small children. The only realistic way to take a baby with a buggy inside was to leave them by the till. I rushed round the packed, enticing shelves of the shop, remembering how I once lingered over which goat's cheese or tofu burger to buy. Now it was speed shopping, quick – eggs, pasta, milk and time to go. Would Jade be crying, feeling deserted?

I got to the till and breathed again. Jade was clapping her hands and making faces at the shop assistant, enjoying this social opportunity while she had him in her line of sight. She hadn't missed me for a moment. I must learn to calm down and just enjoy being a mother, I told myself. As we walked home I wondered if Jade was, deep down, longing for all those smiling, animated Chinese faces, those shop assistants in Xi'an who would rush up to her and pinch her cheeks. What did she make of Britain? The smells, the streets were so different, so much emptier than Xi'an. As we walked home, past the lounging ladies again, I could see them look at her and then at me and unspoken questions passed across their faces.

'Is her father Chinese?' asked a young mother in our local park the next day, as we pushed our babies together on the toddler swings.

I paused, not prepared for this obvious question. 'Er, yes, kind of ...' I answered, and then berated myself for not saying either 'Yes', or 'Yes, and we've adopted her from China', or 'No, her father's British' or something a bit more spiky like, 'Why do you need to know?' I felt embarrassed that her difference was so obvious, yet ashamed that I didn't instantly come out with the fact that she was adopted. Amongst the plane

© Emily Buchanan

Gerald and Jade back in the UK.

trees and the white stucco buildings of West London I hadn't been so focussed on Jade's Chineseness. I wanted her just to be *my* baby and I didn't want to be reminded that she was from another country, born of other parents, that I wasn't, perhaps in other people's eyes, a fully-fledged mother. Often, although not always, the reason for adoption has something to do with infertility, but I wasn't sure I really wanted to share this intimate fact with every stranger I met. Too bad. I realised I was going to have to face up to it; I had to 'come-out' as an adoptive mother. This was where inter-country adoption parted company with domestic placements which could stay hidden from prying eyes. I was also becoming aware that, as I'd been warned, overseas adoption makes parent and child public property.

I remembered what my social worker friend had told me in the café off the Finchley Road: 'It's a huge burden to put on a child. For their whole life other people will be able to see these children were adopted. It's one reason why we social workers are so cautious about overseas adoption. We have to make sure the parents understand what they are undertaking for themselves and their child.' I was beginning to understand what she meant. But then there was an advantage, too, in an adoption that was never going to be a secret. There would be no fateful moment when our child would discover she was adopted. In the past, some adoptees weren't told until they were adults, or not at all. I couldn't imagine what that would do to a person's sense of identity.

....

Jade's first birthday party doubled as a welcome for her into our family. We could offer her no grandparents, but we could give her a doting step-grandmother, an array of aunts, delightful cousins and wonderful friends. Their warmth and admiration for her gave me confidence that she would be accepted here and feel rooted with us. I needed it as I began to discover surprising ignorance in that unfamiliar world of 'other mothers'. I had naively imagined that as I had finally, after so much heartache, achieved the status of 'new mother' I would suddenly enter a great maternal sisterhood. I did find many mothers who were kind and with whom I've made lasting friendships, but I was always taken aback whenever I crashed headlong into cool indifference, competition, even superiority.

Some of my 'child free' friends, with whom I had sweated during months on demanding documentaries, were now off making other programmes with no time to while

© Gerald Slocock

My first party!

away an afternoon with a small child, so I needed to find a new network. The trouble was that I had become an instant mother who had effectively skipped the first twenty months of my daughter's life since her conception: twenty months when I could have been feeding her emotions with love, her body with vitamins and her mind with Mozart. Twenty months also when I could have been breathing, exercising and networking though the National Childbirth Trust. Now here I was, older than most of the mothers around me and, after my somewhat unusual path to motherhood, I didn't naturally slot into their world and I found some of the attitudes perplexing.

Once, at our local swimming-pool, a frizzy-haired woman asked to hold Jade, and Jade went to her easily as she often did, sociable and unafraid. 'Oh, you poor thing, look how she's hugging me now,' said Mrs Frizzy as she cuddled Jade. 'You are friendly, don't you love your mummy then?' The implication was that because Jade wasn't clingy I was somehow less important to her. 'My daughter wouldn't go to anyone at this age, *we* were inseparable,' she added beaming at me.

'I see.' I instantly wanted to seize Jade back, or at least to show that we *were* incredibly close, in fact I wanted to say that I adored my daughter and was quite prepared to die for her. I didn't know how to prove that I knew Jade loved me too. I began to nurture the wicked thought that perhaps some mothers actually connived to keep their children clingy because it made them feel indispensable, and therefore more important.

The adoption naturally became a talking point at parties and most of the time we encountered nothing but encouragement and warmth, so it was strange when out of 'left field' would come an unexpected tactless comment. On one occasion with some journalist friends, a mother watched me bottle-feeding Jade. 'I managed to breastfeed all four of my children. It was *so* satisfying!' she announced, smugly. She knew Jade was adopted.

'Really? Well done you!' I answered.

I lost count of the number of conversations about how early a child had walked or spoken its first word. Beside the wide lawns under the swaying trees of Holland Park there was a small children's playground. As I sat watching Jade digging in the sandpit, a dark-haired, rather tense lady with a determined expression struck up a conversation. After I'd told her about the adoption, she said, 'How old is she?'

'A year.'

'How lovely! My little Bobby walked at eight months, he's been very quick and now he's one and a half and has even started to talk a bit too.'

'That's wonderful, Jade is very easy-going and doesn't seem to be in any hurry to do either.'

'Oh, I'm sure she'll catch up with other children soon. But it's so sweet what you've done, how kind to these poor children. I and my husband wondered about adopting, but we did IVF and it all worked and now we are so happy to have our own little boy.'

Now was I being paranoid, or was that a put-down? I began to feel uncomfortable about being called 'kind'. I knew I was *not* particularly kind at all. We had not adopted out of charity, but because we wanted a child. Our motives were absolutely no different from any other couple who wanted a baby. The really 'kind' people who needed to be given credit were those who adopted older or disabled children.

The clouds swirled overhead and I went over to put a cardigan over Jade's bare arms. She squirmed and threw it off as she dug deep into the sand with her bare hands. She hardly ever felt the cold. I could feel my own insecurity and defensiveness start to turn into a kind of inverse snobbery. Here was my robust Jade with her iron constitution and powerful grip, her solid chest and broad, fearless smile. The Western children in the park looked very sweet, but also puny and pale by comparison. I wondered why people were so obsessed with passing on their own genes; mine were certainly nothing to boast about, afflicted as I was with allergies and asthma. I had been mollycoddled and cared for as a baby, but in any other century I would probably have died. Jade's genes were self-evidently superior, having evolved and been hardened from centuries of toil on that inhospitable, windswept loess plateau around Yulin.

I began to feel particularly sensitive to the position adopted children seemed to have in the public mind: that is, third choice after natural conception and fertility treatment. I couldn't escape the unforgiving logic of this biological hierarchy, but I didn't want Jade to experience it. As far as I was concerned she was as good as any daughter born to me. She was a wonderful girl through and through, and I didn't want her to grow up thinking other people saw her as a 'substitute' child, just as we were categorised as 'substitute' parents.

....

As the months went by, I settled down and found my career-driven urge to get things done dwindled. I got used to living in semi-permanent chaos, and was able to get help from a wonderful part-time nanny who treated Jade with the same common sense she used with all her charges; Jade adored her. She also had a fundamental talent for creating order and it helped me enormously to stay sane. Sometimes adoptive parents are advised not to let anyone else look after their child for the first few months, but I took my sister's advice who, being the main breadwinner, had no choice about working: 'Start as you mean to continue,' she'd said. 'Otherwise Jade will get used to having you all the time and it will be a bigger shock for her when you do go back to work.'

After 'adoption leave' I went back to the BBC three days a week. I did stop touring the world but instead did it vicariously through a programme about global radio called '*A World in Your Ear*' and doing analysis pieces for television news. I was relieved to be able to fit work around childcare, as that was now the number one priority.

By now Jade was relishing her strong crawling ability and showed little interest in walking. She slowly learnt to utter a few words: my favourite was 'mamamama' which she would sing like a continuous hum. The first few times my heart leapt at the miracle that I was actually being a mother to someone. I wasn't interested in the drive to be a perfect parent since I already knew that our family could never achieve 'perfection' in the conventional sense. There was a growing cult, it seemed, of striving, overachieving mothers, known in the US as 'new-momism', where mothers supposedly worried about whether or not they baked homemade cakes or carved carrots into creative shapes for their children's tea. I was already off the scale when it came to competing in these stakes. Adoption was 'parenting-plus' of a different kind.

Franca had told me: 'One of the inescapable truths about adoption is that when you adopt, you are also adopting the world's pain ... you can't live in a bubble and pretend bad things don't happen.' We couldn't isolate ourselves and imagine that our lives had nothing to do with all that poverty and grief thousands of miles away.

It was inevitable that we found ourselves gravitating towards the eclectic set of other adoptive parents with whom we would sit over tea and cakes commiserating on the physical demands of having a small child in our early forties. Wrists and backs bore the brunt of the carrying, eyes were vulnerable from flying fists and pencils, knees ached from sitting on the ground or pretending to be a 'horsy'. We found two families in East London who had girls from the same orphanage as Jade and felt a special bond with them.

Another couple with a Chinese daughter from Henan Province lived a short walk away from our home. The mother, Jenny, had wild hair, warm eyes and layers of bohemian clothing and had once been a punk rocker. Jenny had become a bit of an expert on some of the difficulties of attachment through her experience with her daughter Lily. Amongst the toys strewn around her floor she talked about what becoming a mother had been like for her. 'When we picked up Lily at eight months she gave the impression of not having bonded with anyone. She hadn't been fostered and none of the carers seemed to have built up a real relationship with her. She didn't want to be touched, let alone cuddled. It was very painful for me when I picked her up because she wouldn't look me in the eye, but would look past me and point at something that was more important for her. Most birth babies stare for hours into their mother's eyes and soak up her emotion. They develop total trust. Lily had clearly had to fend for herself and having my face near to hers was probably overwhelming. Often during our first year with her she would actually stab me in the throat with her finger to push me away ...' Jenny stopped and looked out of the window. What could be harder than trying to mother a child who didn't want to get close? 'She used to get really startled too, any sudden noise and she would panic. It's called being hyper-vigilant.'

I was reminded of how Jade sometimes behaved in the park. If she heard a lawnmower or a tractor she would scream. I wondered if those sounds provoked some distant frightening memory and yet her foster father worked next to a bus station, so she should have been used to the sound of engines.

Jenny went on. 'At the same time, Lily seemed intellectually very advanced, it was as if she'd had to sharpen her wits just to survive. I had to work really hard with her. I'd massage her, hold her, cradle her for ages. I eventually took her to a therapist who helped a lot. Gradually she started to trust me. I remember one moment after I'd been holding her for a while, I started to cry with the stress of it all; suddenly Lily saw that I was upset and actually hugged me. That was such a relief, a real breakthrough.'

Lily was leaping up and down off the sofa, trying on some sunglasses and pretending to strum a guitar. It was hard to believe that this confident, beautiful two-year-old, who was quickly learning to talk and sing, was the same child.

....

It was the height of summer and the golden stone walls of Stanway House in Gloucestershire glowed just as they had done on our wedding day. Today was the day of the annual fete, and the cavernous tithe barn that had held our dining tables was now full of stalls selling jam, homemade pottery and embroidered handkerchiefs. Jade was crawling about on the lawn, watching the local fire brigade demonstrate their new engine, and squealing as the firefighters sprayed us all from their hoses. We spotted a couple whose three children looked as if they had not started out in the English countryside. It turned out that the two girls and a boy had been adopted while their Anglo-Colombian parents were living on a farm in Colombia. Because of the violence there they had been forced to move to Britain. Their oldest daughter, an articulate 15-year-old, talked freely about being adopted. She said that sometimes she was teased in the school playground about her mother not being a 'real mummy'. She told us she'd learnt a good answer that stopped them in their tracks: 'I may not have come from my mummy's tummy, but I came out of my mummy's heart.'

We all looked at each other; her wisdom and openness left us dumbfounded. I would never have thought of saying that, but it was *so* true, and I hoped Jade would come up with such robust defences some day.

. . . .

Jade certainly didn't seem to lack confidence. I noticed how her gregarious nature turned her into something of a social passport. On buses she would lean over and start stroking the neighbouring passenger's knee, which was a little unnerving, but nearly always caused a smile even on the faces of the dourest commuters.

I found myself becoming more and more proud of her achievements: her fearlessness in the swimming pool – Gerald would throw her up in the air and she would splash into the water and come up gasping and grinning and asking for more – the way she slept well, even curling up once in a patch of long grass in the Lake District while people gasped at this little figure like a bird in its nest; the way she relished grown-up parties, crawling between the legs of the guests collecting everyone's handbags, unperturbed by the noise and the presence of strangers. Her outgoing nature gradually helped me overcome my shyness about the adoption.

Our first summer with her ended abruptly one day. I was in the middle of writing an audio diary for BBC Radio 4's '*Woman's Hour*' telling the story of adopting Jade, when I overheard a news bulletin coming from a wireless belonging to a builder in the neighbouring house. The announcer said that a plane had just flown into the World Trade Center in

© Gerald Slocock

Anywhere, anytime!

New York. I leapt up and turned on the television to watch the unbelievable events unfold. As the towers collapsed, I strained to see where they were falling, terrified that they might crash into my sister's house which was just four blocks away. I tried to ring her all day but the phones were down. It was only the day after that she was able to call and tell me what happened. She and Steve had been about to vote in the primary elections and were standing in the school playground, just three blocks from the Twin Towers. 'We saw the first aircraft flying right over our heads before it crashed into the North Tower, making this plane-shaped flaming hole in the building. Harrison and Octavia were by then in their classrooms and the teachers were instructed to lower the blinds and carry

© Emily Buchanan

Jade with cousins, Octavia and Harrison.

on teaching. When the second plane hit, we and many other parents rushed inside to pick up our children, and when we got home we found our street covered in layers of dust and debris so we decided to take the family away for a few days. Coming back we had to pass through several military checkpoints just to reach our neighbourhood. It was incredible, the streets still looked like a war zone and there was this ugly cloud of foul-smelling smoke hovering over everything, just filling us with a sense of fear and dread. We discovered the school was being used as a base for emergency vehicles, and all the classes had been moved to a vacant school a little further uptown.'

A week later '*Woman's Hour*' said it needed a 'good news' story after all the tales of death and carnage. They wanted to run my adoption piece. It was strange to think that in this new world which, we kept being told, had changed forever, the simple account of adopting a baby from China could be seen as a brief antidote to the tragedy.

....

One day in the middle of November we visited an elderly client of Gerald's in Hampshire. Not every stockbroker would bring along a Chinese daughter to entertain his clients and I wondered if our presence would be an asset or a hindrance in business negotiations, but luckily the man was charmed by Jade. He showed little interest in the performance of his stocks and shares and spent the afternoon crawling on all fours with her. 'This is the kind of client to have,' I thought. Perhaps as a result of all that exercise, or because Jade thought it was time for a bit of role reversal of her own, when we arrived at the next appointment, she suddenly stood on her own two feet and walked for the first time without being held. We applauded; it was a great feeling, before she had been so wary of letting go of our hands and walking on her own.

We spent Christmas in the French Pyrenees, staying with friends in a small village which clung to the head of a valley carpeted with snow. Beyond it were just mountains, fir trees and miles of loggers' tracks criss-crossed with foot prints of wild boar and deer. At eighteen months Jade was so different from the pale, rotund baby we'd picked up in China. She had lengthened and her limbs were more solid and strong. Her new-found mobility brought a look of permanent surprise to her face. Her mouth would open into a very round 'O' as her

© Gerald Slocock

Call this cold!

head leant forward while her legs obliged by taking her, waddling like a sturdy duck, to where she wanted to go. When she turned, her body tilted precariously but she usually managed to stay upright and avoid crashing into a sharp corner at the last moment. In her padded snowsuit, with her bright brown eyes and red cheeks, she looked just like a Chinese doll, but she was anything but fragile. She had a zest for life and a determined jawline which gave the impression that she knew just what she wanted.

In a local café, an old woman watched her playing with some French children and clucked, '*Pas de soucis, elle sait se defendre!*' (Don't worry, she knows how to defend herself.) It was true: since she arrived I hadn't had to worry about her ability to hold her own with other children. As someone who had been born in the Year of the Dragon she should be lucky, independent and egocentric according to Chinese astrology. The prediction didn't seem wrong so far.

I was discovering too that along with the anxieties and hard work in becoming a mother, there was an antidote, a non-pharmaceutical Prozac that must have been built into children at the dawn of evolution. Jade was not just our daughter but a live-in comedienne as well. Laughter kept us all going even as we were also going grey with exhaustion dealing with her eagerness to get up early and greet each day with a furious demand for our attention. When Jade put her feet into Gerald's size eleven shoes, or when she would hang my bra around her neck or try to hide by concealing her head under the blanket and snorting with laughter when we 'found' her, she forced us to live in the present and to take one day at a time.

On our drive down through France we had stopped off in Bordeaux and taken a couple of tours round the local wineries.

As the very proud guide of the vintage St Emilion cellar was trying to explain to us how egg whites are used to draw the sediment out of wine during fermentation, Jade started giggling. She chortled so much the guide was forced to stop her explanation and wait. We all became mesmerised as Jade's mirth took over and she began to roll on the floor of the cellar as if completely drunk; an unexpected side effect of inhaling the perfume of the fine wines stored in vast barrels around her.

Jade's new-found mobility gave her even more confidence. Instead of needing to be with me most of the time, she often used her legs to get as far away as possible. At a wedding in Holland Park, we were sipping champagne with the other guests, when I turned around and suddenly couldn't see her. I wandered through the marquee and the Orangery, realising with a jolt that she had gone outside to explore the park on her own. She was familiar with it and wouldn't have thought it strange to go searching for the playground. I ran there but began to panic when I couldn't see her. I tottered around the paths in my high heels and long summer dress asking people if they'd seen a little Chinese toddler, feeling ridiculous and frantic. I was about to contact a warden when I spotted her. She was hanging around the queue for ice creams, sidling up to children holding their cones, well out of sight of the wedding. I might have known she would gravitate there.

Children's story books seemed to revel in the 'getting lost' scenario, but the one I found the hardest to read was *Babar the Elephant*. In the first scene Babar's mother is shot by a hunter and dies. Babar flees from the jungle to the city, where luckily he is rescued by a rich old lady who temporarily cures his ills by taking him shopping (it had to be early indoctrination in the value of retail therapy). But as Jade nestled up to me pointing to the pictures, oblivious to the tragedy in the pages, I found myself feeling absurdly sentimental. Tears welled up at the thought of what would happen to her if she lost me.

Then I thought that if my mother had felt like this about me and my sister, then what depth of hell must have driven her to leave us so suddenly and so finally? I couldn't really fathom how a mother could leave her child intentionally, anyway.

I found looking after Jade reminded me of those precious moments I remembered with my own mother. Every time I picked her up and she held her arms stiff so I could get a good grip I would think of how it used to tickle when my mother lifted me up. I realised I was saying the same words, the same baby language that I recalled my mother using. She used to say 'what a lovely day—ee' when we went to school, then she would sing, and I would beg her not to as it was too embarrassing. I wished now that I could ask her more about what I was like at Jade's age. Did I smile a lot, when did I walk, why was I so shy? My whole early childhood was as mysterious to me as was Jade's first year.

One day I showed Jade a sculpture of my mother's head that my uncle had shaped over thirty years before. She looked stern and thin — a sad but true likeness. I told Jade this was her grandmother: 'That's your Mummy's Mummy.' Jade reached for it and kissed the cold nose spontaneously. But how could she possibly understand that this piece of lifeless bronze had once been the person that gave birth to her mother?

I thought back to a time when I was about eight sitting on the sofa; my mother was reading me a story. It was about a child whose mother died and who ended up riding ponies to feel better. I remember saying, 'You won't die, will you, Mummy? You promise.'

'Of course not, darling,' she said. That scene had stuck in my head, because she didn't keep her promise.

. . . .

I found myself becoming more and more curious about my mother's life and realised I had many more questions to ask before those who had grown up with her were gone. The following Easter, when my uncle was over from America staying with my aunt in her pretty house in Gloucestershire, I cornered them and began to probe: 'What was my mother like as a child?'

My aunt was immediately direct and forthcoming about her sister Janet. 'She was extremely unselfish. We used to have our baths together and she was always at the tap end – because it was the uncomfortable end. I was selfish and she always gave in very easily. And she was a tearful child. She lost her confidence completely when we got a new nanny, when she was about one. This nanny was not very kind and was discharged, but during her time with us Jan started to cry very easily. The new nanny found this unprovoked crying rather trying and did her best to distract her but as Jan got older she just got worse, especially whenever anyone sympathised with her. Our father would imitate and tease her to make her laugh but she cried even more. Our mother did her best, but she was very young and didn't know how to make it better.'

I remembered my grandmother as a statuesque, attractive woman whom I respected, but who certainly wasn't the cosy, darning-socks-style of granny. My mother had become extremely critical of the upper classes. Her father, a Conservative and member of Churchill's Cabinet, was shocked when she went as far as publicly joining the Communist Party although he always defended her right to do so. I pressed my aunt for more. 'What was it that made her so angry with the world?'

'She reacted violently against the "deb" life, all that privilege and coming out parties when she was eighteen. She thought a lot of it was silly.'

My uncle sighed and told me how my mother had qualified to become a teacher and taught in secondary schools in Northampton and Croydon. 'She loved her job, but we got used to her always doing something to make herself miserable. She wouldn't have a hot-water bottle when it was cold, she was always punishing herself. Our mother said her life seemed to be a series of onerous duties ...'

Then my aunt added quickly, 'Yes, we were all on holiday in the Isle of Wight once and she was doing the cooking. That night she served just plain sausages and said "you can't expect something fancy every night". It wasn't a joke. When Stalingrad was being besieged during the war, and there was a leak in her kitchen roof, she wore gumboots to show solidarity with those suffering, rather than fix the leak. She always felt she had to deny herself something. She never wore nice clothes. She identified with the underdog. I'm sure that's why she learnt Russian later.'

'Where did all this guilt come from?'

'Some of it was perhaps because she blamed herself that our first nanny had left, or because our parents divorced. She became infused with guilt. I'll never forget a dream I had about her. Did I ever tell it to you? We were going to say "good morning" to our mother and I noticed Jan had blood all over her face. She told me she thought she'd broken the Holy Grail. I always felt the guilt came from something she thought she'd done.'

'I hadn't thought about this before but perhaps because she felt unloved she wanted to back the poor in England, the people whom society didn't love either,' my uncle interjected.

'So what was she like when she became a mother to me and my sister?'

'She was a marvellous mother ... took to it like a duck to water ... an absolutely natural mother, you might not have expected it from an intellectual woman, not doting, but funny with it and down to earth. She was a natural teacher and she could have been great if she'd lived. She even helped me with my homework. A flawed, wonderful woman who could have done so much.'

We continued talking as the late-afternoon sun shone horizontally through the room, the swallows were ducking and diving under the eaves. My mother could so easily have got help nowadays and escaped her self-destructive frame of mind, but instead her life descended into tragedy. I wondered if her self-imposed victim status made it impossible to save herself in the end. My aunt looked down at her hands and then at me. 'She felt you and your sister would be better without her. I do think that. She was frightened she might do you both an injury, apparently this happens with some women. She had a friend at Cambridge, who I think killed her children and then was taken to a mental home and I remember clearly her saying "I thought at the time that was the most extraordinary thing, but now I don't think it's extraordinary any more, I understand exactly", and I know she thought she might do something like that.'

'Because she felt violent towards us?'

'Well, she was losing her mind, you see. She talked about suicide incessantly. But we thought because she talked about it so much she wasn't going to do it. She said "What will happen to the children I do not know." We hadn't realised that she'd stopped taking her drugs. I think the last straw was her worry about protecting you and your sister whom she adored. She didn't think she could protect you so she decided the best way was out. And our mother said afterwards, "I think it was a noble act." People say suicide is cowardice. I think in her case it *was* a noble act.'

The conversation was a revelation. I'd never realised that we had been in danger. I never imagined before that my mother was actually protecting us by leaving us. She could have killed us, but instead she killed herself. I'd always wondered if she could have really loved us if she'd been so prepared to leave. How could a good mother desert her children? But now I was beginning to understand more, and I realised there were strange parallels with Jade. She too could have been killed by her mother, as so many baby girls were in China, but instead she was abandoned. We both had mothers who, for whatever reason, were forced to part with their children. For my mother the coercion came from her depression; for Jade's birth mother the social pressure to have a boy was just as powerful a malady.

There was nothing more to say. I needed time to digest this. Jade woke from her nap. As she sat wriggling on my lap, I prayed I would last longer as a mother for her. I was becoming nervous of returning to dangerous foreign assignments. Would I now really want to hang around under a bridge with the local muggers of Bogota as they woke from their glue-sniffing hangovers? Would I want to fly in small planes over Africa – small planes that I no longer trusted after one had crashed into the Zimbabwean bush with me and my

© Emily Buchanan

The plane that crash-landed in Zimbabwe with myself and the BBC team on board.

colleagues packed into it? Would I want to travel the streets of Mogadishu with their gun-toting gangs? Or fly into the epicentre of the Ebola outbreak in the Congo? They were all things I had been proud of doing and had done eagerly. Now I was changing: I no longer felt like the fearless, or perhaps reckless, foreign correspondent. Now that I had a daughter from a far corner of the developing world, my world was rapidly shrinking.

. . . .

And it shrank even more, once Jade hit two.

I had always regarded the 'terrible twos' as a bit of a myth, and never thought my delightful, friendly, happy child could ever become difficult. How wrong I was.

It all began while we were in Sicily where an Italian friend was getting married. The wedding itself was heavenly, a wind blowing the brightly coloured dresses and large hats of the guests as we stood in front of the stone church overlooking miles of rolling arid landscape. Jade frolicked in the wind, played with a water fountain, and we were all happy. Then we went to an island to the south called Linosa; a quiet, unspoilt place redolent of the 1940s where Gerald thought he could do some fishing. But for us there was to be no peace.

At about two in the morning Jade started to scream. I went to her and she began to bite, hit and kick me. She didn't want to be picked up. I wasn't even sure if she was awake or asleep. She crawled into a corner of the room moaning. Was she in pain? Was she losing her mind? It looked like a kind of mania. I wondered if we had lost our daughter to some local demon, then after several attempts to calm her down, Gerald had the inspiration to put her under a cool shower. Almost immediately it helped and she began to whimper and whine before finally dropping off to sleep. The next morning she seemed to have no memory of it and ran around admiring the bougainvillea blossom. But no sooner had she fallen asleep for her afternoon siesta than the piercing cries began again. The heat of the island was intense and inescapable. We were getting a reputation for having a nightmare child, and even here in child-tolerant Italy we could see the old ladies shaking their heads disapprovingly. When we finally arrived back in London, sleep-deprived and shaken, we realised that the word 'holiday' had been redefined forever.

We knew nothing of Jade's medical history and wondered if her rages were the first sign of some deep-seated mental problem. In fact, we discovered they were simple 'night terrors'

© Emily Buchanan

My favourite game.

brought on by heat, but it marked the beginning of a much more challenging period. Jade's ability to scream with a vocal strength that defied physics was impressive. Chinese people often seem to have strong voices, and can appear to shout at one another, but Jade's voice was superhuman. When a bus conductor asked her to sit down one day, she took umbrage and decided to yell with all her might. I tried to soothe, bribe and placate her, but that only encouraged her. She roared and screamed for half an hour as the long-suffering No. 23 pottered along its route. When we'd finally arrived at our stop, I looked round what had been a packed rush-hour bus to find the whole of the ground floor emptied. 'That's one way to clear everyone out!' I said to the conductor, hoping a sense of humour was in his job description.

Another day, while walking Jade back home from the shops in her pushchair, she decided a good yell was needed. She was protesting first at not wanting to walk and then at having to sit in her chair; she really wanted to be carried. She yelled at such a high pitch that heads turned all down Westbourne Grove. One man remarked that she would make a good opera singer. Others winced and stared at me accusingly.

. . . .

I didn't really want another child at this point. Sometimes I felt bruised by Jade's tempestuous emotions but Gerald, to his lasting credit, was undeterred. For him, her tantrums were like water off a duck's back. If we were out he would just sling Jade over his shoulders and march on, while I was finding lifting her more and more difficult. I also wondered whether putting our futures into the hands of the China Centre of Adoption Affairs once again was perhaps tempting fate too far.

Despite all these misgivings we still pestered our social services department to start another Home Study. Every report and form had to be reviewed, every medical check redone. The irony was that if we hadn't been adopting again the social services would have left us alone without actually knowing how we were getting on with Jade.

The principle challenge this time was a new annual quota imposed by the Chinese, who were struggling to cope with the volume of applications to adopt from all over the world. The UK had a quota of just 126 children in a year; for single mothers the quota was just 6. I met one distraught prospective adopter who had been told she'd have to wait another year before her papers could be processed. The American agencies

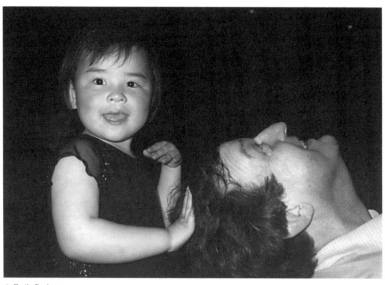

© Emily Buchanan

Drying my hands.

had applied for dozens of quotas so they could continue to adopt over 5,000 children, while our Department of Health had seen no need to apply for more than a single quota.

We were scheduled to go to Panel just six months after we'd started our Home Study, although this time we had to attend in person. Gerald and I were summoned to the red-brick expanse of Kensington Town Hall to be greeted by the Panel's chairwoman. She seemed genuinely interested in international adoption and I prayed the rest of the panel would be as positive. We walked into the large meeting room, and the faces of two social workers, two adopters, an adoptee, three independent observers, one childcare professional, a paediatrician and an advisor to the Panel all swivelled towards us. We sat at one end of the room and they examined us closely. Somehow we had to prove to these people in a few minutes that we were worthy of another child. It felt peculiarly Chinese, this power of the state over the most intimate part of our lives.

'So tell us how the adoption has gone, and why you want another girl from China?' the chairwoman asked. I started talking, telling her about Jade's progress, what the process had been like in China and then my voice petered out. I realised that although they were all 'experts' they actually didn't know much about Chinese adoption. What we'd been through was so far removed from the domestic adoption scene, and it turned out they were shocked to hear how abrupt the 'handover' had been in our hotel room.

The adoptee raised her hand and asked, 'What if the next adoption doesn't go so well? What would you do?'

I looked at Gerald. I didn't really know how to answer that. I realised we'd been lucky, but I couldn't pre-empt every problem. 'We would try and foresee the difficulties and cope as best we could,' was the limp response I gave, feeling that yet again I hadn't done enough homework.

We walked out into the wood-panelled corridor. A few days later we received a letter to say we had been approved. And then there was silence. A couple of months later I began to worry about the quota, and I discovered that our file had been forgotten during a change of staff and our completed reports still hadn't been transferred to the Department of Health. Our social work department remedied it fast, to their credit, and we just made the quota before it was filled up. We then had to have more medical checks, an AIDS test and find guardians for the children. Eventually the bureaucratic wheels cranked over and our papers once again took that slow boat to China.

New British legislation, the Adoption and Children Act 2002, was later intended to streamline many adoption procedures, but some experts remained sceptical about whether it would make inter-country adoption easier. It would still be down to the discretion of local authorities whether to undertake these cases.

....

Jade, who was now three, was oblivious to the lengthy preparations for her to have a sister. All she knew was that she was going to get a 'baby sis sis'. 'Me hug her, me carry her,' she kept saying, imagining perhaps that having a baby sister was like having a new doll. She was speaking a lot more although still struggling to articulate many words. Some Chinese adopted children suffer from speech delays, and she got very frustrated and tearful when she couldn't make herself understood. We would sometimes translate for her; my favourites were 'walletmelon' for watermelon, 'orangine' for orange, 'wawa' for trousers and 'tapo' for potato.

It was heart-warming, though, to see how she was beginning to talk about her feelings. One evening after she had a particularly spectacular meltdown – refusing to have a bath, put on her pyjamas or go to bed – she spoke on the phone to a friend of hers, a little six-year-old boy whom our nanny also looked after. He asked her whether she had had a 'wobbly'. 'Yeah, I had a wobbly, but me calm down now,' she said, nodding her head knowingly. As we were about to embark on the long emotional journey of speaking to her about her adoption, I hoped this kind of openness would stand her in good stead.

There was a little girl who had a little curl ...

She was also beginning to have those childish insights that bring an extra dimension to everyday things. One balmy September afternoon the three of us went to Twickenham to watch the rugby team which Gerald had represented for twenty years, London Irish. We sat high on the packed-out stands; the pitch was emerald, as luminous as the green wigs sported by the fans, while Jade revelled in the party atmosphere. When Gerald shouted, 'Come on, Irish,' she joined in, yelling 'Come on Irish,' too. I wondered what her birth parents would think of her now, a child of the desert steppes on the edge of Inner Mongolia now rooting for London Irish, a team steeped in the wet sod of Ireland. At half time she said, 'Where Irish gone?'

'They're resting,' I said.

She mulled over this and during the second half she suddenly piped up with her clear rising inflection, 'Irish still asleep?'

Everyone around us shrieked with laughter. 'Not exactly,' I said, but in fact she could have been right; they were playing as if they were.

. . . .

It was autumn and a good time to get away into the Spanish hinterland for our last holiday as a threesome. There was an excuse: a friend was getting married there and it meant Gerald would have a chance to indulge his growing interest in golf. It wasn't a game I would have wanted to have been associated with before, with all its inherent 'gender bias' but I wanted to learn too, thinking I could at least show my daughters that women didn't just sit on the sidelines. The trouble is golf is not a good game for people with fragile self-esteem, it's far too humbling, and it certainly doesn't go well with a child. Except on the wildest of courses, a babysitter is essential.

From the walled city of Avila, in the middle of the central Sierra, it felt as if the flat-bottomed clouds were almost within reach as they swept away to the horizon. Over breakfast Gerald, undaunted, took on the task of finding a babysitter, asking a sparky middle-aged waitress if she knew of anyone who could help out. She returned from the kitchen with a round dark-haired woman who said her 18-year old daughter might be free. I wasn't sure this was right. We would never do this in London: ask a waitress if she knew anyone who could look after our child. An hour later, Noellia arrived, a raven-haired, heavily made-up teenager with a large round jewel gleaming from her belly button. Her moustachioed and silent father Miguel sat on a bar stool beside her. We handed Jade over to them. Paranoia kicked in.

'We can't do this,' I hissed. Gerald told me not to be ridiculous. 'But we can't hand over Jade to total strangers who don't speak English,' I continued, convinced she was going to be miserable at best or kidnapped at worst. What if they were child traffickers ready to pounce on naive tourists, ready to lure nice chubby children into a den of prostitution? What if I never saw Jade again? I would be crazy with grief. As they drove off with her I choked back tears. Gerald looked at me and raised his eyes to heaven. I felt even more ridiculous as this was just for a game of golf. I thought of the headline 'BABY LOST FOR A BIRDIE'. I would go down as the most selfish mother ever. It wasn't even as if I was any good at this ridiculous game.

The course was beautiful, even when those fluffy clouds went black and unloaded their rivers of water on top of us.

As we sheltered under a little shack, waiting for the storm to pass, I phoned Miguel. '*Esta bien, esta dormida*,' he said. She was asleep. That was suspicious, no doubt a pretext designed to keep me calm while she was being shipped off to some unknown destination. We finished the game, our clothes were drenched, and we drove to Miguel's red-brick house, part of a modern complex on the edge of the city, incredibly not a false address. Then she came running out: 'Me no cry, me good, me have fun!'

Jade had grips in her hair and was clutching a doll. She was glowing with pride at her independence as she dragged us into the house where we found the whole family sitting around their coffee table. They offered us beer as if we were long lost friends, and said Jade had been angelic. The language barrier had been irrelevant. I felt so foolish at the way I'd allowed myself to become indoctrinated by the diet of fear and paranoia fed to parents in Britain. Needless to say Gerald, the Unworried, hadn't had a moment's anxiety.

On the television that night there were dramatic pictures of floods across Shaanxi Province. We watched terrified people grasping hold of their possessions and huddling into shelters. It made me think again about Jade's birth parents. I asked myself what they would make of her being with us now, sitting in this hotel, warm and dry. Would we ever be able to tell them that she was safe? I wished then I could send them a photograph, write to them, and reassure them. And if I could so easily descend into irrational fears about Jade's safety, what must they have gone through when they gave her up?

. . . .

We'd barely arrived home in London when my friend Jenny phoned: 'The referrals have arrived at the Department of

Health for "Date to China" November 02, that's yours, isn't it?' Parents were batched together according to the date their papers left the Department of Health and were sent to the CCAA in Beijing.

'What, already?' I said. We'd been expecting them later.

The sudden acceleration in processing time sent the email adoption grapevine into paroxysms of joy. First-time parents were ecstatic. 'After nine years, at last I'm a mum!' exulted one. 'Yippeeeee, after all the hurdles ... I can't wait for the post tomorrow!'

I too became glued to the front door, waiting for our postman to call. At 11 a.m. the doorbell rang. It was our loyal builder who'd brought a skipping rope and a book for Jade while passing by to see what kind of tiles we needed to repair a patch of wall in the kitchen. Then the doorbell rang again, and I rushed to answer it. Jade was right behind me, having got into the spirit of anticipation; the postwoman said she'd never had a door answered so quickly. I signed for the brown envelope and Jade immediately snatched it away. The phone rang and it was my producer from a News 24 discussion programme I was presenting wanting to talk about the weekend's show. 'I've just had our referral from China and I can't talk now!' I protested.

Unfazed, he started to discuss the theme of how effective our intelligence agents have been in providing accurate information on Iraq, and Tory leader Ian Duncan Smith's big idea about how to reform public services. I tried hard to concentrate, knowing that the brown envelope was now somewhere else, possibly being ripped open by Jade and its contents strewn around the kitchen. I managed to make some quick notes, promised to call back later, put the phone down and went into the kitchen to find Jade – not destroying the brown envelope, but practising skipping with her new rope. It had a built-in aerobics chant. 'One, and two, and three, and four ... up and down, up and down,' went the electronic voice. Our loquacious builder started talking about the tiles but at this point I had to interrupt. I reached past him and tore open the envelope, searching for the photograph.

And there she was. A tiny round face, a bit like Jade's had been. There was the same anxious, forlorn look and slightly wrinkled eyebrows. They could easily have been sisters: there was the turned-down, glum mouth, the wide round face and pale skin, but she looked in better health than Jade had done in her picture. There were two other photographs in which she looked rather surprised, not realising how much her expression would be analysed by her future parents. In one she was in a bright blue baby walker, almost drowning in her large red cardigan; in the other picture she was nestled into a wicker basket, a bunch of crimson silk peonies and roses in her lap. Her name was Rong Min Ying, a revolutionary name meaning 'hero of the people', but to us she immediately became simply Rose. She was living in the Xiushui Social Welfare Institute in Jiangxi Province.

I reached immediately for our guidebook. Jiangxi was a completely different region of China to Jade's province. It was south of the great Yangtze River, north of Guandong; once it had been prosperous with the development of silver mining and tea growing but it had gone into steady decline and was now principally famous as one of the old Communist guerrilla bases. The provincial capital, Nanchang, had been the site of their historic uprising of 1927. It was followed by several years of war after which Chiang Kai-shek's army finally encircled the Communist troops who had been based in the so called 'Jiangxi Soviet'. But the Communists made a dramatic breakout in 1934, marking the beginning of their heroic Long March. Mao's 80,000 troops trekked for a year over 6,000 miles of hazardous country. The overwhelming majority of them perished along the way while the rest regrouped in Yan'an in Shaanxi Province. I desperately wanted to find links between my two daughters and here already was one. Rose had been born in the province where the Long March started, while Jade was from the province where it had ended. Perhaps their families could boast of strong revolutionary credentials. The Long March established Mao as the key military leader of the Communist forces; he called it 'a manifesto, a propaganda force, a seeding machine'. He would be turning in his grave to think of capitalists like us coming seventy years later, indeed being invited by the Communist government, to take away Chinese girls, the granddaughters of his hard-won Revolution.

Xiushui was a town in the mountainous area to the north of Jiangxi Province. Strangely, the Shaanxi renegade Li Zicheng who had toppled the Ming dynasty had finally ended his days in that same region. The story goes that after he was driven out of Beijing, he had ended up hiding in these mountains where he died, either by suicide, or as some recount, by being beaten to death by peasants from whom he was trying to steal food. Here was another serendipitous connection between the two provinces. There were bound to be many more.

....

I showed everyone the picture; at work the make-up ladies got first glimpse, and they 'ooed' and 'ahhed' as did any other colleague I bumped into. But however much I looked at Rong Min Ying's serious, round, angelic face, I still felt detached from her. I should have been whooping with joy but instead I wondered if this time I would have to *learn* to love my child. My heart was already stretched to the limit by the demands of a powerful, entrancing but sometimes difficult three-year-old. I now felt like a 'real' mother, and having a second daughter wasn't going to enhance that. This thought made me feel guilty; perhaps I should own up that I had hit the glass ceiling of my maternal instinct.

I think I feared that the experience of loving Jade had been a fluke. We had been so lucky; surely we couldn't be that lucky again. What if this little girl didn't take to us, what if she'd been badly traumatised? I wondered if I really had the emotional energy to devote to her. I sat at our long wooden kitchen table, ingrained with wine stains and crayon marks, swirling in a soup of doubts and uncertainties, when I casually opened *The Guardian*. The headline stabbed at me:

DO THE FOREIGNERS WHO ADOPT OUR GIRLS KNOW HOW TO FEED AND LOVE THEM IN THEIR ARMS AND HEARTS?

. . . .

What had I just been thinking? Of course we loved them, totally and unconditionally. The author of the article was a Chinese writer, Xinran, who'd written extensively about the suffering of women in her book *The Good Women of China*. Now, it seemed, she had also spoken to women who had actually abandoned their baby girls. She described talking to some near the banks of the Yangtze River:

> Did they not want to find out where their babies were?
> 'I would rather suffer this dark hole inside me if it
> means she can have a better life. I don't want to disturb
> my girl's life,' said one. 'I am very pleased for a rich
> person to take my daughter, she has a right to live a
> good life,' said another. One of them asked me: 'Do
> you believe those foreigners who adopt our girls know
> how to feed and love them in their arms and hearts?'

....

I read that over and over again. I thought of all the adoptive families I knew, doting on their longed-for daughters. How could anyone think we didn't adore them? This was a stark reminder that while we wallowed in the emotional luxury of wondering whether we were good mothers, these women were living every day with a void inside them, having absolutely no idea what had happened to their children.

I read on. Xinran described passing a public toilet one cold winter morning in Zhangzhou back in 1990: 'A noisy crowd had gathered around a little bag of clothes lying in the windy entrance. People were pointing to it and shouting, "Look, look, she is still alive".' Xinran had picked up the bundle to find a tiny baby girl inside, barely a few days old: 'She was frozen blue, but her tiny nose was twitching.' Xinran took the baby to a nearby hospital, but found no one was in a hurry to save her. As a well-known radio presenter, she then took out her tape recorder and started reporting what she saw. 'Immediately a doctor appeared and took the baby to the emergency room. A nurse came up and said, "Please forgive our cold minds. There are too many abandoned baby girls for us to handle. We have helped more than ten, but afterwards no one has wanted to take responsibility for their future." ' Xinran broadcast the story on her show, and then ten days later she got a letter from a childless couple wanting to adopt the baby girl. She also received a message on her answering machine, recorded with a weeping voice:

> I am the mother of the baby girl. She was born just four days before you saved her. Thank you so much for taking my daughter to the hospital. I watched in the crowd with my heart broken. I followed you and sat outside your radio station all day. Many, many times I almost shouted out to you: 'That is my baby'!

. . . .

I needed to know more, much more about these poor women, and I knew I had to meet Xinran, but not yet, not with our second daughter waiting for us, there was too much to do first.

Our translator this time was a young student called Jane. Chinese people sometimes adopt English names when dealing with foreigners. The first thing I asked her was whether it would be possible to visit Rose's orphanage. 'It is a very rough road to get there and the orphanage director fears it may trigger re-entry trauma,' she replied emphatically. Yet again, our longed-for goal of actually seeing where our child came from was being held tantalisingly out of reach.

While we made the preparations I began reading a book called *Siblings without Rivalry* which argued that the reason brothers and sisters quarrel so much is that a new sibling feels the same as if a husband were to take another wife. So while everyone was saying, 'How lovely for Jade to have a sister', we realised it would probably be the most emotionally threatening development she'd had to face since we adopted her. For the moment she was oblivious to the downside, looking forward with rose-tinted spectacles to the idea. When her teacher asked her what she was doing at half-term she replied eagerly, to the amazement of the rest of her class, 'Me going to China to get my baby sister.'

....

Although I had given up my role as Religious Affairs Correspondent to work part-time, I was called on to cover Pope John Paul II's twenty-fifth anniversary and watch Mother Teresa be put on the first step to sainthood. It was my first assignment abroad since Jade's arrival and part of me was thrilled to be in my old job again. We stood on the platform at the back of Rome's St. Peter's Square – a stage set if ever there was one, built 350 years ago but still carrying maximum impact in the television age. Its curved colonnades and cobbled piazza, steadily sloping up to the great Basilica and holding a couple of hundred thousand worshippers, was magnificent. The ranks of red-robed cardinals, the bishops in their purple, the choirs, all made a rich backdrop for a performance of Tamil dancers dressed in luminous orange robes and garlands of marigolds. There were offerings of Mother Teresa's blood, a giant tapestry of her was unveiled and Indian music echoed round the square. When it was time for communion, priests carrying shining white parasols walked through the crowd; it was as if the Church was giving His Holiness a touch of Hollywood. The Pope quoted Mother Teresa's firm stand against abortion and in favour of adoption: 'If any woman doesn't want her baby I will look after it.'

As the words rang out, I looked over the fluttering banners to the statues of saints silhouetted against the clear blue sky and thought of those women in India I had met, the ones who had had one abortion after another in their desperate attempts to have a girl, particularly one woman in the Punjab who'd had fourteen abortions and eventually had a son. These were terrible cases, with a woman's so-called 'right to choose' perverted so that she was forced to choose abortion simply because of the sex of her child. On the other hand, wasn't abortion actually the lesser of two evils in these societies obsessed with sons? Could a mother be expected to give birth to one daughter after another and cope with having each one taken away, even if they were to be adopted? It was the same question for China, as the birth-control policy forced thousands of women to abandon their girls so they could try for a son; perhaps it was more humane to let them terminate one pregnancy after another. Anyway, in spite of the appeals of the Catholic Church, there seemed to be no end in sight to the killing of baby girls – sex-selective abortions were on the rise right across Asia.

On that glittering day, as the priests walked back with their white umbrellas, the music died down and the colourful display of Church unity and power ended, I felt so grateful to those brave women who for whatever reason didn't abort their girl children, but gave them away. Their sacrifice saved their children's lives and had given us, thousands of miles away, such overwhelming joy.

. . . .

Back home events sped up. Within days our ornate Invitation to Travel dodged a postal workers strike and arrived safely, guaranteeing us our visa. We also narrowly avoided a baggage handlers strike at Heathrow before we finally took off for China.

As we sat on the plane to Beijing I began to read *Astonishing Splashes of Colour* by Clare Morrall. It was about a young woman whose mother was killed in a car crash when she was a child, and was now unable to conceive. One line leapt out of the pages at me:

> I can't decide which is worse, to not have a mother, or
> to not have children. An empty space in both directions.
> No backwards, no forwards.

I sank into the seat and watched Jade wriggling on her father's lap, pulling his nose, and then throwing her head back with a full raucous laugh as he tickled her tummy. Thanks to this man and this child, my 'empty space in both directions', my past and my future were being healed.

As for our two girls' birth mothers, it was just too cruel to imagine what sort of futures lay ahead for them. I could only pray that we could send them both a message through the wind to tell them their daughters were safe and well.

- Chapter Six -

Little Dragon, Little Horse

Our bags were smoothly checked through from Beijing to Hangzhou, China's 'tourist capital', in spite of just a half-hour turnaround between flights — a feat of efficiency European airports had long given up. After sixteen hours travelling, and with Jade exhausted, we opted for the first hotel offered to us by a smart young woman in Arrivals. It turned out to be an anonymous glass-fronted establishment in the town centre, but inside it was buzzing with all the glamour of 'New Silk Road Model Look World 2003', a kind of junior models' international congress. It also seemed to be hosting three simultaneous weddings; we had to skirt three brides in brilliant white gowns hovering around the entrance, along with their bashful-looking husbands. It was possible these were models dressed up in bridal outfits, I wasn't quite sure.

We squeezed into the lift with our bags, pressed against the sides by a large lady in a voluminous red ball gown. We had truly landed in 'glitz' city, just a hundred miles south west of Shanghai, the first leg of a week's tour to show Jade some of her motherland before we picked up her sister. It was to be a tall order taking a three-year-old round China, but as usual we didn't want to make things too simple, preferring to seize the chance to see more of this fascinating country with which we felt an increasing emotional bond.

The hotel was on the so called 'Champs-Elysées' of Hangzhou, a wide street flanked by designer-label shops stretching down to the celebrated West Lake. But as we walked out to explore, it was our nerves rather than our credit cards that took the strain. Jade decided to protest over some minor irritation as if the end of the world had come. She moaned, cried and kicked her legs all down the street attracting astonished stares. This was her re-entry into China, and she wasn't going to do it quietly. I once read a book called *Don't Sweat the Small Stuff* and realised it was meant *par excellence* for our darling daughter. At one point she got out of her pushchair, sat on the pavement tantalisingly too far from the elegant lake-side pagodas we'd come to see and wouldn't budge. We were stuck. Gerald already had a bad back, and I worried about crippling mine too by lifting her. So we just stood there, while a small crowd gathered.

I wanted to say something, but I just kept struggling to recall those few Mandarin classes we'd squeezed in before our departure. The phrase that kept coming to mind was, '*Ni jie hunle ma?*' – 'are you married?' – but that didn't feel quite right for the situation. The crowd grew as more passers-by peered over to look at this strange group: two 'big noses' with a little red-faced girl screaming furiously on the ground. I flipped through the phrase book which offered any number of potentially useful sentences for the situation like, 'Could I have a bottle of beer?' or 'Show me the best restaurant where I can eat Peking Duck'. I nearly plumped for 'Please exchange this!', looking at this turbulent bundle of emotion on the grey pavement and then thought better of it. I could have said, '*zhe shi wode huzhao*' or 'this is my passport': after all Jade was a kind of passport into Chinese culture, but I thought the double entendre would be lost.

In the end I managed, '*Ta shi san sui*' – 'she's three years old' – shrugging and looking up at the sky, not as if I expected any help to come from that direction. There were immediately understanding grunts and nods of acceptance from the assembled throng, but no one moved. This was clearly the best entertainment in town.

Under pressure from so many interested faces, Gerald eventually gave in and put Jade on his shoulders, despite his troublesome back. Her emotional tempest calmed into a broad grin within five miraculous seconds. The speed with which her most tormented cries could transform into joy still amazed me. I always wondered whether she had really been as miserable as she appeared or was the entire performance put on just to turn the heat up on her tired parents. The change of mood was a relief for her and the patient citizens of Hangzhou, but the means by which it was procured proved disastrous for Gerald's vertebrae. By the time we'd returned to the hotel, he was almost bent double and we had to make an urgent call to their massage service.

A woman with iron-strength fingers came to our room and proceeded to pummel and press into Gerald's torso for half an hour. After being flattened into the firm hotel bed, Gerald eventually prized himself off it, and managed to totter to the hotel restaurant. The elegant room, hosting tables of a dozen diners each, sparkled with loud voices and laughter. We began to recover our energies slowly as we were greeted with a magnificent dinner of West Lake panting fish, spinach, chicken and chestnuts with fried crunchy vegetables. Jade romped between the tables with some other Chinese children, occasionally running back to us clutching a rose, a lollipop, a balloon or some other booty.

I began to relax and drink in the thrill of again being in China: the joy people took in children; the energy and dynamism; the sense of this huge, unpredictable country which was still so obscure to us – and the culmination of another epic journey to find a child.

But the next morning, before we could begin sightseeing, we had to sort out Gerald's back. 'The local back hospital is five minutes away next to the Xinhua bookstore,' the giggling receptionist told us. Easy, except that Xinhua wasn't in English lettering on the road sign. So, a full twenty minutes later, down a small alley with 'pavements mined for incautious steps', as my father used to say about uneven surfaces meant for pedestrians, we found a Red Cross sign in front of a tatty door.

Once inside the dark and grimy entrance hall we hesitated over where to go: to the right were the steaming kitchens, the other way led down a dark corridor. A young man saw us and waved us up some worn concrete stairs, past the unmistakable sharp smell emanating from some traditional Chinese toilets – the ones where the user squats over a tiled gutter, with half-doors to give just a hint of privacy – and then opposite we saw a large room in which several patients were lying on tables, their exposed backs being rubbed and kneaded, their necks twisted and cracked by doctors in white coats. A woman winced as one doctor put pressure on points on the souls of her feet while another chatted on her mobile phone oblivious to the two acupuncture needles, heated by ultra violet lamps, sticking up on each side of her spine.

The contrast between the quiet yet informal professionalism of the doctors and the shabbiness of the building was striking. The floor was unpolished wood, thick with dirt; there were black, peeling blobs of damp on the ceiling and walls, the wiring was held together with black tape and an old skeleton was lying as if asleep on the shelf, next to a calendar showing two Chinese dancing dolls.

The most senior doctor, Mr Wu, told us he had qualified at the Hangzhou School of Traditional Chinese medicine seventeen years before. He had a pale, sensitive face, a kind smile and small but very strong hands. He told Gerald to lie down and began rubbing his back, sticking half a dozen needles into points around his spine, before he was joined by two other practitioners. They pulled his legs while Mr Wu massaged and burrowed with his elbow. Gerald tried to distract himself by reading out loud an irrelevant section in our phrasebook called *Pass the Pepper*: 'A Chinese cure for diarrhoea that actually works is to eat black charred meat covered in spicy red capsicum ...'

Meanwhile Mr Wu looked over to Jade. 'She's very beautiful.'

'She's from the north, Shaanxi Province,' I said.

'So she'll be very strong too!'

The treatment lasted nearly an hour and at the end we were only charged the equivalent of £8. We were deeply impressed by the service, but after just one session there wasn't much chance of a miracle cure.

We hobbled back to the hotel to begin planning the next few days, for which we needed that rare commodity, accurate travel information. In spite of the express train to modernisation China was taking, straightforward facts were still in short supply. For decades people were used to being told only as much information as the state felt they should know, so an inquiring mind was not encouraged. It meant that, even now, those in charge of travel information often couldn't find the simplest information. We wanted the times of buses, not to some obscure temple, but to one of the biggest tourist attractions in China, Huangshan Holy Mountain. No one at reception had any idea how long that journey would take, so they called on the hotel manager. A sprightly young Belgian was at our side in a moment, sporting a black-leather heavy metal jacket, black trousers and a large gold chain as well as an in-your-face black metal cross hanging on his bare chest. He wasn't quite sure whether it was four, five or six hours by bus, and as for the times – well, that would be the preserve of the travel desk which was shut at that moment. It was difficult to concentrate on his answers until he explained that his outlandish outfit was part of the fashion show. There was a special celebration that night in which the hotel staff were entertaining the models of 'New Silk Road Model Look World 2003'. Failing on the bus times, he invited us to join him for dinner instead.

A conference-room stage had been adorned with a red drape embroidered with the words 'Sunny Appreciation Party', while a mock catwalk was set up, reaching into the centre of the dining tables. Dozens of models from all over the world were there, eating pigeon-sized portions of food. They squealed in horror as one at a time they were invited up on the stage to be blindfolded and then offered glasses of drink that had been doctored with condiments like tomato ketchup, mustard or vinegar. When they spat out the foul-tasting liquid there were roars of laughter, and later a prize was awarded to the model who guessed correctly what the adulterating substances were.

Then it was the turn of the hotel staff to take to the stage. First we were serenaded by the golden tenor voice of the besuited Head of Hotel Security. Miss Wu Lan from the Food and Beverage Department was next, in a slinky two-piece skirt adorned with red and blue ribbons and silver ornaments. Her little black top left plenty of slender midriff showing, which she stretched and twisted to the music. Several young women from the Housekeeping Department strode on after her, dressed in more sober black trousers and tops, and then slunk, sullen and very model-like, up and down the catwalk. Other young girls from Housekeeping came on in very plain black tunics with white shirts, and they too managed to look stylish and coordinated. The Chinese hotel manager then danced rather awkwardly as he was escorted down the catwalk by a tall, blonde Miss Ukraine. The idea behind it all, we were told, was to make all the hotel staff feel valued and part of the team.

The music was very catchy, with lyrics something like, 'I want to dance, cha, cha, cha' and it certainly made Jade feel completely part of the team. She began waving her arms about and before I could stop her she had sprung up onto the stage and begun jumping up and down, dancing to resounding applause from all the young models, hotel staff and assorted local journalists. Encouraged by the response, she pulled Miss Russia onto the stage with her and tried to imitate her, rocking her hips with her hands at her waist, to more hoots and applause. Jade carried on prancing around before scampering back to us, grinning with excitement and sitting down to guzzle a plate of spring rolls, rice, mushrooms and mashed potato.

The whole episode had obviously given her so much to think about that she couldn't sleep that night. I ended up giggling and chatting with her in our bed until at least four in the morning. We eventually slept but all woke up jet-lagged and weary. Gerald's back was stiffer than ever. We opted for a quick tour of the National Silk Museum before resting beside the West Lake admiring the old wooden pagodas, the giant black cormorants swooping over the water, and listening to the quiet clink, clink of the mah-jong players.

At the Buddhist Temple of Inspired Seclusion we bribed a tired Jade with chocolate-filled wafers to walk up the slope against the flow of pilgrims coming the other way. A man on a penny whistle created a gentle mournful sound, his fingers doing a soft vibrato which soon dissolved Jade's complaints. She was entranced, too, as the monks began to chant, their voices echoing down the long path up to the main gate in front of the Hall of the Four Heavenly Guardians. As we arrived at the temple itself Jade stood calmly, her thumb in her mouth, warming her back against an urn where worshippers were burning incense. The rich colours, the steady pulse of the chants with the sharp strikes of the gongs, reminded me of our days in Putuoshan. This was a timeless and reassuring scene as we embarked on yet another of our mad adoption adventures. Inside the hall Jade stared at the great laughing Buddha who is said to be able to 'endure everything unendurable in the world and laugh at every laughable person in the world'. He must be having a good chortle at us, I thought.

Then I thought about Rose and her round, delicate face. Did she know we were on our way? We were longing to see her; it was only a few days before we'd be able to hold her and squeeze her tight. Meanwhile Jade was showing herself to be an adventurous traveller who was as curious about China as the Chinese were about her.

Her skirt was black from the soot she'd wiped off the side of the urn; in fact it matched the charcoal coating around the beggar's chicken which we later tucked into in the Louwailou Restaurant. Using an ancient recipe, the cooks there coated the chicken in mud and lotus leaves before baking it. The idea supposedly came from a beggar who stole a chicken earmarked for the emperor and secretly cooked it while buried underground. The waiters cracked open the package in front of us, revealing what looked like nothing more than a lump of dried mud, but inside was the cooked, steaming chicken soaked in all its juices, succulent and delicious.

A table of seven Chinese men next to our table kept giving us the thumbs up sign as they noticed Jade. To them she was a curious mixture. 'She doesn't look Chinese any more,' one man grunted as he chewed on his pork slices. 'You have made her Western.' Jade certainly didn't appear Chinese to the Chinese. At home with us for two-thirds of her short life and she'd become like a foreigner. It wasn't just the fact that she didn't speak Mandarin; it was her mannerisms, her dress and hairstyle that made her look Western. 'Look at the way she is confident and going up to speak to those people over there; Chinese girls are taught to be more quiet and are usually more shy,' another man said.

For the moment the Chinese seemed happy that we were taking away their daughters, to them they were simply a big social problem. But I couldn't help wondering how they might feel in twenty years' time. I had met Koreans who were now embarrassed that so many Americans came and adopted their children; perhaps the Chinese will feel the same. I wondered if they would then be hostile to these Chinese expats who were a living testimony to an uncomfortable past.

Back at our hotel it took us two days of enquiries to find out how long the journey would be from Hangzhou to Huangshan Holy Mountain. After much scouring of the tiny print on the bus timetables the earnest young ladies on the travel desk said it would be twelve hours. Then they made some phone calls and said it was seven hours. With a three-year-old child that didn't seem possible and we thought we'd have to abandon the idea but, after another day of persistent questions, Gerald found out the journey was in fact just four hours.

. . . .

The West Bus Station hall was cavernous; buses were lined up outside at separate entrances, their times on electronic notice-boards, while women in blue uniforms announced departures into microphones. We climbed on board glad to have seats, as the bus was packed. I sat with Jade and read *Monkey Puzzle* to her at least twenty times. It was rather poignant, a story of a monkey who couldn't find his mother. Every time a butterfly announces that she's found her, it turns out to be another animal and not the monkey's mum. Jade wanted it over and over again.

For the rest of the journey she slept and I felt so close to her, and proud: proud that this brave, adventurous girl was taking it all in her stride. Would she remember any of this? Perhaps not, but at least she would have a general feeling that being in China was fun. I wanted so much for her to associate China with good experiences, to act as a bulwark against the truth of her own past which she would gradually come to understand later on.

The bus rolled past the outskirts of Hangzhou: a sharp contrast to the wealth in the city centre. It didn't take long to be reminded of how China's burgeoning wealth was not yet trickling down to most of its vast population. We passed smoky factories and dilapidated outbuildings interspersed with muddy fields, shabby roadside shops and cigarette kiosks. The pop video on the bus, showing a seductive female singer wafting around a rose garden in a white dress, couldn't have been more at odds with the dreariness of our surroundings.

The urban sprawl gave way to villages in which wooden huts were being replaced by buildings covered in white tiles; around them herds of cows grazed on steep hills covered in flowering chrysanthemums. Bizarrely, as the landscape became more beautiful the bus's video changed to a thriller with dark scenes of murder, shootings and prison cells.

This was Anhui Province, one of the poorest regions of China. Out of the window I saw a man so laden under piles of straw at first I thought this moving haystack must be a donkey. Another walked beside the road trying to keep his little flock of ducks and ducklings under control. I could see men and women labouring by hand in the fields; some carried water in buckets hanging on a pole across their shoulders. The sun was setting, a golden orb through the mist. I wondered where, in these picturesque scenes, baby girls were even now being silently abandoned. The pressures on these labouring, farming families would have made having a son essential. Anhui is notorious for girl abandonment. There are thought to be over 50,000 orphans scattered throughout thousands of small child welfare institutes and many are eventually sent to the capital Hefei. Foreign funding has improved conditions enormously and it now has one of the highest rates of international adoption in China.

There were villages here where nearly all families lived in small, dark, damp mud houses, tilling the soil by hand, and yet with their meagre earnings they were still expected to pay a variety of taxes and fees to the local government. One brave man in a village somewhere in this hinterland had a few years earlier challenged the corruption of local officials and their excessive taxation, but even though he made a formal complaint through all the correct channels, he was beaten to death inside a police station.

As tourists we couldn't have been aware of the seething anger of local peasants, although even our guide whom we picked up in the bright lights of Tunxi was pretty candid about daily life. He called himself Steve, and as this was a tea-growing region he whisked us straight out to a street devoted entirely to shops selling different kinds of tea. Jade was taken in hand by a woman who carried her around feeding her little nuts tasting of chocolate. As Steve chewed and cracked them, and we sat sipping the delicious, jasmine-flavoured green tea, he explained that Anhui, along with Shaanxi where Jade is from, were the two most deprived provinces in China. 'It means there are three things that are most important for us: get a house, get married and have a son, which explains why there's so much construction, you would have seen all the new houses in the villages, and why a lot of girls do get abandoned here.'

The next day we drove to the Holy Mountain itself, taking lunch in a small roadside restaurant on the way. We were advised to choose the local delicacy, stone chicken, which duly arrived bubbling in a bamboo casserole dish. The soft, tasteless flesh swimming amongst some boiled mushrooms certainly didn't taste like chicken, and the spotted skin gave us a clue. The girl serving us brought over a dictionary and pointed at the word 'frog'. I looked at the leg on my plate and didn't feel so hungry after that. Jade, all along, had wisely decided to stick to rice.

Nearby we walked over a perilous swinging bamboo bridge slung across a river so we could take a ride further downstream on a raft. We passed wooden houses with great bunches of green leaves, a kind of Chinese spinach, hanging outside while women with sunburnt faces, wearing grey jackets and straight trousers, came out of their kitchens to look at us. Life looked simple, tough and unforgiving.

We clung to the wooden chairs strapped to the bamboo raft while a jovial elderly Chinese man wearing a cloth cap and glasses regaled us with tales of how he'd emigrated to Taiwan and then America after World War II. When I told him Jade was from Shaanxi Province, he laughed: 'Do you know what they used to say about Shaanxi people? They only have three baths in their life – one when they're born, one when they marry and one when they die.' He threw his head back in mirth, rocking our fragile craft. It was just like the old Home Counties snobbery towards uncouth northerners in Britain.

November weather is unpredictable and we had been lulled by the warm, balmy sunshine. Overnight the clouds came in and gripped the mountain in a cold vice. Suddenly it was winter, and the cavernous restaurants of our mountain hotel were unheated and icy. We sat in our thickest sweaters and hats, picking over the breakfast of boiled rice and spicy green beans which did nothing to thaw us out. The heavy cloud cover looked inauspicious for viewing 'most spectacular mountain scenery in China' but it wasn't just the weather that was against us.

We drove to the base of the cable car and were about to get on when Jade threw one of her most powerful 'wobblies'. As she pulled away from me and I tried to stop her getting close to the tracks, she suddenly complained her arm was hurting: '... like *before*, Mummy.' I knew at once it was serious. She'd dislocated her elbow once in London and the only solution was hospital. So, shrouded in freezing fog, we had a minor medical emergency on our hands. I flipped the pages of our phrasebook, and eventually tracked down the word *'tuojiule'* or 'dislocated', showing it to anybody who would stop, and pointing at Jade who was looking cold and miserable. Eventually we found the path to a nearby hotel, where a Scottish anaesthetist studying acupuncture in Shanghai was sitting in reception, disgruntled that Highland weather had stymied her visit to the Holy Mountain for the third time. She helped us organise a taxi, in fact a mini-van with no suspension and no windows, which rushed us down the back-jolting road to the town's hospital. It was a relatively new building, and we were ushered into a room where a doctor was treating a woman lying down with a leg in plaster. He turned to us and after some more pointing to *'tuojiule'*, he took Jade's arm and imperceptibly twisted it back into place. It was our second taste of the surprising speed and efficiency of China's chronically underfunded medical service.

Travel plans with a three-year-old were always going to have to be flexible. Instead of the 'most spectacular mountain scenery in China' we ended up seeking comfort in the municipal swimming pool, which we had to ourselves. Fed by the steaming waters from nearby hot springs, it looked as if it hadn't been renovated since the Revolution, with pale green paint peeling off the damp walls and an eerie deserted atmosphere as the hot vapour rose from the water. We ate lunch in a café next door in our overcoats, and stayed wrapped up for dinner at the hotel. The brochure did its best to cheer us up: 'Dining is a mixture of physical joy and mental happiness. Every delicious dish offering is our rejoice ...' But all we could feel were the gales howling through the glass front doors.

As a compensation for not seeing the mountain, the next day Steve took us to see some well-preserved 'traditional' villages set in valleys of paddy fields and surrounded by wooded mountains. He was determined to give us a lesson in Chinese philosophy at the same time. In the first village, called 'Xidi' or 'Western waterflow', the Confucian sense of order was paramount: 'Everything here is based on good *feng shui*. Look at this room, what do you see? There's a clock, a mirror and then over there a vase. In every room there are these three objects. It's to show it takes "time" to plan and "reflect" before designing any beautiful object. Too many people do things first and think afterwards, that's how you lose money!'

Symbolism was everywhere: a leaf carving pointing downwards meant retirement and the return to one's roots; a Ming Dynasty wooden door with jagged panels criss-crossed to look like broken ice represented hard times; opposite was one with bats carved on it, meaning prosperity and a good harvest. Calligraphy hanging on silken scrolls spoke of respect for parents. There was no mention of daughters; the inhabitants would have lived by a Confucian world view that destined girls into subservience. 'Women and people of low birth are very hard to deal with, if you are friendly with them they get out of hand,' Confucius had written. He upheld a social system based on male lineage in which land and money was passed from father to son. A son was expected to work the land, continue the ancestral name and care for his parents in retirement; having a son was the only way to ensure a comfortable old age. Although so much of this old order was smashed during the Cultural Revolution – we saw carvings of noblemen which had been decapitated by the Red Guards – the lowly position of women in peasant families was still much the same as it had been for 2,000 years.

The time for our night train to Nanchang was approaching and there was just a short while to eat supper at a roadside restaurant back in Tunxi. The hotpot of duck, beans and peppers simmered on the charcoal stove. As we tucked in, sitting on precarious metal stools round a tiny table, Steve said, 'You know, my mother was adopted. She had been left in the street in 1938 and picked up by a family who had five boys and now wanted a girl. I am very sad never to have known my biological grandparents ... by the way, for this adoption do you have to pay any money?'

'There is a standard fixed fee of $3000 which officially is a donation to the orphanage, although we actually hand it over to the Civil Affairs Office.'

'I'll give you *my* daughter for that!' Steve couldn't believe we were again coming so far and spending so much money for a daughter, or for any child, for that matter.

....

We shared our berth on the train with a Beijing businessman and an orthopaedic doctor. I was able, using the businessman as a translator, to ply the doctor with questions about Jade's dislocated elbow. I also asked him about some gymnastics classes we'd seen in Hangzhou where children were achieving improbable feats of flexibility: holding one leg up vertically so their foot rested on an ear and then bending away in an arc. The last time I'd seen anything like it was amongst the Shaolin Monks. He said these children were often enrolled for very early training. 'The parents sometimes force them to do it,' he said, 'so that they will end up earning money for them.'

Jade slept like a lamb in the top bunk with Gerald, while I lay on the bottom bunk, listening to the slow clunk, clunk of the wheels. This felt like the most romantic way to travel to our new daughter. It was calming, steady and inevitable. The track stretching into the night towards Nanchang already linked us physically to her. I thought about Rose in her cot, having her last night at the orphanage, unaware of the big change that was about to hit her. I remembered my nerves at first meeting Jade, and realised I'd been avoiding dwelling on my lurking anxieties about whether this daughter was going to take to her new parents.

....

The next morning was Remembrance Day and for us, too, a day to remember forever. I felt sick as a dog; my stomach was in revolt. Supper the day before had taken its toll. If it wasn't the hotpot, then perhaps the rice had not been fresh. The weather was now bitterly cold and wet, and Nanchang Station looked uninspiring in the grey early morning light. I just didn't feel up to the task ahead.

We had booked into the Jiangxi Hotel, a modernised 1960s building with spacious, inexpensive rooms. We looked out onto a wet car park and a jumble of concrete buildings. Gerald fiddled with the TV remote control looking for world news and the Rugby World Cup, while I tried not to think too hard about my abdominal cramps. I really didn't want to meet my child in this state. Then I thought about giving birth: that put my stomach ache into proportion. Surely I could put up with a bit of pain and nausea, wasn't this how women usually felt as their child arrived?

....

Jane, our translator, took Jade downstairs to be ready to meet Rose when she arrived. A few moments later the door to our room opened. Jade bounced in first: 'Look, Mum, this is my baby sister. Mum, Dad, look!'

But Miss Rong Min Ying was in no mood to be introduced. She was red faced, distraught and crying her eyes out. The head of the orphanage, Mr Rong, put her on Gerald's lap and in her nappyless state she instantly peed all over his trousers. She was miserable, inconsolable. Gerald lifted and hugged her and her tears flowed ever faster. I tried to make soothing noises but I actually sounded tense. She screamed even louder when I went close to her and she buried her face in Gerald's sweater.

Mr. Rong sat on the corner of our bed oblivious to her cries. He had given all the girls his surname, and indeed he looked an archetypal kind father, in his early fifties with a handsome, sensitive face. He told us what he knew of Rose's past, while Jane translated. 'She was left at five in the morning outside the old people's home in a small town south west of Xiushui, called Zhencun. Dawn is a favourite time for babies to be left as it means the mother, if it is her, can leave her child under cover of darkness, and it's the shortest wait for the baby before she is found. Sometimes parents will set off firecrackers to alert people that a baby is there. There was no note attached to Min Ying, so they had to estimate her birthday, but she appeared from the state of her umbilical cord to have been about a week old when she was left.'

'What happened to her after she was found? Did she stay in the orphanage?'

'We didn't keep her long before we placed her with a foster family, they were looking after three other girls at the same time.' I was so preoccupied with trying to find information about Rose that I completely forgot to ask the names of the other children there. And I couldn't quite concentrate as I glanced over at Gerald struggling to comfort our wailing child. What was going on inside her little round head with its wisps of black hair? How much she must have been missing her foster mother and the three other little girls. I didn't feel instantly that she was *my* child. She clearly belonged to someone else and I almost wanted to ask Mr Rong to take pity on her and return her to her foster mother. This was too cruel. On top of that I wasn't feeling well and couldn't gear up any intense emotion at all. The decibel level kept rising as Jade began to add her complaints to Rose's, but Mr Rong battled on against the noise. 'We have sixty girls at the Xiushui Social Welfare Institute. There are no boys. Most of these girls will be adopted by foreign couples and a good number are now being fostered.'

'Do you really think it is a good thing for foreign couples to be adopting these children? Shouldn't there be more domestic adoption?' I asked, wanting so much to see what he really thought about us.

Jade piped up: 'Mummy, Mummy ...'

'Wait a minute, Jade, just let me talk to Mr Rong.'

'Yes, we think foreign couples can create a better situation for the baby ... we think that a developed country has a better chance to care for the children. If Chinese people had the ability and the income we would like Chinese couples to adopt more. But Chinese adoption law is very tough and a lot of families are too poor to do it.'

'Are the number of babies being abandoned going up or down?'

'Definitely down, sometimes we only get sent one a month, at other times two or three.'

'Mummy, *Mummy*, I want to feed her ...' Jade's tone was rising to a high pitch.

'Xiushui is a very poor mountainous county, near the border of Hunan, Hubei and Jiangxi Provinces. Boys mean labour for the land. Families are allowed two children in rural areas but only if the first one is a girl.'

'Mummeeee, where's her bottle?' Jade whined. Gerald made up the feed and gave it to Jade.

'For families in your area, if their second child is a girl, then are those the ones that are most likely to be abandoned?'

Mr Rong laughed. 'I have no idea.'

I was beginning to hit a brick wall. 'There must be too many boys and not enough girls in that part of China?'

'I don't think that problem has arisen around Xiushui.'

My head was spinning, I felt unable to think clearly. There was so much I wanted to ask, yet I could see that Mr Rong was beginning to tire of my questions, and the perpetual crying of poor Rose was becoming unbearable. We let Mr Rong and the other orphanage staff leave.

....

Rose carried on crying as Jane took us out of the hotel across the road to a small photographic shop. Unlike Jade, who had been so immediately cheerful, no amount of clucking from the photographer would change Rose's expression for the official picture. She cried as we entered the shiny, newly built Civil Affairs Office and carried on wailing as we put her foot into the familiar pad of red ink. She stopped crying for a few moments while Gerald let her look out of the window and stare at the modern office blocks rising out of clusters of cramped tenements, and she paused in her tears when he put her in a little supportive frame on wheels, a kind of baby walker, in which she waddled up and down the corridor like a little dalek, perhaps finding some distraction in the presence of a familiar toy.

Jade was now in a buoyant mood and was determined to play with her, pushing her up and down the corridor, past a room filled with a couple of dozen Americans adopting their children. I peered in and was curious to see how organised it was, down to the slick video presentation. I watched them for a moment cooing and laughing over their new children, still feeling strangely distant from this whole process. My stomach was continuing its rebellion over the previous night's dinner and my emotions were somehow tangled up, unable to switch on my maternal light bulb.

Jade had no such qualms, and was already showing signs of being protective and possessive. 'This my baby sister and no one going to take her away, Mummy.'

'No, darling, of course, she's yours.'

Meanwhile Rose didn't know what to make of this new family of hers. She looked bereft, avoiding eye contact with me and gazing at every female Chinese office clerk who passed by with longing, no doubt looking in vain for the face of her foster mother.

As we waited for our documents to be ready, Jane showed us the photographs Mr Rong had taken for us of Xiushui and Rose's foster family. This was priceless instamatic film to link us with our daughter's past. Here was a young, attractive woman in a beige sweater with black horizontal stripes, her long black hair tied back into a ponytail revealing a slender silver ornament waving from her right ear. She was standing in front of a line of low stone houses surrounded by a privet hedge, holding Rose up to the camera. Rose was looking serious and expectant in her bright yellow jacket, blue trousers, and pink and purple shoes.

In another picture was a row of smiling foster mothers showing off a dozen other children. We were told they worked for free, just being given milk and clothing for the babies. They looked such warm and kind people, doing this job for the love of the children. How can they bear giving up these girls? I later learnt that Rose's foster mother had soon afterwards moved away from Xiushui. Perhaps she couldn't stand the grief of giving up this child whom she had loved for a year.

We looked at scenes too of Xiushui town: the grey blocks of flats, the modern concrete bridge straddling a wide river nestling into wooded mountains. As for the orphanage, downstairs was apparently dedicated to care of the elderly and the disabled, while upstairs lived the babies. One picture showed a touching scene of these two worlds meeting: Chinese wisdom in action. Grey-haired men and women, wearing their traditional blue 'Mao' jackets, could be seen grinning and laughing as they bounced tiny babies wearing luminous orange and red sleepsuits on their knees. This didn't look like a sad institution at all, but a place full of smiles and community spirit. Some Chinese orphanages had clearly come a long way since the grim days of the 'Dying Rooms'.

Jane brought out, too, the 'Finding Announcement' she had dug up from the Jiangxi Business Newspaper. Every three months they published a list of abandoned babies and their photographs to give biological parents a chance to claim them. There were 202 tiny mugshots arranged over two pages. All were of infants just a few months old, being cared for by eight Social Welfare Institutes of Jiangxi Province. Twenty-five were from Xiushui. Sixth down, in column one, was our daughter:

> Rong Min Ying, female, born 2002 Nov 19. Picked up at the entrance of the old people's institute at Zhencun Town. At that time she was big-sized, fat and round faced.

....

We scanned the others. Some were described as 'thin and long faced', others were 'square faced and medium size', one had been left at the local Civil Affairs Bureau, another at the County Hospital, another at the bus station, another in a square — all public places where a little human bundle was bound to be spotted. Their parents were given sixty days to claim their child, but, we were told, they seldom did.

Our guide book said Nanchang could be miserable on a cold wet day, and on that cold wet day it certainly was. Icy winds took our breath away as we rushed from one government office to another, clutching our two children. I couldn't feel the warm glow that had swept me off my feet when we adopted Jade. I wondered if I was really up to this and whether this sweet, melancholic girl would ever get to like me.

Rose did bond well with Gerald, nestling into his broad chest and padded ski jacket as we squashed into one taxi after another. Jade was making sure my lap was almost permanently filled, insisting on sitting on my knee at every available opportunity. Although pleased to have a sister, she didn't actually want to leave Rose an iota of physical or emotional space to begin to attach to me. She demanded my undivided attention, finding an excuse to chat and, if I looked at Rose, pulling my face towards her. 'I don't want to share Mummy,' Jade said with her emphatic logic.

'I completely sympathise with Jade,' my sister said when I phoned her in New York. She remembered my arrival, when she was three and a half, with dismay. 'Life was never so much fun any more. I had been at the centre of everything and then you were this sweet little baby whom everyone doted on.'

Rose slept well that first night. It was a relief to be able just to watch her, to see how all the unhappiness of the day melted as her eyelids, laced with their long black lashes, rested shut. Her pink, tear-stained cheeks became pale, her mouth relaxed into a perfect rosebud shape. I knew I just needed time.

....

The next day we asked Mr Rong to help us spend a donation from an enterprising couple in the UK who had adopted a baby from Xiushui a year earlier. They'd swum the length of Derwent Water in the Lake District and raised £500 which they wanted us to give to the orphanage. So we sped over the vast modern toll bridge to go milk shopping in Nanchang's Economic Development Zone. This city, which our guidebook described as 'a nondescript capital of a province that sees little in the way of foreigners', was clearly transforming itself at lightning speed. Thriving engineering, textiles and paper industries were leading, as the brochures said, to 'Nanchang city striding forward to a modern, civilised and picturesque future'. Unlike so much of China's communist rhetoric, this didn't seem like an exaggeration.

The Jiangxi Bright Hero Dairy Company was guarded by an imposing electronic metal gate which opened onto a series of warehouses and processing plants. They manufactured a hundred tonnes of powdered milk a day. We bought twenty-eight cases of infant formula milk powder – about two months supply for the orphanage – but then discovered we had to go to another office in town to pay for it. A member of the Dairy's staff piled in the taxi with us to show us the way. 'Very rowded in here!' said Jade who had trouble with the letter c.

I was pinned next to Mr Rong and took the opportunity to ask him how the orphanage was funded. It was a bit of a mystery what really happened to the $3000 we handed over. 'We get no state funding at all,' he said, 'so we have to rely on these foreign donations. We are going to use the money we receive from the Civil Affairs office to build a new orphanage. Private donations and foreign adoption has meant that over the last three years I have been able to look after 150 children. Before that the Social Welfare Institute didn't exist.'

'What happened to the babies then?'

'I don't know, they may have gone to other homes, or had nothing ...' Mr Rong wouldn't elaborate.

After a protracted session paying and getting a receipt for the milk powder, we took Mr Rong to Wal-Mart to buy some hi-fi equipment for the orphanage as we felt strongly about the benefits of music. It was a daunting task as the shop was on several floors, each the size of a football pitch. One part was franchised to shops selling expensive furniture and designer clothes without a customer in sight, another was the real Wal-Mart in all its glory – shoes, children's clothes, hi-fi, household goods, all fighting for space. The combination of loud videos competing with each other, the overheating and the crowds deadened our minds. We bought the present for Mr Rong, who by now was completely exhausted, and he left for the bus station. I wanted to go with him and see Xiushui, but with the girls it just wasn't practical. That trip would have to wait until they were older.

We met up with some other couples who were adopting at the same time; they seemed to be in the same rather dazed state as us, just trying to cope with it all. One attractive, fair-haired lady said her social worker had told her to be sure to bond with the baby and not let anyone else carry her. What a pressure that was. Should I be forcing Rose to bond with me? I didn't think so. I wanted to give us both a chance to get used to each other. I saw a hint of wide-eyed curiosity when she looked at me but she would quickly avert her gaze. It made sense that she would be bewildered when presented with this strange woman with red hair and told 'this is your mother now'. When she looked at me with those deep, dark, melancholic eyes as if to say, 'Who are you? You aren't my mama,' I felt she was right. I wasn't her mother, yet. I couldn't force it, especially as I knew it had to come naturally. At least two years before, when my emotions were far more raw and unready for rejection, Jade had been ready to leap in and accept me immediately.

Over the next few days, I quickly discovered that food and baths were a way in to Rose's heart and guaranteed to make the glummest expression vanish from her face. Three days after we had her, I was splashing warm water over her in the tub, when she suddenly giggled out loud for the first time with me. It was like music.

....

The pace of development in Nanchang was rapidly displacing the atmosphere of old China, but we did get a flavour of it one afternoon during a stroll amongst the leisurely crowds in Bayi Park, which nestles on the banks of a large lake. The privations and upheavals of previous decades were written into the ruddy, rustic faces we saw, aged and shrivelled from a lifetime outdoors and the fierce struggle to survive. This older generation was so much shorter than the new generation of young, well-nourished Chinese in the cities. They looked like the creaking remains of the Revolution and its privations. Many still wore simple blue 'Mao' suits as they smoked over chess and cards. Through the trees I could see a solitary lady in a red tracksuit practising t'ai chi. A group of old men and women were waving their arms lightly up and down in a session of qigong. At last: here was China not packaged for official viewing.

I thought everyone would have had a story to tell about the last fifty years. This would be the same generation as Rose's grandparents. They and their children somehow survived the Great Leap Forward – Mao's disastrous economic experiment in which peasants were grouped into people's communes, mobilised off the land to build vast irrigation projects or melt down iron for industry in thousands of blast furnaces. The resulting lack of manpower in the fields combined with bad weather led to severe crop failures in 1959. While vital grain was still being exported to Russia, over the next few years more than 20 million Chinese died of starvation. By 1963 half of

© Gerald Slocock

Chess in Bayi Park, Nanchang.

those dying were children under ten – the Great Leap was supposed to strengthen the nation but had ended up draining away its lifeblood. In Nanchang it was apparently so bad that corpses would be left lying in the street. There was a story of a peasant who'd made a fortune picking up these bodies and boiling soup out of them. He had finally been caught when a customer found a human finger in the bottom of his bowl.

In this very different country, we watched several hundred heroic survivors of this turbulent past gather round a solid-looking lady who was brandishing a bunch of plastic roses. She was belting out a folk song that could have been tuneful if the amplification hadn't made it tooth-shatteringly discordant. We sat down beside the river to listen from a distance, only to find that a small crowd followed us. Without Jane to translate – she was busy dealing with our documentation – we were grateful to find one of them, a businessman, who had a few words of English. I asked him and his wife what they thought of foreigners coming here to adopt girls. 'I think it's a good thing; we have a son anyway and we are happy, what does my wife think? She thinks it's OK too for the girls to go. They will have a better life so what's wrong with that?'

'In the countryside, in the villages is life getting easier or more difficult?'

'Nanchang is getting rich but it will take a long time to change things in the villages,' he said. 'Life is very hard, and we still need boys to work the land.'

I couldn't help worrying about whether these overseas adoptions were helping or hindering the crisis facing baby girls. Did our presence make it easier for a husband to reassure his wife that her baby girl would be well looked after in some rich foreigner's home, so that he could persuade her to give up a daughter? I had no way of knowing. Here, though, there seemed total ignorance of overseas adoption, and once it was explained people accepted what we were doing, or perhaps they were just too polite to indicate their displeasure.

The park had its own fairground and Jade was in dodgem heaven as she drove Gerald around beaming with pleasure. I was so busy watching them that I didn't notice at first a sad, spaced-out young woman hovering beside Rose's pushchair. I couldn't work out whether she was drugged or just depressed. Had she given away or lost a child? Was she now staring at every baby she saw adopted by a foreigner to see if it was hers? A fantasy, perhaps, but I felt the spectre of all those grieving mothers lurking behind her curious face.

That night we slumped on our bed; Jade was sleeping, almost lost, in the other huge double bed, while Rose was curled up in her cot. We watched anything that moved on TV. It turned out to be golf. I felt emotionally drained. I could scarcely imagine what it must be like to have children easily or to live without them and spend spare time going for long walks or to the movies. Other parents' lives at that moment appeared so uncomplicated in comparison to our mad journey. 'Do you have any regrets about adopting? Things could have been a lot simpler and cheaper without it, couldn't they?' I ventured, knowing Gerald's answer, knowing we adored our children, but feeling ragged and in need of reassurance.

'No regrets,' Gerald said. 'Look at that shot, it's going to be a birdie.'

'So you wouldn't go back and do things a different way, like just not bother with children at all ...?'

'Not for all the tea in China,' he said smiling and turning to me.

'Not even if I gave you all the jasmine-scented green tea from Tunxi?'

'No!' We hugged each other tight and the tears rolled, yet again, down my cheeks. Gerald was so free of angst; thank heaven — one of us needed to be.

. . . .

Day four with Rose, and along with the sunshine her smiles came out in force. She even said 'mamama' and reached out to me. She waved and clapped her hands and crawled, in her one-sided bottom-shuffling way, to stare out of the hotel window. She gripped my fingers in hers, with that telltale vice-like hold: I had yet to meet a Chinese child who didn't have strong hands. I fed her, changed her and she accepted me without protest.

Over the next few days, Rose became more relaxed, she ate like the 'horse' that she was in Chinese astrology. I was beginning to feel the stirrings of a true bond between us. 'She *is* becoming our daughter,' I told myself. When she put her upturned cereal bowl on her head like a hat and laughed at us, I experienced a surge of love for her shiny black eyes, wide-open mouth, the dimples in her cheeks and the determined, humorous personality inside her diminutive body.

Although the Xiushui Social Welfare Institute was just out of reach, Nanchang's SWI was permitting visitors. It was the largest in the province, and offered care and treatment for dozens of orphans, many of them disabled or with serious illnesses like Hepatitis B and meningitis. We were shown one two-year-old girl who lay pale and motionless with an enlarged swollen head, apparently suffering from hydrocephalus, a complication of meningitis where the brain swells with excess fluid. There was also a primary school in the grounds which educated hundreds of children, some graduates from the orphanage who now lived in long-term foster care.

This building was clearly benefiting from its foreign donations; there seemed to be an abundance of carers and conditions were good. Even so, the sight of the two baby rooms upstairs was a shock. They were light and airy, their windows and walls were decorated with brightly stencilled decorations, just like a baby ward in a western hospital – but the difference here was that all the babies had been abandoned. Twenty-two of them, all under three months, lay on their backs in cots in neat rows in the centre of the rooms. They were each wrapped up tightly in swaddling clothes, with just their tiny faces showing. Most were girls, with a few boys categorised as 'disabled' – this sometimes meant having small birthmarks or cleft palates. Half the girls, we were told, would be adopted by overseas couples and half by locals. Some of the 'disabled boys' would also be adopted abroad, the others would remain and be looked after in the Institute.

I wanted to pick up and hold each of these vulnerable, tiny children. I tried to imagine Jade and Rose like this, eight months before we adopted them. I'd never experienced them as fragile, tiny babies and it hit home how easily their lives could have been snuffed out. I pulled back the blanket on one cot to see a little girl, her eyes tight shut, sleeping soundly. I showed her to Jade. 'Look, this is what you were like once.'

This was clearly a showcase orphanage, and while we were there a large group of American adoptive parents filed through. Yet even though conditions were exemplary, no amount of stuffed teddies and plastic toys on display could hide the raw and uncomfortable fact that this building received several dozen abandoned girls every year.

....

On a day off from form-filling and dwelling on the miracle that had brought Rose to us, we decided to take the two girls up to the mountain resort of Lushan 'along the road with four hundred bends'. We rested at a temple, drank tea, then dipped our hands in Yellow Dragon River to guarantee that we would live for ninety-nine years, before taking a cable car up the vertiginous slopes of the mountain, complete with spindly fir trees clinging precariously to the rock face. Their silhouettes against the sky were reminiscent of Chinese paintings through the centuries.

On a pagoda in the middle of Flower Path Lake I asked Jane what young and educated women of her generation felt now about giving birth to girls. 'Parents think that a girl will marry and leave home and not look after them in their old age, which is one reason they want a boy, but I think nowadays women are becoming more responsible for their own parents. I personally would rather have a girl than a boy.' We kept in touch with Jane − and almost exactly a year later, in Beijing, she did give birth to a baby girl, to the delight of both her and her husband.

Jane went on to tell me that although it was illegal for pregnant women to have sex-determination tests and then abort a female foetus, it was widely practised. There were places in China where the number of girls being born was diminishing fast compared to the boys: places like Hainan Island off the south coast, where there were 135 boys being born for every

100 girls. The average in China was 117, whereas the norm should be about 105 boys for every 100 girls born.

Rose perched on Gerald's shoulders as we walked down a stone path through a pine forest apparently planted from the air by the forces of the Nationalist general, Chiang Kai-shek. Nearby was Lushan, once called Kuling as it was built and named by a nineteenth-century English missionary as a place for 'cooling off'. Clusters of stone houses developed into a summer retreat and in the 1930s the rich and powerful Chinese moved in, including Chiang Kai-shek. He and his family lived in the Meilu Villa, set into the side of a hill, surrounded by now rather dishevelled gardens, overlooking the valley. Although simple by Western standards today, it boasted the best plumbing then available; we saw the original bath, bidet and lavatory as well as the family's old kerosene-powered American refrigerator and an upright piano.

Near the Meilu Villa is a large concrete conference hall that has witnessed pivotal moments in Chinese history. It was here that General Chiang Kai-shek planned his final campaign against Mao's Red Army, the campaign that forced Mao into the Long March to Shaanxi Province. It was also the venue for the now notorious Lushan Conference twenty-five years later.

Jiangxi Province is famous as a hub for the early stages of the Communist Revolution, and here on Mount Lushan, Mao later entrenched his political powers. Inside the hall, the stage was adorned with a portrait of Mao hanging above a table covered in a white cloth and flanked by ten red flags. The defence minister and hero of the Long March, Marshal Peng Dehuai, had dared to write a letter telling Mao that the latest inflated statistics for agricultural production suffered from the 'wind of exaggeration ... which cost the party a great deal in

© Emily Buchanan

Rose bonding with her new father on Mt Lushan.

© Emily Buchanan

And with her new family on Mt Lushan.

prestige.' Mao distributed his letter to all the delegates and watched as three other senior members of the government came out in agreement. Mao then unleashed a fierce attack on these critics, calling Peng a 'Right opportunist' and purging him. Within a few months, the Great Leap was extended with catastrophic results for the Chinese people. Peng Dehuai died in 1974, after many years of violent interrogation and imprisonment.

A video commemorating Mao's political coup played over and over in the empty conference hall. A few tourists wandered in and out, gazing at some black and white photos of their once Great Helmsman relaxing between meetings. It was chilling to think that from such a characterless, mundane building, in these green peaceful mountains, so much destruction had been unleashed.

To the south of Mount Lushan is the vast expanse of Poyang Lake, the result of the merging of the Gan River with the mighty Yangtze. It was described in the brochure as 'extending to the end of heaven'. We heard it was one of the most important wetlands in the world and worth dragging the girls on another journey with us to see. We drove out of Nanchang, passing through Wucheng township: a place Jane said had a similar income level to Rose's home town of Xiushui. Most of the population relied on fishing and rice growing, and everywhere there were signs of hardship – a group of men struggling to put out a fire in a brick factory, street after street of ragged, ramshackle houses which eventually gave way to a long, flat, dusty causeway across the dried-out lake.

Along this slow, bumpy earth road we passed water buffaloes pulling carts. One of them had stopped while a farmer and his wife piled it high with grass that they'd use for burning in

© Gerald Slocock

Rose with farmers en route to Poyang Lake.

their stove. We asked them about their attitude to girls; they had their pretty ten-year-old granddaughter with them. They said they had a son and four daughters and were happy with girls; they had all been born before the One/Two Child Policy had begun.

In a village entirely made of dilapidated wooden houses a group of peasant women with bright red, wind-burned cheeks told us they loved girls even more than boys. I had no idea whether to believe them; as transient visitors asking questions on a highly sensitive subject we were unlikely to be told what they really thought. A girl looking remarkably like Rose stared at us from a window. I looked down at Rose in her pushchair, shaking her chubby legs and gurgling at some little boys who were poking fingers at her. What if she had a twin or even an older sister in a village like this? What if one day they found each other and compared notes about their upbringing? What if ... it was useless to speculate.

We moved on and the landscape opened out to flat grassland dotted with small lakes. Cotton buds hung onto dried-out bushes while the wind blew the white plumes of the long grasses. A huge wide river ran past the road, the same river that went through Rose's town. This was our link with her birthplace. A fisherman waded in the water bringing out little minnows which he laid out on the earth to dry. Dust blew up all around us as our car crawled and slid over the earth, until at last we saw the great expanse of water and marshland ahead.

In the rainy season Poyang is the biggest lake in China but in November it is a small fraction of its original size. In summer we would have taken a boat, but now the water had retreated so far it was barely visible from the sandy escarpment. Shrimps, snails and clams that thrive in the lake were exposed by the retreating water, attracting thousands upon thousands of birds. At first we couldn't see much, and then through the binoculars we could only gasp with the beauty of it all. Soaring white cranes, taking refuge from the Siberian winter, were taking off in groups of two, three and sometimes even a dozen or so. Their stretched-out, snowy wings with black tips flapped in apparent slow motion; their dark sword-like beaks, tinged with pink, sliced the air. It was as if a Chinese painting had actually come to life.

Jade ran about shouting into the sky and peering through the binoculars, while Rose was transfixed by the wild antics of our hair. The wind buffeted us constantly as we stood high on the earthy escarpment, gazing at the distant glassy water and the beating wings of these elegant creatures. Amidst the cranes we could also see flocks of tundra swans, white storks and black geese. Spoonbills, pelicans, grey cranes, lake gulls and mandarin ducks added their voices to the cacophony of calls and cries. There were simply thousands upon thousands of birds here from as far away as Russia, Mongolia, Japan and Korea.

We were told the white cranes only laid two eggs a year, and when they hatched the chicks fought each other until one died, so they were used to a one child family long before it became mandatory for humans. The brochure from the local museum showed a picture of a white crane and her child: the title, predictably, was 'Mother and Son Enjoying Family Happiness'. The cranes lived sometimes until they were seventy and stayed with one partner, so for the Chinese they symbolised longevity and conjugal bliss. Amongst the museum collection of stuffed birds and mammals we noticed a picture of Prince Philip at the lake from 1986 fulfilling his role as President of the World Wildlife Fund.

It must have been the river shrimp for lunch that did it. The next day I was crippled with stomach cramps and diarrhoea. 'Me too have slight diarrey,' said Jade. The dark and putrid loos in the Hanchang Market, loos which a lady was daring to charge for entry, were enough to drive me back to the comfort of our hotel. We later managed a visit to the Tengwang Pavilion, a modern reconstruction of a Tang Dynasty structure, where Jade dressed up in an ornate empress's outfit for a posed photograph. She smiled slightly and her headdress was tilted a bit, but otherwise the picture looked remarkably authentic.

....

And then it was time to whisk Rose away from her roots and go to Beijing for her British visa. At Nanchang airport we perused a bookstall spread across half the check-in area which left no doubt about what were best-sellers. There were dozens of titles along the lines of *Management by Proverbs*, *Making Achievement of your Life*, *Do What You Want To Do*, *Success or Never* and *Success Depends on the State of Mind*. It was cheering to see that women were part of the target market: there was *The Capital of Woman* and also *The Woman with Capital*, *Men and Women Should Have Different Jobs*, *Source of Elegance*, *The Question of Woman* and, tantalisingly, *English Lover*. The trouble was that although the titles were translated, the rest of the books were all in Chinese so we had to guess at the contents.

Rain and fog cloaked Beijing as we landed, and were met by our friend, the burly, handsome accordion teacher who ran the Little Angel Art School for the performing arts that we'd visited three years earlier. He drove us along the wide ring roads, now even more clogged with traffic than before, to his family's flat in a southern suburb. It was in a new development area, where low-rise blocks surrounded a children's playground. We took the two girls to play there, shivering in the winds which whistled between the concrete buildings, and immediately noticed an elderly couple wrapped up nose to toe in padded clothes, sitting on the see-saw, going up and down completely expressionless as if drugged or bored or traumatised or all three. Perhaps the repetitive movements were their reassuring escape from a new, fast-moving China they couldn't begin to keep up with.

Inside our host's flat there was a striking picture of him with his attractive wife taken in the 1960s; they were looking into the distance, the wind blowing in their faces — it looked as if they were two comrades at one with the ideals of the Revolution. Nowhere on their faces was written the truth of what they must have been suffering at the time, each with a father facing a long prison sentence for being a threat to the Cultural Revolution. In those days a performing arts school would have been forbidden. It never ceased to amaze me how people like this, indoctrinated to hate the West, couldn't have been kinder to us. They particularly adored Rose and after a few days, Rose even began to call our hostess 'mama' and appeared confused about who was whom. She'd had a lot to take in, and here were more new people showering her with attention. I badly needed some time with her alone.

....

On the flight home, there were no more distractions. It was a chance to sit and hold our youngest daughter, to stare into her big black eyes, eyes which no longer automatically swivelled away from me. I wanted to cuddle her and stroke her soft head to make up for lost time. I had felt confused, and she had too, but now we were travelling in one direction just beginning to get to know each other, going home. I lay back in the seat as the information screen up ahead announced that there were 64 mph headwinds, and we had 3,560 kilometres still to go. A good metaphor for adoption, I thought. Although our family was complete and our journey to Jade and Rose had finally ended, there was still a long way to go on the next leg: coping with the dynamics of having two children, working out what to do about their Chinese past and how to begin to repair the torn threads of their history.

- Chapter Seven -

From Nanchang to Notting Hill

On Rose's first morning in Britain, the excitement of having her home had to compete with the Rugby World Cup Final and a dawn stabbing in our street. Jenny and Lily came to call, along with an assortment of police officers asking for witnesses to the crime outside. Gerald and the policemen became glued to the television, shouting and screaming as England triumphed, while Jenny and I ogled over Rose, blissfully oblivious to this great moment in sporting history. Our new daughter was getting her first taste of 'gender bias' in our family, but she seemed to cope remarkably well.

Competition on the rugby field that day was as nothing compared to the territorial battle that developed between the two sisters. Jade began to take a passionate interest in anything that Rose decided to focus on. So if Rose chose a book to look at, Jade suddenly wanted it desperately. If Rose picked up a toy cup, it was that particular toy cup that Jade needed and snatched from her. Jade would end up clutching an armful of objects, almost glued to Rose who crawled around the room calmly looking for something else to play with. Jade wanted so much to be in charge, but she just couldn't control this 'dolly' who was very much alive and had a mind of her own. Rose's patience did snap the odd time, and her two sharp front teeth sank into Jade's arm, resulting in howls of pain and indignation.

Jade was naturally distressed to find her new sister not only sleeping in our bedroom, but taking a lot of our attention. She became increasingly mischievous and determined to be noticed, even waking at two in the morning, switching on lights and dragging chairs around the kitchen. It was sometimes impossible to calm her down unless we lay with her in her bed, or she came to ours. There was one night when she wriggled, chatted and kicked until dawn as her 'why's' became ever more insistent: 'Why you get up and comfort me? Why, Mummy? Why me crying? Why Rose sleeping? Why me *not* sleeping, Mama?' I so wanted to reassure her, calm her turmoil as she adjusted to her new sister. I comforted, held her and kissed her cheeks while I couldn't help but feel my emotional tank was running dry. I was trying to be a good mother while my body was rebelling against the daily exhaustion and sleep deprivation. If I was going to suffer from post-adoption depression this would, I am sure, have been the moment. Some adoptive parents can feel very low and then guilty at the same time as everyone thinks they ought to be blissfully happy. I was lucky to have escaped my own mother's tendency to black moods, and I soon found myself distracted by the more pressing needs of our new arrival.

The following afternoon, Rose developed a slight fever, and she fell into a deep sleep after lunch. I had to wake her when it was time to pick up Jade from nursery school, but as I lifted her out of her cot her eyes rolled upwards and she began foaming at the mouth and shaking. Suddenly my precious child whom I was just getting to know disappeared behind a

© Jenny Matthews

Pulling together.

bizarre, quivering body. Frozen with alarm, I sat on the bed holding her and praying she wasn't going to stop breathing. I'd never seen a fit before and had no idea whether it was going to cause brain damage. Then as quickly as it had started, it stopped and she fell into a deep sleep.

Our doctor later said that perhaps the shock of coming out of China, along with her fever, had triggered the convulsion. I felt acutely the yawning gap in our knowledge of her medical history. I checked with our translator, Jane, who was now back in Beijing, whether this had ever happened before. We had not been told she was prone to fits, or perhaps she had never had them in the past? A message came back from Rose's foster mother via the children's home that she'd had no fits during her time with her. I had nothing else to go on, and had to believe it.

Gradually the children settled down and we moved Rose's cot next to Jade's bed. Our nights became less active and the burning rivalry toned down slightly, although there were often intense bouts of sibling squabbles. Ferocious snatching and loud arguing would alternate with moments when Jade would become extremely protective, even maternal, to Rose: 'I Rose's Mummy, not youououou ...' she would chant at me. Rose remained remarkably unperturbed by the see-sawing emotions in her older sister. She was very self-contained, perhaps more used not to being the centre of attention, as she had been fostered with three other children.

Sometimes in the morning I would find Jade had joined Rose in her cot and I could hear them chatting and giggling with each other. When I came to find them, Jade would ask for a blanket to be put over the cot like the roof of a cage and the two of them would growl and scratch at the bars pretending to be baby tigers. 'Me good, me playing with Rose nicely now,'

Jade would say proudly: giving me a tantalising moment of such motherly bliss I wanted to laugh and cry at the same time.

I felt immense satisfaction watching Jade develop her relationship not only with her sister, but with other children as well. Her current 'best friend' was Eugenie, the only other girl in her class at nursery school. They were inseparable and egged each other on in their mischievous pranks. One day they were playing together in Jade's bedroom, while Eugenie's mother, Mary-Lu, was telling me her anxieties over her pet tadpoles. 'I let the sun shine on the tank, and one died – to think that I've cooked a baby frog! How could I?' Mary-Lu was distraught.

'That's terrible, and you're a wildlife expert!'

'What's more, I crushed my stick insect the other day.'

'How on earth did you do that?'

'Well, I'd let it out for some exercise and I was doing the washing up and just didn't notice where it had gone. Then I heard a crunch under my sandal and it was too late, I felt awful about it for days.'

We became so preoccupied with her zoological fatalities, at the same time as enjoying a moment of uninterrupted conversation, that we had not been aware of how silent our daughters had become. Then suddenly we heard piercing squeals. We leapt up to find the two girls had emptied out every single toy and article of clothing from the cupboard onto the floor and were using the shelves like bunk beds. The tiny bedroom was knee-deep in toys, clothes and chaos. We scolded the girls while trying hard not to smile.

Jade's other 'best friend' was Lily. One morning Lily was visiting, and as Jade munched on some toast she piped up out of the blue, 'My Mummy in China couldn't look after me.'

I really do want a bunk bed! Jade with Eugenie Bakker.

'That's what happened to me, my Mummy couldn't look after me either,' chipped in Lily with a very serious face. We were amazed. Here were two four-year-olds comparing their experiences, no doubt just the beginning of a lifetime of discussions about their past and their sense of identity.

Jade had begun to show an interest in the story of her origins. We had told her over and over about how we had come to China to find her after her parents had been unable to look after her. We recounted how she'd been left safely in a children's home and that we had travelled all the way from Britain to pick her up, how we had been so excited to see her and what a beautiful baby she was. She'd ask, 'Did I talk like this? Wa, wa, wa wa?'

'Yes, you were a baby, you couldn't even stand up.'

'Why I a baby, Mummy? Tell me over and again, Mummy.' And I would start the story again.

....

'The adoption starts as a kind of fairy story, but around the age of eight, children will begin to understand that they had a mother once who couldn't look after them, who left them, and the pain really sets in.' It was a week later, and Franca Brenninckmeyer was speaking in the airy modern treatment room at the Post-Adoption Centre in North London. I thought it was about time I checked out how children's understanding of their adoption develops as they grow up.

'What will be the symptoms of this "pain"?' I asked.

'They can get sulky, withdrawn, have more temper tantrums. There can be a lot of anger with the birth mother which can get projected onto you, the adoptive mother.'

'What will we be able to do to alleviate it?'

'Treat it like any grieving process and don't try and fix it. Say to them, "It was sad and I'd be sad too if that happened to me." Talk about it, even suggest writing a letter to the birth mother that you keep somewhere safe, to treasure because of course you can't send it to her. Imagine a name for her, imagine what she looks like. Show the girls their reflections in the mirror and talk about whether their birth mothers might have had the same colour hair, or eyes.'

'I suppose it feels a bit threatening to discuss their birth mothers ... adoptive parents like myself can have a fear that their child will want to leave them.'

'That's the big misconception. Discussing and being open about the birth mother will only strengthen the bond with your child. If you share the experience with them, they will feel even closer to you. The birth mother can never recreate that primary parental experience that the child has with you ... the looking after you do, the daily routines, all the care and fun. That history you've had can never be replaced. Even if an adoptive child meets and befriends their birth mother she can only become in their mind part of the extended family, like an aunt or a cousin. They can love her but you are and always will be their mother. You can't lose them, because the childhood attachment is to you.'

'Then what happens after that, when is the next hurdle?'

'Well, you may go through a phase that is somewhat calmer, when they are just enjoying growing up, experiencing all sorts of new things, learning new skills and making real friends. When puberty sets in, things can get tricky again. They begin to ask lots more questions, they start wondering who they are going to be like when they grow up, and therefore they want to know more about their background. As information and understanding about their adoption story increases, feelings of loss and grief may intensify. And then you're into the teens which is another stage, with more profound questions around identity, both their own as well as their birth parents, including racial and cultural identity. "How do I fit into the world?" can become a more pronounced question – even though not often verbalised. The wish to search for the birth parents may become stronger at this stage, as it is often felt that "knowing who they are" could help fill the gaps in their sense of self.'

I hoped that somehow the children would grow up emotionally stable and confident in spite of their background. To me the big question for the future was whether they would be able to forgive their birth parents for abandoning them. For that they would have to understand the dreadful social pressures that existed at the time of their birth. I wanted to investigate those pressures, tour the Chinese countryside, ask questions, get to know Chinese women, but I had two small children to look after and couldn't become the roving journalist again, and even if I could have travelled, this kind of research was severely restricted in China. All that would have to come later. For now all I could do was talk to some of the people who *had* probed the dark, secretive world of child abandonment.

I wanted to try and imagine the women who gave birth to Jade and Rose; their daughters had become mine by a cruel quirk of fate and I wanted to try to understand their world. Somewhere in or near Yulin and Xiushui two women must now be grieving over their lost daughters; two women who continue their everyday lives with a gnawing hole in their hearts. Perhaps one had already had a daughter and hadn't been allowed to keep her second, perhaps by now she had been lucky and had a son. In Anhui Province, for example, the American anthropologist Kay Ann Johnson and her researchers found that most children given up for adoption were second or third daughters. Perhaps the other invisible woman in our lives was simply a single mother who couldn't bear the shame of having a daughter outside marriage. Either of these women could have killed their baby girl but chose not to. Jade and Rose could also have a sister or a brother who had not been rejected. This would be a harsh realisation to accept later on.

. . . .

The first thing I noticed in Xinran's flat was a large pair of green Wellington boots with two twisty tropical plants spiralling out of them – the Orient meeting the green wellie brigade, perhaps the ultimate symbol of East meeting West. Xinran was eager to talk about Chinese culture, being perpetually astounded at how little Westerners know about China, but this was not the occasion for a colourful conversation about the Chinese arts or the media. Ever since I'd read her article about the Chinese mothers she'd met who had given up their girls, I had wanted to ask her what more she could tell me about daily life in the countryside, in particular about the prevailing attitudes to the birth of a female child.

Sitting on her broad, green leather sofa sipping tea, Xinran began slowly to recall the horrors of what she'd observed. She told me how, as a journalist, she had gone many times into rural areas to talk to peasant families. In 1989, she travelled round Henan interviewing local peasants about birth control, and over the next seven years she met dozens of families across central China. As late as 1996 she found that attitudes to girls had changed very little, even in the richer areas of the south.

She described one village on the borders of Guangdong and Guangxi Provinces in southern China where women welcomed her into their homes, eager to teach her the skills that were passed down to them over the generations. One of those essential skills was how to kill a baby girl. 'One old lady said to me, "You must learn this. Girls have to know about this before they get married." She showed me some wet paper. In the countryside they have this thick paper made out of dried grass — ordinary paper was always very expensive — it's very coarse, it's called *ma fen zhi* because it looks like dried horse manure. The lady said, "You put it in the water and cover the baby girl's face just for a few seconds and the baby will die." And she said that when the baby is born ... I find it very difficult to say this ... normally they have a pot of hot water to clean up the mother after the birth. But what they do is check if the baby is a girl and if she is, they just put her straight into the pot and let her drown. They were doing this in a village that was actually quite rich and I could see that many families there had more boys than girls. Before the birth, the nurse or midwife is told by the family that if she finds the baby is a girl she is allowed to take her away.'

'So it's agreed beforehand with the mother?' I asked.

'Yes. And also I was told that when the baby is born, normally they have a kind of liquid in their throats and usually they are turned upside down so the baby cries and can start breathing. But if the baby is a girl they don't clear this liquid out, they leave her upright so it stays in her lungs and she can't breathe. So they don't even give her the right to cry in her short life.'

'Do they say afterwards that the baby died naturally?' I asked.

'They just say, "it was a girl", or they say "there was no child", and then everybody knows it was a girl. It's very, very normal, unbelievably normal.'

'So if you're pregnant and you go off and have your baby and come back with no baby then everyone assumes it was a girl, and asks no more questions?'

Xinran sighed and nodded. 'In many places in the country-side even when you're pregnant, everything you make is with the assumption you will have a boy, and you hang the things up outside the house. You don't see any clothes for a baby girl being made there.'

'So there are no little pink suits for girls hanging up?'

'No, no flowers or anything, unless the family has a boy already, and then the mother may prepare for a girl. But the father will often say "Don't be silly, why waste time doing these kinds of stupid things for a girl?"'

I asked Xinran if she herself had ever witnessed the killing of a baby girl.

She looked into the distance, as if recalling a memory she had long tried to suppress, and told me what she had seen back in 1989 in a village near the town of Yuanyang in Henan Province. It was a poor area where the yellow earth was stony and dry, and yielded only meagre crops of red sorghum. She was sitting outside a little mud-brick house. Inside was the family's one room – the *kang*, typical of northern China – which was used as a kitchen and living room by day and a bedroom by night. It was tiny and held all the tools and stored food they needed. A woman was giving birth inside and the family had hung up some coloured clothes for 'birth luck'. The husband was obviously nervous. What Xinran told me happened next is too horrific to write here. Suffice to say it was just one example of the everyday hidden murder of baby girls in Chinese villages. She said that for the locals it was nothing unusual; few cared or seemed to notice.

Infanticide is thought to occur across whole swathes of the country from Gansu, Ningxia and Shaanxi in the west through Henan and Hubei and then into Anhui and Jiangxi in the east. I cast my mind back to the women of South India whom I had met years before; for them too killing a girl was a necessity of life. This was no different.

Xinran went on. 'Several years later in 1995, while I was in Shandong Province, near a mountain called Yimeng, I found some families who would just throw the baby girls out of the house as soon as they were born. I could sometimes see partially eaten corpses lying on the ground. They didn't treat them as human beings. This is why I often wonder whether women in China really belong to the human world. You don't feel they do. Whenever I tried to tell them this was wrong, they just hated me and thought I was stupid.'

I thought about Jade and Rose, chubby and loved; Jade's sparkling grin and Rose's dimpled cheeks. It was hard to imagine the kind of desperate existence that led to a baby girl being hurled out like a piece of rubbish or drowned in a bucket of water. How far would China need to develop for daughters not to be thrown away? The problem was that it wasn't just the government's One Child Policy which had pushed families to abandon their girls; there were also ancient feudal traditions that had laid waste to girls' lives long before the idea of population control.

'Village law is often very cruel to women saying that not only must you have a son, but your *first* child has to be a boy,' said Xinran. 'Otherwise the family tree is seen to have gone wrong. So the pressure to get rid of a first daughter is enormous and village elders feel they have the right to kill a woman who disobeys this law. It's the same if a girl is raped, abused or touched: everything is her fault, not the man's fault, so she has to be killed.' Xinran said she had become so angry about all this, and tried to get help from the local police and the local government, but villages were like little kingdoms where they felt they had the right to do this kind of thing.

I thought about the two birth mothers with whom I had a lifetime's connection. I wondered what miracle had made them decide not to kill their girls.

'If the family is a bit richer, they might keep the baby girl,' Xinran continued. 'Then they don't think it's a waste of food to feed her. In some villages they will keep the girls to feed them up and to sell later or exchange for a brother's wife. That, in some ways, is even worse, because the little girls have to do lots of housework such as collecting firewood, carrying water, cleaning the yard. From five or six years old they become a kind of slave in the family, I have seen some having to walk barefoot carrying potatoes for six hours a day. This is why some of the mothers don't care if they kill their baby girls because they don't want them to repeat their own life. Dozens of people told me the same thing: "If my daughter is going to have the same life as me, I would rather she died without knowing anything".'

I imagined Rose's delicate little feet and Jade's strong broad feet, both pairs so perfect and so soft. Both had giggled uproariously when a young student friend had painted their toenails pink. They had talked about it for days, and kept thrusting their toes into my face so I would say again how pretty they were. To think of these girls carrying heavy loads, walking barefoot for hours on end ... Sometimes I could barely get Jade to walk at all when she was tired, she would just sit down on the pavement and refuse to move. What might have happened to her iron strength of will, her confidence and humour if she'd been turned into a domestic slave?

Xinran had more to tell me.

'Some mothers really don't care what happens to their daughters. I was shocked when I met some near Wuhan, nearby the River Yangtze. They were planting rice. I went and did planting there with them. I was nervous of the fish and that I'd be bitten. But luckily one of the women said I could just look after the tea water and the lunch, and mind the cow, which was a relief. This middle-aged woman had a terrible problem, a growth around her neck like a goitre, a huge swelling. As we sat watching the other women working, some were washing clothes on the flat stones, carrying their babies on their backs, I asked her about daily life. She said for the women doing the planting it was very hard work, the water was very cold, and they had bare feet: "We don't want our girls staying in our village, we would rather they went to a better place. When they are teenagers we can easily sell them to rich families and get cows or tools back. They'll be well fed for two or three years before they are married off to the sons in that family." I thought she was teasing me, so I said, "If you can't sell, what do you do?" She said, "We can check when they're born and if there's something wrong, or they don't look good, we'll just kill them." So I asked her what she meant by "if they don't look good." '

'She replied, "We have a special lady who can judge very well from the nose and the eyes if they are good looking or not good looking, if this is a lucky girl or not a lucky girl. Also you can go to a special master who will analyse the birth date and time and who can say if she is going to bring good luck or not." I asked, "Then if it's the wrong date you will kill her?" "Yes, because otherwise she will bring bad luck to our family." They really did believe this. I asked about her, how come she survived, and she said "I wasn't born in this village. Let me tell you the truth, in my village, my mother killed seven of my older sisters. This is why my nickname is Number Eight. After another two girls, my mother finally had a son but unfortunately he died, and everyone thought it was my fault because they'd kept me so I'd brought bad luck."'

'So I asked her now that she was a mother herself what did she think her own mother had felt for her children? She said "What's the difference between cats and dogs and these kids? Tell me what the difference is?"'

'Then I asked her, "You are number eight, did your mother tell you that you were Number Eight, that she killed your sisters but kept you because eight is a lucky number?" She didn't answer the question but simply replied that it was easy to kill a child. She showed me how you hold the baby's neck, and you can kill her just like a snake. She showed no emotion at all.'

....

I couldn't believe these women didn't feel something. Surely it wasn't possible that they were so stone-hearted. I wondered if it was the only way to survive. If they had shown their feelings, even to themselves, their suffering might have become too painful to bear.

Xinran said she had long been baffled by the lack of emotion displayed by so many of the rural women she met.

'It's something I've been wondering about since coming to the West seven years ago. My own mother said that as people get more educated they can understand feelings better, but without any education as was the case for some of these women, they just switched off their emotions. This is one of the factors that has contributed to the high suicide rate for women in China. As more and more people are allowed to travel and see other parts of China, more women are questioning what they've done. They see advertisements and television, they see women looking smart in the cities and they are hit by great feelings of pain and guilt. They ask themselves, "If my girl hadn't died, she could now be grown up and beautiful. Why did I let her life go like that, why did I give her up?" The guilt becomes overwhelming.'

I asked Xinran if she had ever met a woman who had given up her daughter for adoption, and who might now be pining for her. She told me about one case of a doctor whom she was sure was suffering to this day.

'I was in hospital in a little town in Shandong Province. I was suffering from very low blood pressure. As I was lying on my bed, a drip in my arm, I saw lots of young couples coming in for abortions. The doctor treating me had a round, calm and intelligent face, she was in her forties and I felt I could talk to her about them. She told me that sometimes these couples come in two or three times a year. She drew for me the shape of a pear and tried to explain to me how the wall of the womb gets very thin. It's very dangerous to have too many abortions; you need time to let the womb lining grow back.'

'I asked the doctor, "Why are they doing it? Is it because they are having so much sex, or because they're not using birth control?" She said, "No, no, the pill is easily available. But I still help them. It's no good trying to teach the women not to do it. You have to teach the men, because it's the men who force the women to have abortions because they want to have a son." So I asked more: "Since you are a doctor, shouldn't you try and advise them not to?" She answered: "You have no idea what kind of a life I've had. I became a doctor here because I myself had to give up two baby girls." '

'This doctor had been educated in the city, but while she was a medical student her parents were sent to the countryside by Mao during the Cultural Revolution and she had to follow them. They ended up in a little town which was short of doctors, so she decided to stay and work there. She married another doctor and although he was very educated, she was still terrified that his family might force her to give up any baby girl she might give birth to. She said, "I was frightened of them, so when I became pregnant I decided to give birth on my own. Can you imagine how difficult that was?" The husband's relatives had waited outside the room which adjoined the communal family courtyard. When she finally had the baby, and her husband came in and saw it was a girl, the first thing he wanted to do was to hide it. He said, "Don't tell other people, just say this is an unhealthy girl and we had to kill her." The whole family was waiting. Her husband didn't even allow the girl to cry. Then she'd implored him: "On my life I beg you not to kill her." Her husband did listen and used the quilt to cover the baby so she was able to cry and clear her lungs without being heard. He was a doctor so he knew how to do it safely. Then he wrapped the baby up and hid her in the cupboard, telling the whole family that the baby died, it was all over.'

'The next day the woman doctor got up early in the morning and took her girl out of the cupboard. She held her close to her while she slept soundly. She went out of the house and walked to the police station and put her child gently on the ground; the baby seemed to know and started crying immediately. "Xinran," she said to me, "you've no idea how agonising that was for me. I had to go away quickly otherwise the policeman would arrest me." She left the place and heard the baby crying and crying. Then she went back three or four times to comfort her and each time she left, the child would start crying again.'

Xinran stopped talking and we looked at each other in silence. This poor doctor's heartbreak hung like a shroud around us. It was that terrible moment of abandonment, that breaking of the total trust between mother and child. I thought about my mother and her leaving us all those years ago. However many times I thought about it, it never got any easier. My eyes filled with tears and I looked up to see that Xinran's were as well. She herself had been through a traumatic family break-up during the Cultural Revolution. Red Guards had burned her home, she was effectively 'orphaned' and sent to live in a prison camp with her baby brother. She didn't see her mother and father for many years.

It was several minutes before she was able to continue. 'These are very painful memories for me. I remember the doctor repeating over and over again, "It was as if my little girl understood me. I went back to her, then left her, went back and left again. I thought she must be a genius because she understands me; she knew when I was there and when I was gone."'

When it came to the second child the doctor made an agreement with her husband. She said, "If it's a girl please don't kill her. I will go on having other children until you have a son, for your family tree, but if you kill the girls I won't give you any more children at all." So they had a deal. Her husband wasn't a bad man, and when her second baby turned out to be a girl, this time he helped her. They were both frightened because people in the town where they lived disapproved of having a girl as a first child. As the second pregnancy came to term, her husband said he wouldn't allow her to see the baby if it was a girl. As soon as the child was born, her husband simply looked at the newborn and said to her, "Forget it". So she knew at once it was a girl. Her husband gave the baby to a friend. Then she was lucky, her third baby was a boy. She told me she couldn't allow this to happen to other women, so she helps girls to have abortions because it's less painful than having to endure what she went through. That was in 1995, and I am sure she still thinks about her daughters every day.'

I still was no nearer having any idea of what kind of women the birth mothers of my daughters were. Did one have her new baby snatched away under a prearranged marital agreement? Did the other leave hers on the steps of the Social Welfare Institute and watch trembling to see if someone found her?

Xinran seemed to read my mind. 'It's very important for your Chinese daughters not to be hurt in the future and they mustn't think, "my mother didn't love me and gave me up". This is just not true. And even if the mothers seemed to be callous, seemed not to feel anything, they are still human beings. It's not their fault. They were living in their times and in this kind of ignorant period.'

I often wondered whether there was any chance that a birth mother would be able to track down her abandoned children. I had heard that sometimes babies carried marks on their bodies, a sign from their mothers who might one day want to identify them. Jade had that mysterious jagged scar on her thigh which no one had been able to explain to us.

Xinran didn't think it was an identifying mark. 'In peasant homes they often use candles or oil lights during the birth, and when they want to check if it's a boy or girl they sometimes put the candle or oil light very close so they can see, and the hot oil or wax can drip onto the baby. This happens very often to both girls and boys. I remember reading about one case in the papers when a midwife checked and the candle wax dropped on this boy's penis and hurt it and the family was very upset. So they had a big court case and went to the lawyers about it!'

....

There were many barriers against the chance of a reunion with the birth mothers. Chinese law was clear. In 1992 the government had inserted a special clause within the Protection of Rights and Interests of Women which said:

> Women's right to life and health shall be inviolable. Drowning, abandoning or cruel infanticide in any manner of female babies shall be prohibited; discrimination against or maltreatment of women who give birth to female babies or women who are sterile shall be prohibited ...

The women who abandoned their babies knew they had broken the law. Even if one day there was a general amnesty, it would take enormous courage to come forward and admit what they had done.

....

'You can say that we are an emotionally abused people,' Xinran said. 'It will take a long time to get over it. Of course a lot of what I'm talking about many Chinese people just don't believe. Life in the countryside and in little towns is just another world from our booming cities.'

I was learning more about what it really meant when people talked of China being two countries in one. The experience of the rural poor was from another era compared to the lives of the women we had met on our travels: the beautiful, fashion-conscious models in Nanchang, or the dancing girls who'd sung to us in the day-care centre in Xi'an. Xinran acknowledged that, of course, millions of families in China are devoted to their girls, and often the ideal family is presented as one boy and one girl. We too had met Chinese women who expressed a preference for girl children. There was a feeling growing that girls were more likely to stay at home and look after their parents, while sons had to travel far afield to find work. But, even so, there were still large areas of the country where girls were being rejected, if not after they were born, then beforehand through the spread of ultrasound technology.

I walked home, the grey sky heavy with rain. Xinran had painted a bleak picture of the kind of fate my children had narrowly escaped. Part of me wanted to forget that all of that existed and concentrate on their lives right now, but the gaping hole in their pasts still gnawed at me. Short of travelling to China, which was not yet practical, I wanted to talk to anyone within reach who had visited the places they were born.

....

My search took me no more than half a mile away where there lived one of China's leading dissident writers. Ma Jian fled the People's Republic under threat of arrest in 1983. He settled first in Hong Kong and then London where he wrote up his travels through China's hinterland in his book *Red Dust*. I had read his account of arriving in Jade's region:

> When I step onto the high plateau of northern Shaanxi I feel I am walking towards my ancestors' heart. This land covered by fine dust blown from the Gobi Desert is the cradle of Chinese civilisation. The fertile banks of the Yellow River here have been cultivated for over eight thousand years. I have come in search of my roots.

....

And I had come to Ma Jian in search of Jade's roots.

Ma Jian is seen as something of a hero for disaffected Chinese artists and writers and his house has become the centre of what his wife Flora described as a 'maelstrom of people and activity'. With Flora translating, and their baby son asleep in his pushchair, Ma Jian showed me photographs of Yulin. There was one of himself looking like a pensive, windswept Confucius standing above the frozen Yellow River with the jagged, dry, golden landscape behind him. Another was taken from lower down, at the water's edge, which showed how the raging floodwaters had frozen in mid-flow to create an eerie white landscape complete with motionless icy waves. 'There's a feeling of being at the edge of China, a frontier land,' he said. 'Beyond Yulin there's just desert and Mongol lands. It's one of the very poorest parts of China where farmers live at subsistence level relying on their crops of wheat, sweet

© Ma Jian

The loess plateau around Yulin.

potatoes, corn, apples and dates to live. In summer the rains often fail and farmers are left in the grip of terrifying drought. Women will then have to walk hours just to get their daily supply of water. Crossing to a neighbouring village can be arduous as the soft loess earth has been carved up by rivers over the centuries and is now divided by steep ravines. Some people live in cave dwellings which are actually houses built into the soft rock. They are cool in summer and warm in winter, and are in fact an ingenious, cheap way of coping with the inhospitable climate.'

He told me how in the year after Jade was born there was a severe drought. Frequent crop failures put extra pressures on parents to have a son to guarantee their survival. To have to feed a daughter who couldn't work the land could literally have meant starvation for the family. 'The poorer the villages the more they need boys in the fields, and the worse the gender imbalance. Sometimes, I was told while I was there, if a man can't find a wife, women are kidnapped or bought for 3000 Yuan, about £230, and then if they don't produce a son they are beaten up or dumped. Some women are sold and then chained to the house so they don't escape. I went to one village near Yulin where husbands actually rented out their wives to other men who wanted sons.'

I could hardly believe what I was hearing. Did Jade's biological mother have to endure an environment like this? If she did, has she survived?

'If the wife is known to be good at producing sons her husband will rent her out and if nine months later she produces a son, he gets 8000 Yuan, or about £600. If she ends up producing a girl they will try again or else just get rid of her. There was even a story in the newspapers when I was there of a father who had rented out his 14-year-old daughter to another man to see if she would produce a son. Life is very precarious and by the end of the year most of the peasants are in debt to the government. The tax burden is very heavy. There's just not enough money for education or medical treatment, and either of these is often seen as a waste of money for girls. Sometimes a girl will go to school if the family wants to keep the son at home to work in the fields. Teachers, though, often don't get paid and the fees parents pay go straight to the local government.'

Even though he now lived here in the West, I was surprised to see how much Ma Jian still simmered with anger over what he saw as the failure of the Chinese government to help improve peasants' lives. 'When the government was faced with the problem of mass poverty, instead of first solving the economic problems they laid the blame on overpopulation and introduced the draconian One Child Policy. On top of that they sucked the peasants dry with taxation so in poor areas like Yulin, people are driven to desperate measures to survive, that's why it's such a hot-bed of dissent.'

We talked about the case just a few years earlier of a peasant lawyer from northern Shaanxi, Mr Ma, who had dared to take the local government to court for overtaxation. He became a hero, garnering support from tens of thousands of farmers, but he ended up in prison. Then a few years later, eighteen months after we had adopted Jade, 80,000 peasants had apparently rallied in Yulin for an 'anti-taxation and anti-exploitation' conference, threatening a 'revolt' if the central government didn't act.

Ma Jian felt that the depth of poverty in the countryside around Yulin meant that it would have been very difficult for a peasant woman to travel to the city's Social Welfare Institute to leave her baby. He thought Jade was more likely to have been born to someone on the outskirts of the city. If she had been born in a village her mother would probably have found it simpler and cheaper to let her die. He himself had had a conversation with a woman south of Yulin which to him summed up attitudes to girls there. He recounted it in *Red Dust*:

I watch a woman feed her baby with a piece of bread from her mouth, and ask her how many children she has.

'None,' she says, looking at the track behind me.

'Isn't that yours, then?' I say, pointing to the baby in her arms.

'Doesn't count, it's a girl.' The baby's mouth is smeared with wet dough.

'Women are equal to men now, haven't you heard?' I say. I watch an insect land on the baby's chapped cheek then fly away again. The mother tuts and rolls her eyes to the sky.

....

I wondered if Jade too was seen as a non-person when she was born. 'How long is all this going to go on?' I asked.

'Politics is the problem, the terrible living conditions of the people. The mass of peasants have very little idea of city life. It's an irony that the Revolution and half a century of communism hardly improved their lives at all. In fact, in some areas, the peasants are worse off now than they were when the communists first came to power. Of course now many Chinese are heading to the cities in a headlong rush to make money, but solving the social problems of the country is not on their minds.'

....

I rushed home in time to pick Jade up from nursery school. As she bounced out, I thought back to her performance in the Nativity Play. She had played both a sheep and a shepherd, which meant being dressed throughout in a fluffy white tunic with black tights, having floppy white ears attached to her head and her nose painted black. She had come tentatively on stage and searched the faces in the audience. When she saw me and Gerald, her eyes had lit up like beacons, and she grinned and waved furiously at us. Tears of pride had rolled shamelessly down my cheeks. When she had to squat around the pretend campfire on her travels to Bethlehem, she had beckoned to me and hissed, 'Come and join me, come *here*, Mummy!'

'I can't!' I mouthed, hoping she wouldn't leap off the stage to get me, and interrupt the other three-year-old angels who were about to start their enchanting rendition of 'Twinkle, twinkle, little star.'

However many snippets of information about Yulin I could gather, I could only ever have a superficial idea of what life really felt like for Jade's birth mother. And even if I could understand the social conditions, the big, gaping question was unanswerable. What was she really like? I was a mother of children whose personalities had been shaped by two women I would never know. Was Jade strong-willed, stubborn, sociable and engaging because of the genes from her parents, or because of how we were bringing her up? Which bit of her was down to being adopted? Was Rose's bright, independent, mischievous personality a product of her first parents, her year in foster care with three other babies or her life in London? The nature/nurture debate was for us even more unfathomable than for most parents.

....

Eventually the girls will go back to China when they are old enough to ask their own questions. Life in the poor areas may well have been transformed by then – or perhaps not as much as one might think. When I went to visit one of Britain's leading anthropologists of China who'd specialised in the phenomenon of gender discrimination in Asia, I discovered that social attitudes were not developing at the same accelerated pace as China's tiger economy.

Dr Elisabeth Croll was sitting in her spacious office, packed floor to ceiling with books, at the School of Oriental and African Studies in London. She herself had not observed at first hand any cases of girls being abandoned or female infanticide in rural China, but the statistical and andecdotal evidence suggested to her that these practices still occurred. 'We know that there is female infanticide in China and that there is sex-selective abortion although quite how much and on what scale is not clear. What we do know is that there is a preference for boys and not only in rural areas, and that the statistics on the sex ratios of birth suggest that these practices not only continue but are actually increasing,' she said. 'It is really important to recognise that these practices are not confined to China with its One Child Policy, but they also occur and are increasing in neighbouring East and South Asian societies such as India, Pakistan, Korea and Taiwan which don't have such a rule. So we can't hold the One Child Policy entirely responsible.' She did, however, say that it had exacerbated the preference for girls in China.

I was intrigued by this. I asked her if girls would still be abandoned or aborted if the population policy was lifted altogether.

'Yes, I think that girls, and especially second daughters, might continue to suffer. This is largely because the rapid decrease in fertility across East and South Asia and the widespread preference for fewer children have resulted in a trade-off: fewer children but still one son. In addition, parents want to raise and educate their two or three children well so that the children can earn a good income and support them in their old age. It is much more expensive to have a child nowadays; expectations are higher and governments encourage parents to want the best for their children. We all know that it is much easier to give the best to two or three children at most than to four or five children which was the previous norm. One of the main reasons parents prefer to have a son is that there is little or no social security or pension provision especially in the countryside – hence this is not down to some backward prejudice; there are good economic reasons still to want a son.'

Beijing has long tried to counteract this discrimination, while blaming old-fashioned feudal thinking, rather than its population-control policies. From the early 1980s, the government charged the Women's Federation with the task of persuading parents that girls were just as valuable as boys. Posters and education campaigns were launched to raise the status of the girl child. In 2004 there was a recognition that more needed to be done to avert a crisis, with warnings that millions of 'missing' girls could become a destabilising factor in years to come. The State Family Planning Commission launched a campaign entitled 'Care for Girls' which aimed to improve the value attached to daughters. Families were to be given extra incentives to persuade them to keep their girls and there was a crackdown on ultrasound tests. UNICEF too supported this fight against sex-selective abortions, female infanticide and discrimination against girls.

Growing prosperity, particularly in the big cities, has also improved the perceived value of a girl, but it doesn't guarantee that families have less of a desire to have a boy. Centuries of discrimination don't disappear overnight.

....

It wasn't even as if the Western world could boast of being free of it. In Britain we had our own long history of 'son preference' with Henry VIII being one of the most high-profile examples, dispensing with wives who didn't give him a male heir with total ruthlessness. Prejudice and discrimination didn't end in the twentieth century either; there were still families that preferred to have a son to take over property or a business, and which saw girls as inferior, except in their ability to marry well.

I thought back, too, to a sultry summer day which I'd spent with the two other families I knew in East London who had adopted from Yulin. We had met half way between us, in Coram Fields, a park built exclusively for adults with children, near the British Museum. As the three girls played in the wet sand, spraying water over each other and forming the beginnings of a kind of Yulin sisterhood, I had mused on how old Captain Thomas Coram might have looked down on us and approved. He was an eighteenth-century philanthropist who lived at a time when British society cared little for the plight of unwanted children. He was deeply affected by seeing young children exposed, sometime alive, sometimes dying or dead, in the streets of London.

In the twenty years between 1730 and 1750 records showed that three-quarters of all the children christened in the capital were buried before they were five. Terrible failures of social policy along with the rise in gin drinking contributed to this lethal period for poor children. There was one court case recorded of a woman who had fetched her child from the workhouse, strangled it and then left it in a ditch in Bethnal Green in order to sell its clothes and buy gin. Many mothers with illegitimate children were afraid of being charged with infanticide and so abandoned them in the streets instead. The Poor Laws were woefully inadequate, while the parish workhouses simply became death traps, with nearly 100 per cent mortality rate for the infants in them.

After a lifetime as a shipbuilder and sailor, Thomas Coram became so horrified by the poverty and brutality in the capital that he established the Foundling Hospital for the care of abandoned children. He faced opposition from those who associated the word 'foundling' with 'bastard', and who thought the hospital would encourage vice and licentiousness. But many prominent artists and musicians of the day were inspired by the idea and became enthusiastic patrons, including Hogarth, Gainsborough and Handel.

....

Nearly three centuries later, there are parts of China today struggling with another social crisis with dire results for children.

As I continued my search for news of that remote Shaanxi city of Yulin, I did find one Yulin resident now living in London: a doctor who had actually seen the discrimination against girls first hand. Dr Xuebin Dong, now involved in tumour gene therapy, had been brought up in the Yulin region and worked there in the late 1980s. He lives with his wife and son in a flat south of the Thames.

His description of the area around Yulin was beginning to sound familiar. 'The locals call it the "hairless land", because the yellow earth is so dry and so alkaline nothing, not even grass, grows. Sometimes it's so chalky the earth is actually white. I used to work in the Surgical Department at a county hospital where we shared a ward with the gynaecology and obstetrics department. I witnessed a couple of occasions when a woman gave birth to a daughter and then said to the midwife, "We don't want the baby; can you find a home for her?". Legal adoptions were very restricted so she would try her best to find a family for her. Sometimes it was easy, for instance I remember a nurse had asked me if I could get her a "good" girl, so I was able to pass one of these babies on to her. I knew several of my colleagues were doing the same thing. Once the child was taken by the new family there would be absolutely no contact with the birth family. Adoptions were nearly always kept secret as the adoptive family feared that the natural parents would later on claim the child back. They couldn't bear to think of losing the child after many years of living together.'

It was fascinating to hear that people had actually asked for girls to adopt. It reminded me again of Kay Ann Johnson's research, which showed that it was often the need to have a son, rather than automatic rejection of girls, that was the driving motivation for abandoning a female baby. Indeed there were cases hitting the newspapers of girls being trafficked from one part of the country to another to supply families' desire for daughters. In one incident, twenty-eight female infants, all younger than three months, were found in nylon bags aboard a long-distance bus. It turned out this was part of a trafficking ring, selling girl children from central China to couples in Anhui and Henan Provinces in the east, both provinces where girl children were also being abandoned or aborted in large numbers.

. . . .

A few months later Dr Dong decided to go back to Yulin to see his parents, his first visit for five years. I seized the opportunity to give him some photographs of Jade for her foster family.

We had already exchanged some letters with them but I wanted to hear so much more about Jade's early life.

When he arrived in Yulin, Dr Dong could hardly recognise his home city. Much of the old town had been rebuilt; narrow streets had made way for white-tiled blocks and large modern squares. He described how the city was now filled with restaurants and shops, while taxis, cars and motorbikes raced in all directions. 'It was like being in the gold rush. Everybody was in a hurry, there was too much pressure, and it was too hot and chaotic for me. But I did manage to find Jade's foster father. We met up outside his small shop which sold motoring lubricants near Yulin's main bus station.' Dr Dong showed me the photograph he had taken of himself standing next to the squarely built, grey-haired man I had seen before in other pictures we had been sent. 'I told him Jade was being well looked after. He seemed a really kind, decent man, salt of the earth, who told me that he and his wife had been devastated when they had to give up Jade. He had lost ten kilos from the stress of it. They had adored her and had even wanted to adopt her themselves but were told it was too difficult and expensive.'

This was a revelation as I'd been told previously that Jade's foster parents had long forgotten her and had very little information to give me. And here was another family who already had a son, but who had desperately wanted to have a girl. 'They said the orphanage gave them a small fee which barely covered the cost of clothes and milk, but they did the fostering "out of love",' said Dr Dong.

It was such a relief to know that although this wasn't her birth family at least these warm-hearted people had genuinely loved and nurtured Jade for her first year. I always felt she must have been well cared for, and now they would be a treasured link to her past when the time came to take her back to her home town. I was later able to contact the adoptive parents of the other little girl they had fostered at the same time as Jade; they lived just west of London, and sent me a photograph of both the babies sitting, camera struck, on a big bed – baby Jade in a red dress and crimson leggings. It hit home to me, then, that when Jade came to us she lost not only her foster parents, but her foster sister as well. This was an invaluable glimpse into her life before she was our daughter, and another small, precious piece of the jigsaw.

An amateur American historian took me a few steps closer to Jade's simple foster home when he was able to visit it and send me some brief video footage. Brian Stuy has made a small

© Brian Stuy

The main gate of Yulin Social Welfare Institute.

business out of visiting orphanages and foster families around China on behalf of adoptive parents. His film also showed Yulin's ornate Buddhist temples carved into ochre rock faces, miles of crumbling sections of the Great Wall, statuesque pagodas and everywhere the dry, dry land. The city's streets looked very typical of many Chinese cities but with hints of the countryside nearby, such as peasant women driving donkey carts loaded with vegetables. I was already familiar, from earlier pictures, with the elaborate gateway to Yulin's Social Welfare Institute, but what I hadn't seen before was the gate to the baby-room complex further down the street. This was the place where most of the children left at the orphanage were actually discovered. The plain functional gateway in a brick

© Brian Stuy

The gate to the baby-room complex, Yulin SWI.

wall, with dirty white metal doors, held such intense symbolic significance for us, although to anyone else it would be unremarkable. I could imagine Jade's mother leaving her baby on the cobbles, perhaps beside the door or under a nearby tree, knowing she would be bound to be picked up by the staff inside and kept safe. Perhaps it was dark, so who knows how many hours Jade waited alone, listening only to the sound of traffic, before the gate was opened.

....

Some adoptive parents had already returned to their children's Chinese roots. One couple we knew had taken their eight-year-old daughter to see her orphanage on the east coast of China, only to find she wasn't very interested, complained about the smell and wanted to return home. Rose's orphanage was more accessible than Jade's and adoptive parents were beginning to pay visits there. One British mother came to see me hot from her time in Xiushui, thrilled by the welcome she'd received. 'We were treated like royalty. Because I am so tall, people thought I was actually from the north of China, and some distant cousin to Mr Rong, the orphanage director.' She showed me a photograph of the exact spot in the middle of a courtyard where her baby, wrapped up in a basket, had been left. The foster mother of her daughter had also been so distressed when she had to give the baby up that she'd vowed never to foster again. These foster parents, too, weren't paid but did the job for 'love'.

I received a letter from Mr Rong telling me that Rose's foster mother had sold her house and moved to Guangzhou, so it meant my trail to her past life was already going cold. Perhaps this kind woman had found giving up Rose and the other babies she fostered just too painful. An American documentary about adoption from Jiangxi Province showed a desperate moment when a foster mother was prevented by a simple misunderstanding from seeing her charge for the last time. She broke down in uncontrolled weeping. I was beginning to realise that we had to grieve for the foster parents as well as the biological ones.

The whole transition from foster to adoptive family was sudden and tough on all parties involved, not least the children. Perhaps it should be much slower, more graduated and take more account of the psychological trauma. It looked as if the process was streamlined to suit the groups of overseas adopters, many coming from the United States, who preferred to operate on a strict timetable. The speed and efficiency of our time in China was convenient for us too, but I for one would have been happy to spend more time getting to know my children before we took them from the only home they knew.

....

'Now, what will you be doing about bi-cultural socialisation?' A question our social worker had asked.

'About what?'

'Teaching your children about their culture and heritage. And will you be learning Mandarin?'

Remembering a friend who had been turned down for her third Chinese child by a social worker who accused her of not having sufficient 'depth of cultural feeling for China' I knew this was an explosive question. I answered, 'Of course, we will try and do what we can.'

I didn't actually think Gerald and I could teach our children much about Chinese culture. We'd accumulated some

Chinese silk pyjamas for the girls, there were the glass perfume bottles we'd bought — one with a dragon and one a horse painted on the inside — we read them the odd Chinese fairy story, enthusiastically drank Chinese tea and Gerald was adept at a stir-fry, but somehow this didn't seem enough to foster the girls' cultural roots.

We had grouped together with other adoptive families a few times to celebrate Chinese New Year. At the last party, Jade had galloped about holding a paper dragon over her head. Some families had gone further, enrolling their children in Chinese nurseries, or learning Chinese cooking, including how to make fortune cookies. For all of us it was uncharted territory, all we knew was that some kind of positive relationship with China was essential, but how Chinese we should try and make our children while they were living in the UK was a dilemma. Somewhere there had to be a balance between them fitting in with other British children, while not losing a sense of pride in their heritage.

We had wondered about getting a Chinese au pair, but the Chinese students I interviewed, being 'only' children, had no experience of young babies. One arrived for an interview wearing stiletto patent leather boots and a miniskirt, and looked very perturbed at the idea of changing nappies. Many young Chinese students in Britain also carried high career expectations from their parents and they didn't have much room in between their MBAs or their music diplomas to look after children.

At first, we just continued with our Chinese language lessons, and to make them as painless as possible we invited our teacher to do them over Saturday breakfast. The last thing we wanted was an atmosphere of 'Oh no, not Mandarin today'. Jenny and her husband would come over with Lily and her new, recently adopted sister and we'd tuck into coffee and croissants while struggling to remember a word of what we'd learnt in the previous lesson. Jade was partially interested, and took a logical, if rather dogmatic approach. When the teacher pointed at some broccoli and said what it was in Chinese, Jade adamantly disagreed and said 'No! That's not *ganlan*, that's broccoli, silly.'

Eventually we graduated to a new Chinese school that was just starting up. We found our needs coincided with the many Chinese mothers who had married Westerners and who still wanted their children to learn Mandarin. Jade and Rose began to go every Sunday morning, and started to learn rhymes like this one, yet another to be sung to the same tune as Frère Jacques:

Liang zhi laohu,
Liang zhi laohu,
Pao de kuai,
Pao de kuai,
Yi zhi mei you yanjing,
Yi zhi mei you weiba,
Zhen qi guai!
Zhen qi guai!

Two tigers,
Two tigers,
Running very fast,
Running very fast,
One without eyes,
One without a tail,
How very strange!
How very strange!

Meanwhile our patient teacher would try and drum some words into us weary adults at the same time.

I was touched, many times, by the positive reception we had from the Chinese community in London. We often found people were very interested in the adoption and it wasn't difficult to start to make friends. One attractive media consultant and opera singer from north-east China told us how her own father had always regretted that she wasn't a boy, and made her feel constantly inferior to her younger brother whom the family doted on. She struggles to this day to feel confident about herself, and feels driven to work harder and harder to prove to her family that she is doing well. To her, the sight of Western people like us adopting baby girls affirms their value and sends an important message to all Chinese women.

Xinran too thought the adoptions were a valuable way to save children's lives, but she worried about how our girls would feel about China when they grew up. When I met her over coffee one day she told me she passionately wanted to do something to prepare for what she saw as the potential problems ahead. 'In the 1950s and 60s some of the children adopted from Vietnam, Korea and Japan had very difficult lives, separated from their culture of birth, and some even committed suicide when they themselves became mothers. There was no help for them in those days. We have to give these newly adopted children of today the roots and connections to their culture. I would like them to be proud of being Chinese and different, in an interesting way.'

She decided to throw her considerable energies into setting up a charity called 'The Mothers' Bridge of Love' aimed at giving Chinese adopted children all over the world a means to keep in contact with their country of birth. At the same time she wanted to communicate to women back in China the stories of what happened to children once they were adopted. She thought as more Chinese people learnt about overseas adoption, the more it would help the cause of women's rights in China.

After questioning how realistically we were going to build some Chinese foundations into our children's lives, it was such a relief to find this dynamic woman wanting to take the first step. I became a trustee of Mothers' Bridge while Xinran recruited a group of women helpers in Beijing. They put together a programme of cultural education along with plans for helping the poorest of Chinese children. Some of the cultural material would come to us via a website and a Children's Journal, then in years to come, ours and other overseas Chinese children would be able to travel, either to Nanjing – for a stint at a Children's Music and Arts Centre – or to the regions they were originally from and stay with families there. I loved the thought of Jade and Rose making friends with other children their age from Shaanxi or Jiangxi provinces. Eventually the idea would be for them to do voluntary work in the poorer villages so they could learn about the conditions their parents' generation lived under. I could just imagine them in their 'gap year', if they were drawn to it, helping to build a much-needed school or teaching the children there about the West.

When we had first thought about adopting these Chinese girls, with my scant knowledge of the country, I had never imagined how much we would feel we wanted to adopt a part of China too. If we couldn't find our daughters' birth parents, the least we could do was to offer the girls an enduring sense of their motherland.

. . . .

They were going to need all the confidence they could get.

The press image of overseas adoption as essentially a trade in babies was already filtering down to the playground. Some adopted children had already been asked by their classmates whether their parents had 'bought' them.

'BABIES FOR SALE,' screamed the headline in the *Daily Mail* above an article about adoption from China. 'BUYING HAPPINESS,' was the caption under one of the photos of parents handing over their $3000 to the Civil Affairs Office. There was, of course, a terrible trade in some parts of the world; I had seen it in action in Paraguay, and we couldn't guarantee that some corruption didn't creep into the adoption system in China, but to reduce every overseas adopter to being a 'baby shopper' was a gross perversion of the truth. Parents paid fees to the Civil Affairs office, but we also paid fees to our own Social Service departments. I wondered if people expected the whole process to be offered for free.

While the problem of corruption in Romanian adoptions was in the press, I went to a piano recital and was introduced to a lady by my host as someone who had two girls from China. Although well educated, she still came out with an extraordinary remark: 'I've just been watching the news about Romania. Are your children stolen too?' It beggared belief. What answer did she expect me to give her? The emphasis in our Home Study on how much we understood about racism was beginning to make some more sense.

I did worry that in any transaction where money was involved, corruption could fester. I had pressed Professor Elisabeth Croll when I saw her, putting it to her that no one seemed certain about exactly where the $3000 'donation' was spent. She thought there was a danger that some corruption or exchange of money for favours might occur, as in many other comparable situations in China today. But she also felt it was very likely that much of the fee was used by the orphanage to meet its running costs and care for the children who stayed behind. Fees like this are vital for local institutions, which get very little central government money. Professor Croll drew a parallel with the use of ultrasound scans which are outlawed for the purposes of sex identification. However, cash-strapped local health services are only too happy to use the fees the scans engender to supplement their funding.

And weren't there also huge dangers that inter-country adoption might even encourage the trafficking of female babies? In fact, she thought it was sons rather than daughters who were more likely to be kidnapped and trafficked for the domestic market. There were cases, of girls being trafficked, most probably for domestic adoption, such as the ones found on the long-distance bus, but there was a larger market for boys than girls as they commanded a higher price.

I had another concern too, that overseas adoptions might become too permanent, well after the need for them had gone. After all, in the long term abandoned girls should be able to find homes within China. All signs are that they will continue, with the China Centre of Adoption Affairs paying its first visit to the British ministry now dealing with adoptions, the Department for Education and Science. The Director of the CCAA, Mr Lu Ying, and several of his colleagues came to the offices in Waterloo and met some adoptive parents and their children. He thanked us for our kind assistance and support and for giving Chinese children a new life. 'I hope that China will become your second home, and to see you all in Beijing,' he said.

When I asked him how long they would continue looking for foreign adoptive parents, he replied, 'South Korea started overseas adoptions in 1953 and they are still going on. Of course domestic adoption will always be the major pillar of adoption and we follow the Hague Convention on the Rights of the Child which says that domestic adoption should be satisfied first, before inter-country adoption.' As to the risk of corruption, he argued that the reason the $3000 donation was in cash meant that it could go straight to the Social Welfare Institute, without being paid into provincial social welfare funds. If anyone tried to spend dollars on the black market they would be noticed, so he thought fraud was minimal. At least it seemed the Chinese government was keeping a close eye on the system. I'd heard of one case from Sichuan Province, where an orphanage director and his accountant were put in prison because they had been caught embezzling adoption funds and going on shopping sprees to Hong Kong.

An official at the DfES said he had a 'warm glow' after the meeting and felt the Chinese delegation cared deeply about the welfare of the children leaving their country. There was no longer a quota and the number of Chinese adoptions to the UK was now creeping up. The British government was also introducing better regulation aimed at improving the lot of all adopters.

Some people have expressed to me their worries that inter-country adoption could all be part of a strategy by the People's Republic to spread Chinese influence round the world, creating a pool of parents sympathetic to their nation. Even if it is, I do know that influence works both ways: the flow of Western money and personnel going to orphanages in far corners of the country will be shaping China's destiny too.

In America there's a substantial infrastructure, private agencies organising around 5,000 adoptions a year. When I expressed my anxiety about this 'institutionalisation' of overseas adoption to Amy Klatzkin, an American adoptive mother who has written extensively on the subject, she replied, 'I worry about this a lot. A few years ago Wang Liyao of the Anhui Academy of Social Sciences conducted research in urban and rural China surveying people's views of international adoption. Urban people by and large had heard about it and thought it was great good fortune for the kids but worried about the adopted children's ability to be proud of their Chinese heritage. Rural people, by contrast, hadn't heard about international adoption, and many respondents thought it was an awful idea. The good news from that is that, unlike the situation in Korea and many other countries, international adoption is not (yet) a reason that Chinese birth parents relinquish children. They are not doing it so their kids will have a "better life" in a rich country. The pressures are all internal, and the expectation is that their baby will be taken in by another rural family and raised in the Chinese countryside. That's what happens to most abandoned infants, and rural people know that ... Once international adoption becomes a reason for abandonment, it also becomes part of the problem. For the moment I don't think that is the case in China, not for most female infant abandonments, anyway.'

So we, as adoptive parents, have to be vigilant and continue to ask difficult questions to make sure that the system that sent us our children doesn't become discredited.

....

We were invited out to dinner with a business friend of Gerald's; my producer friend Ian O'Reilly was also there. The house was decorated almost as if it was a stage set; it was packed with exotic ornaments and a heavily embroidered silk tapestry adorned the dining table. I sat opposite a large bubbly lady with blonde hair who turned to me just as we had started to eat some delicious Thai green curry: 'I've been hearing from your husband about your two little girls. They sound wonderful! Do you know that Rose had a twin, and that the twin died? That's why she is such a powerful personality; she is really two people in one. I can see it was very cold when she and her sister were born ...'

I was speechless.

'Rose's mother already had a little girl, so when the twins arrived her husband was horrified. They had hoped at least one would have been a boy. The mother wanted to save them so she gave some money and food to some people, intermediaries who took them away. They didn't love them or feed them properly, and en route the twin died because she was so much weaker. Rose screamed and screamed for lack of milk. They didn't look after her umbilical cord either. They buried the twin and took Rose to the place where she was found.'

Now I was dumbfounded. Rose's tummy button had looked quite swollen when we met her. I couldn't really believe this, it was surely pure invention, and the thought of Rose having a little twin who died was too dreadful to contemplate.

None of this was based on anything, except that this woman happened to be a celebrated clairvoyant called Sally Morgan, and she claimed to have a kind of sixth sense and be able to tune in and see things most of us can't. I wasn't sure I wanted to hear any more, but then I thought, why not ... Surely with the girls' past so unknown, even the speculation of a medium was better than nothing. So I showed her photographs of the girls. 'Oh, look at this one, Jade, is she? She's the double of her maternal grandmother. She was born probably outside a house. I see a large slab of concrete or stone. Her mother was from a family leading a nomadic lifestyle, moving from place to place. She was a teenager, about eighteen and not married, who had hidden the pregnancy all the way through and got her mother to help her give birth. She had only been out working a few minutes before.' Then she drew a plan on a napkin showing me where she thought the birth had taken place. 'Here's a road, but with no cars, a dirt track, there are bits of shrubbery and rocks ... she's leaning against this door ... it was daylight, she could even have been outside. She tried to give birth silently, frightened that she would be heard. She put her baby in a woven rope basket and carried her away.'

'And what about the scar on Jade's leg?'

'That was where they cut the umbilical cord — it would have been between her legs — and whatever they used to cut it, a piece of glass or metal, cut her leg too. The mother then took the baby herself on a bus or truck to the orphanage and left her there. She is now no longer with the same boyfriend.' I glanced at Ian. What was a BBC journalist doing delving into the spirit world for information? I should just dismiss it. Gerald was listening, transfixed. Sally needed no encouragement. 'Does Jade have trouble speaking?'

'It has taken a while for her to talk fluently and she still struggles sometimes.'

'It's her palate, does she have quite a big tongue?'

'I'm not sure, I think so, I'll have a look.'

The next morning I asked Jade to stick out her tongue and the tip reached down to the bottom of her chin. Neither Rose nor I could do the same with ours. Sally told me many other things and I shall simply file them away knowing they could be either fact or fantasy. As the years go by, I will just wait and see if any of her predictions come true.

....

Jade has just started primary school. She earned herself 'pupil of the week' in her second week there for being caring to other children when they were upset. I glow with pride, and think of all those schools that didn't want to make room for an adopted child. I go to collect her. She waves to her classmates: an exciting mix of nationalities including Bosnian, Algerian, Egyptian Coptic, Dutch, French, American and even Mongolian. Jade skips alongside me and proceeds to jump up and down every step we pass as we walk slowly to the park. Rose is in her pushchair waving her legs and grinning. I ask Jade whether she thinks she is Chinese or English. She replies, 'Chinese,' and then two minutes later, she grins, 'Mum, actually I'm English.'

Maybe she is simply both. Her and Rose's whole relationship with China will be an adventure that we will travel together over the next few years. For now, though, the first phase of this long journey is done.

Now the girls run off across the grass, pick up a stack of twigs and then race back. Jade's thick brown hair bounces from side to side, her cheeks are pink, her eyes radiant as she throws her arms around me. Rose follows, her hair popping up from her head in a top-knot like a small fountain, running as fast as she can with her determined toddler legs flailing and calling 'Mama, Mama!' like a little sheep.

I think back to the tortuous adoption process, the agonising over my maternal abilities, the fears and insecurities, the

© Gerald Slocock

Rose.

attempts to grapple with a gigantic country: now it all seems so absurdly obvious that this was the right thing to do. The shadows of doubt have no hope against this cascade of limbs and laughter. I hug the girls tight, as they wriggle in my arms, fighting as ever for the prime position on my lap. 'Don't push! One knee each!' I tell them.

These girls have shattered the biological hierarchy; I have almost forgotten that I'd once wanted to give birth. Now Jade and Rose are simply *my* children.

....

I think of how every morning for the last three weeks, Jade gets out of bed, and within minutes asks with a broad grin, '*Please* can I play doggies, Mummy?'

'Yes, of course.' I know the routine: 'Go and lie in your basket then and eat your bone!' She crawls around on the floor and pretends to chew. I throw a ball for her and she collects it in her mouth. My stepmother has two cocker spaniels and Jade has become fascinated by them and their mannerisms.

But then she says something else. 'Mummy, Mummy, I want to be born.'

I know, by now, what she wants me to do. I stand up and she crawls behind me, then through my legs. I lift her up and say, 'What a lovely new puppy-dog, so beautiful!'

'I'm weak, Mummy, look, my legs are all shaky.'

'There, there, puppy, you'll be strong soon.'

'Mummy, the big dogs are coming to get me, chase them away!'

So I wave my arm and chase the other dogs away. After repeating this little routine over several days, I ask her, 'Why do you want to be born, Jade?'

'Because I like it and I want to be like other doggies.' She may be imitating the dogs she knows, or has watched too many wildlife programmes or, since many adopted children practice similar rituals, perhaps there is something much deeper going on. One time she actually lies down and says, 'I'm a baby doggie, come and pick me up from China, Mummy!'

All I know is that while once I yearned to have a baby, now I find myself giving birth every morning. I am sure it's healing for both of us.

Rose has watched this game day after day and now insists on taking part. 'Born, born,' she cries, and then she too crawls through my legs, although sometimes she decides to turn round and go back again, or else lies down half way through the operation and refuses to move. I don't dare speculate on what that symbolises.

. . . .

I find it fascinating how these girls, springing from families I can barely imagine, are now becoming part of us, shaped by our accumulated experience handed down from our parents and grandparents. It's as if they are grafting themselves onto our families, like plants that started off separate, but grow as one. And while we influence them, they bring to us their own family histories embedded in their Chinese roots; opening our minds and hearts to another civilisation.

When I think back to losing all my other tiny, barely formed babies, I still feel pangs of sadness, but at least now I can share in the joys of a friend's pregnancy. My girls have more than filled the void. Now, all I really wish is that my own mother could have seen her beautiful grandchildren. They've taught me how to love, how to revel in the present and most of all that children, wherever they are from, bring with them limitless supplies of happiness. They would surely have given her a good enough reason to stay alive.

....

And as Jade and Rose grow up, if they ever ask me whether I see them as second best, I'll be able to scoff at the mere suggestion. They are the most enchanting daughters any mother could possibly ask for. Of course, it'll be for them to decide whether the mother they were given matched up.

© Jenny Matthews

Selected Bibliography

Archer, Caroline for Adoption UK, *First Steps in Parenting the Child Who Hurts – Tiddlers and Toddlers*, Jessica Kingsley Publishers, 1999

Buchanan, George, *Possible Being*, Carcanet New Press, 1980

Chang, Jung, *Wild Swans*, HarperCollins, 1991

China, Lonely Planet Publications, 1998

Chennells, Prue and Chris Hammond, *Adopting a Child, a guide for people interested in adoption*, British Agencies for Adoption & Fostering, 1990

Cotterell, Arthur, *The First Emperor of China – the story behind the terracotta army of Mount Li*, Penguin, 1989

Croll, Elisabeth, *Endangered Daughters – Discrimination and Development in Asia*, Routledge, 2000

Croll, Elisabeth, *Fertility Decline, Family Size and Female Discrimination: A Study of Reproductive Management in East and South Asia*, Asia-Pacific Population Journal, June 2002

Evans, Karin, *The Lost Daughters of China – Abandoned Girls, Their Journey to America, and the Search for a Missing Past*, Penguin 2000

Faber, Adele and Elaine Mazlish, *Siblings Without Rivalry*, Piccadilly Press, 1998

Fry, Ying Ying and Amy Klatzkin, *Kids Like Me in China*, Yeong and Yeong Book Co, 2001

Furedi Frank, *Paranoid Parenting*, Allen Lane, 2001

Hessler, Peter, *River Town – Two Years on the Yangtze*, John Murray, 2001

Hughes, Frieda, *Stonepicker*, Bloodaxe Books, 2001

Jian, Ma, *Red Dust*, Vintage 2002

Johnson, Ian, *Wild Grass – Three Stories of Change in Modern China*, Pantheon Books, 2004

Johnson, Kay Ann, *Wanting a Daughter, Needing a Son – Abandonment, Adoption, and Orphanage Care in China*, Yeong & Yeong Book Co, 2004

Lisle, Laurie, *Without Child – challenging the stigma of childlessness*, Routledge, 1999

Menzies, Gavin, *1421 – The Year China Discovered the World*, Bantam Press, 2002

Morrall, Clare, *Astonishing Splashes of Colour*, Tindal Street Press, 2003

Perry, Elizabeth J. and Mark Seldon eds, *Chinese Society, 2nd Edition – Change conflict and resistance*, RoutledgeCurzon, 2003

Regan, Professor Lesley, *Miscarriage – what every woman needs to know*, Bloomsbury, 1997

Spence, Jonathan D., *The Search for Modern China*, W. W. Norton and Company, 1999

Winchester, Simon, *The River at the Centre of the World – A Journey up the Yangtze, and Back in Chinese Time*, Penguin 1998

Xinran, *The Good Women of China – Hidden Voices*, Chatto & Windus, 2002

Useful Web-sites:

Department for Education and Skills – www.dfes.gov.uk
British Association for Adoption and Fostering – www.baaf.org.uk
Overseas Adoption Support and Information Service –
www.adoptionoverseas.org
Overseas Adoption Helpline – www.oah.org.uk
The China Centre of Adoption Affairs – www.china-ccaa.org
Children Adopted from China – www.cach.org.uk
Families with Children from China – www.fwcc.org
The Mothers' Bridge of Love – www.motherbridge.org
Australian Society of Intercountry Aid for Children – www.asiac.org
For adoption books and free parent guides – www.emkpress.com